D0077109

Unless Recalled Earlier

DATE DUE

ǂ 4 ǂ-94			
NOV 1 7 1997			

DEMCO 38-297

Empirical Studies
in Field Instruction

RECEIVED

AUG 1 0 1990

MSU - LIBRARY

Empirical Studies
in Field Instruction

Miriam S. Raskin
Editor

The Haworth Press
New York • London

HV
11
.E54
1989

Empirical Studies in Field Instruction has also been published as *The Clinical Supervisor*, Volume 6, Numbers 3/4 1988.

© 1989 by The Haworth Press, Inc. All rights reserved. No part of this work may be reproduced or utilized in any form or by any means, electronic or mechanical, including photocopying, microfilm and recording, or by any information storage and retrieval system, without permission in writing from the publisher. Printed in the United States of America.

The Haworth Press, Inc., 12 West 32 Street, New York, NY 10001
EUROSPAN/Haworth, 3 Henrietta Street, London WC2E 8LU England

Library of Congress Cataloging-in-Publication Data
Empirical studies in field instruction.

    "Has also been published as Clinical supervisor, 6(3/4) 1988" — T.p. verso.
    Bibliography: p.
    1. Social service — Field work. I. Raskin, Miriam S.
HV11.E54   1989   361.3'072   88-24670
ISBN 0-86656-869-7

1852 2825

10/19/90 RB

To Ira, Seva and Xan

ABOUT THE EDITOR

Miriam S. Raskin, EdD, ACSW, is Associate Professor of Social Work and Director of Field Instruction at George Mason University, Fairfax, Virginia, a position she has held for the past 14 years. Her research interests include field instruction, child welfare, and women/family issues. She is active in the community and serves on social service agency boards and county commissions. Dr. Raskin received her MSW from the University of Maryland School of Social Work and Community Planning and her EdD from Virginia Polytechnic Institute and State University.

Empirical Studies
in Field Instruction

CONTENTS

EDITOR'S COMMENTS

It is with great pleasure that we are able to publish this collection of articles edited by Miriam Raskin. I have been acquainted with Miriam and her work in field instruction for many years. Miriam has been truly dedicated to the field instruction component of social work education. When she proposed to us the idea of a volume devoted to field instruction, we eagerly pursued organizing it. After much hard work on the part of many, especially Miriam, we are now able to present this volume.

Carlton E. Munson, DSW

About the Contributors

Donald R. Baker, PhD, has been with the undergraduate Social Work Program at Illinois State University's Social Work Program since 1981. Dr. Baker has organized and presently teaches within the practice methods and research sequences of the program. Prior to coming to I.S.U., he was Director of the undergraduate Social Work Program at Tarleton State University. Dr. Baker has conducted research in the areas of psychosocial oncology, sociobehavioral casework, medical interviewing, and scholarly productivity. He is a graduate of the University of Texas at Arlington School of Social Work and the George Warren Brown School of Social Work at Washington University.

John C. Behling, PhD, has been Professor of Social Work and Sociology for the past 26 years. He has been practicing research in a variety of areas in the human services.

Cynthia Brownstein, PhD, is Assistant Professor at the Graduate School of Social Work and Social Research, Bryn Mawr College. Her interests include practice research, professions and mental health policy and research. Current research involves the liaison role and social work practice in the organization.

Caroletta Curtis is Associate Professor in the College of Social Work, Ohio State University. One of her areas of interest is field instruction as it impacts on student growth and development as a potential professional social worker.

Anne E. Fortune, PhD, is a faculty member at Virginia Commonwealth University School of Social Work. She teaches practice, human behavior and research and has been liaison and field instructor.

Sara Ann Foster has practiced for eleven years primarily in child welfare. She has served on the board of the National Association of

Social Workers, the State Professional Standards Committee, the State Personnel Committee, and the State Licensing Committee. She teaches in the College of Social Work at Ohio State University with a special interest in women's issues and health care. She served as a member of the House of Delegates, Council on Social Work Education representing the undergraduate constituency for eight years. She is a member of the Ad Hoc Committee in Columbus, Ohio on planning a series of workshops on Women, Men: Roles in Transition for the local community and the state. She co-authored two articles: Student and Faculty Perception of Women's Content in Social Work Curriculum, published in the *Journal of Education for Social Work* (1979); and *Scarce Resources for Retirement Planning: A Dilemma for Professional Women* published in *Gerontological Social Work* (1983).

Barbara Stemerman Friedlander, MSW, graduated magna cum laude from the State University of New York at Albany with a BA in Sociology. She completed her MSW at Virginia Commonwealth University, graduating with the Community Service and Leadership Award. She is currently Counseling Program Coordinator for Jewish Family and Children's Service of Palm Beach County.

Margaret Schutz Gordon, MSW, is Professor Emerita, School of Social Welfare, University of Kansas, where she served for 13 years as Director of Field Instruction. She previously was Director of Field Instruction at the George Warren Brown School of Social Work, Washington University, St. Louis, where she also taught practice and research. Her practice experience was at Washington University Medical Center, St. Louis. She has presented numerous papers and published on both medical social work and field instruction. Long active in the Old American Association of Medical Social Workers and Medical Social Work Section of the National Association of Social Workers, she served as President of the Kansas Chapter of NASW and on several national committees of that organization. Together with W.E. Gordon, she has long worked at refining and clarifying the practice frame of reference first described in the FIRP Report and they have published and presented papers on this.

William E. Gordon, PhD, is Professor Emeritus of Research at the George Warren Brown School of Social Work, Washington University, St. Louis and Adjunct Professor, School of Social Welfare, the University of Kansas. He was founder and Director of the Doctoral Program at the GWB School of Social Work. In addition to teaching and supervising student research, he focused his work on the development of a scientific basis for social work practice and published articles on that theme in *Social Work* and the *Journal of Education for Social Work* and elsewhere. He is a former Board member of the Council on Social Work Education and 2nd Vice-President of the National Association of Social Workers, and a committee member of both, and frequent presenter at annual meetings. He is the first recipient of the Richard Lodge Prize of the Adelphi University School of Social Work "for his contribution to the development of social work theory for the enhancement of professional practice."

Beverly Hartung Hagen, PhD, is Associate Professor of Social Work at the University of Nebraska at Omaha. She teaches graduate social work methods courses and serves as a liaison to practicum instructors and students. Dr. Hagen has contributed to the human service practice literature on subjects such as working with groups, rural social work and women's issues.

Reva Fine Holtzman, DSW, with the rank of Professor, currently is Educational Director of Field Instruction at the Hunter College School of Social Work, CUNY. Prior to this title, she served since the School's inception in 1956 as the Coordinator of Field Work. She also is the Director of the Center for Field Instruction, a relatively new endeavor being developed to promote the education and training of field instructors who are experienced and who have taken the Seminar for New Field Instructors. Her major role has been in the education and training of field instructors through the seminars for new field staff that are conducted; and has been active in developing and maintaining standards and guidelines for field instruction placements at Hunter as well as for creating and developing innovative field programs. She has presented at many regional and national conferences on field instruction, on such topics as "Evaluation and Assessment of Student Field Performance,"

"Developing Advanced Education and Training for Field Instructors," etc. She also is Project Director of an NIMH Division of Aging grant for an innovative geriatric Alzheimer/Family Caregivers training model in collaboration with the Long Island Jewish Medical Center.

Allie C. Kilpatrick is Associate Professor at the University of Georgia School of Social Work. She has been Director of Field Instruction for the school since 1982. Prior to that she was Director of the Off-Campus Learning Service Center in the Middle Georgia Area where she worked intensively with students and staff in practicum agencies. She is committed to the provision of educational direction for the practicum and has done additional empirical studies on field instruction with John Turner and others.

James P. Love, PhD, is Associate Professor and Director, Office of Field Instruction, with the School of Social Work at Florida State University.

Linda I. May, MSW, ACSW, received her MSW degree from the University of Georgia School of Social Work. Her professional experience includes practice as a social worker in mental health and medical settings, and as an independent consultant. She is an active member of the Georgia chapter of NASW. The research for the article, "Stress of Self-Awareness in Clinical Practice: Are Students Prepared?" was conducted while she was an MSW candidate at the University of Georgia.

Patricia Campbell Ramsey, DSW, is Assistant Professor and Coordinator of Field Instruction at North Carolina Central University, Department of Sociology, Social Work Program, Durham, North Carolina. She has been a faculty member at Meredith College, Raleigh, North Carolina, and the City University of New York, Borough of Manhattan Community College. A native of North Carolina, Dr. Ramsey received a BA from North Carolina Central University, MSW from New York University, DSW from Yeshiva University, Wurzweiler School of Social Work, and a Post-Doctoral Certificate in Rational-Emotion Psychotherapy from the Institute for Advanced Study in Psychotherapy, New York City. She has experience in private practice as a counselor and psychotherapist, social work consultant, trainer, and court expert witness. Her practice experience in public agencies has been in the areas of family and children service, medical and health care, and job training programs. On the local level, she is active on a number of boards such as Operation Breakthrough, YWCA, United Way, and Human Relations Commission.

Miriam S. Raskin, EdD, ACSW, is Associate Professor of Social Work and has been Director of Field Instruction at George Mason University, Fairfax, Virginia for the past 14 years. Her research interests include field instruction, child welfare, and women/family issues. She is active in the community and serves on social service agency boards and county commissions. She received her MSW from the University of Maryland School of Social Work and Community Planning and her EdD from Virginia Polytechnic Institute and State University.

Susan R. Rook, MSW, completed her degree at Virginia Commonwealth University. Her concentration was in the area of mental health. She was previously employed for eight years as a child protective service worker with the Department of Social Services. She is now employed by the Department of Mental Health as a Mental Health Therapist by Southside Community Services Board in Virginia. This is her third year at the Brunswick Mental Health Center, a rural mental health setting located in Lawrencesville, Virginia.

Dina J. Rosenfeld, DSW, is Clinical Associate Professor at New York University School of Social Work. She is Consultant to the Multiple Sclerosis Society and the American Short-Term Therapy Center.

Rita M. Scrimenti, MSW, is presently employed at the Daily Planet, Inc. in Richmond, Virginia. The Daily Planet is a multi-purpose center that provides mental health and social services to chronically mentally ill adults, the homeless, street people, and others in need of survival and support services. She is a program director responsible for the growth and socialization components of the program. Besides providing supervision to staff, she also is a field instructor to students enrolled at Virginia Commonwealth University and Virginia Union University. Students are placed at the agency or in adult homes as part of the agency's outreach project to adult home residents.

Constance Hoenk Shapiro, PhD, ACSW, is currently Associate Professor and Director of the Social Work Program at Cornell University. She served as fieldwork coordinator in the program from 1973-1980 and currently teaches courses in the methods/fieldwork sequence. Dr. Shapiro's research efforts are primarily in the field of human sexuality. In addition to dozens of articles, she is the author of two books: *Adolescent Pregnancy Prevention* and *Infertility Counseling*.

Louise Skolnik, is Assistant Dean for Academic Affairs at the Adelphi University School of Social Work. She formerly served as Director of the School's Social Services Center, a multi-service agency operated by the School which serves as a field placement site for 40 undergraduate and graduate students per year. She has also been Adelphi's Assistant Director of Field Instruction. In 1984-85, as a doctoral intern at the Council on Social Work Education, Professor Skolnik staffed the Council's special project on field instruction.

Susan L. Smith, ACSW, has been Coordinator of Field Instruction in the undergraduate Social Work Program at Illinois State University since 1981. Prior to coming to I.S.U., she taught human behavior and field courses in a social work program at South Carolina State College for seven years. Ms. Smith has conducted research in the areas of child abuse, adoption disruption, interracial relationships, and scholarly productivity of social work faculty. She is a graduate of the University of Tennessee School of Social Work, having practiced in child and family service agencies in Tennessee and Illinois.

Karen M. Sowers-Hoag, PhD, ACSW, is Assistant Professor at the Department of Social Work, Florida International University, N. Miami, Florida. She is currently Coordinator of the undergraduate Social Work Program and Chair of the Research Sequence.

Bruce A. Thyer, PhD, is Associate Professor with the School of Social Work at the University of Georgia. Dr. Thyer was formerly Associate Director of the Office of Field Instruction with the School of Social Work at Florida State University.

Nai-Ming Tsang, BSc, DipSW, MPhil, is Senior Lecturer in the Department of Applied Social Studies, Hong Kong Polytechnic. He has been a fieldwork supervisor for social work students for over ten years. His MPhil thesis is on "Students Perspectives of Field Instruction in Undergraduate Social Work Education in Hong Kong." A paper based on this thesis was presented at the 22nd International Congress, International Association of Schools of Social Work, July-Aug. 1984, Montreal, Canada. He is now a PhD candidate doing research on the application of experiential learning theory an social work education.

Julianne Wayne, MSW, EdD, is Associate Dean of Academic Affairs, Boston University School of Social Work and former Director of the School's Field Education Department. In addition to her interest in supervision, Dr. Wayne is a social group work teacher and consultant and has authored many articles on group work practice. She received her MSW from the Boston University School of Social Work and her EdD from Clark University.

Melvin Williams, PhD, is a recent doctoral graduate of the School of Social Work at Florida State University.

Preface

The importance of field instruction in social work education is axiomatic. Conceptualized early as apprenticeship training, field instruction has matured to take its place as one of the core components in professional social work education at both the undergraduate and graduate levels. Curiously, however, the concept of field instruction as an educational experience, central to the student's understanding of the interface of theory and practice, has not developed as have other components of the curriculum. A number of possible explanations can be offered: lack of understanding of how to systematize experience into academically sophisticated units of study; absence of appropriate methodology to collect and analyze data about learning outcomes and those variables which are critical to them; expectations that the person administering and directing field work would have the time and/or background both to conceptualize field curriculum and to deal concurrently with the complexities of the actual placements; the sheer amount of energy required to place and monitor problems and experiences of large numbers of students, confer with their field instructors, and evaluate agency settings; and the lack of academic recognition and reward of field experience as equivalent in status and rigor to traditional coursework.

Field instruction tends to be viewed as a monolith, undergirded by a number of assumptions culled from practice wisdom about what makes a good professional social worker. While such assumptions may have validity, this perspective tends to obscure the complexity of components that comprise the field experience. Among these are the history of the agency and the school, and the interaction of the two; the politics of agency life and those of student placement; the experience and knowledge of the field instructor, the experience and commitment of the liaison faculty, and the administration of the service agency at any given point in time. Academics

© 1989 by The Haworth Press, Inc. All rights reserved.

have limited understanding of field instructors and what they have to offer. Each of us considers ourselves expert in what students need to be exposed to, what they can handle, and how they should be prepared. We stand our ground in spite of very limited understanding of what makes for the change from a student who is exploring how to practice into a practitioner capable of developing new dimensions of practice. In fact, we don't have a body of knowledge that is backed by solid analysis of hard data.

This is an important volume. It is provocative and controversial in that it challenges a number of assumptions long-held. Indeed, the volume is organized into sections each of which defines as a myth. We have not paid sufficient attention to field work and those faculty and field instructors who are responsible for what happens within it. Yet, students look back upon their field experience as that portion of their education that caused them the most excitement and pleasure, or conversely, the most struggle and pain. Field instructors and liaison faculty are largely without voice, however, and are not speaking well for themselves. The transition from agency apprenticeship to tutorial supervision seems to have developed largely without a guiding conceptual framework and tested theory. It just grew.

Research questions might begin with exploring the purposes of field instruction as an activity that meets the needs of agencies; provides experiential learning of social work content; and/or provides opportunities for students to test out what they have learned. It would be instructive to know, for example, what changes were made to support the shift of model from apprenticeship to tutorial supervision. The articles in this volume begin to pose some critical questions which must be addressed if we are to rely on tested knowledge of what makes for a good learning experience in our profession.

It is particularly important that the need for empirical research in this component of our core curriculum has surfaced at this point in time. Perhaps it is simply that we can no longer ignore it, given the changes that have taken place in human services which directly affect the professional lives of the social work community. I note the number of social workers who find themselves working in settings where other professions are dominant. I note the trend toward increasingly specialized practice with the expectations of in-depth expertise acquired in the two years of graduate education. I note the competition among social workers who are agency-based professionals as compared to private practitioners. I note third party payments and their impact on supervised and independent practice in single or multidisciplinary settings. I note the increased demand for student placements in a single community and the issue of quality control. I note the tension frequently seen between the worlds of practice and education. And I note the significant turnover reported among field instructors and the change of perception about that activity as a natural outgrowth and dimension of professional obligation.

Major thinkers in our profession have raised field instruction as a critical concern and have challenged the social work community to produce empirically-based knowledge about practicum activity. From proposals suggesting that we emulate the medical model of teaching hospitals with students doing residencies upon completion of their academic work, to laboratory classes, to teaching agencies affiliated with universities, the models proliferate.

Basic questions endemic to any model, however, remain to be answered. They include critical turning points in the experiential teaching/learning process, education contract development, students/supervisor matching, differential task learning in curriculum design, and much more. Field and classroom faculty are challenged to focus on the needed research to give us better understanding of what is and is not valid in designs of field instruction that work, and upon which we can rely with some confidence. This volume is an important first step in insisting that attention must be paid in a rigorous and responsible way to this fundamental aspect of social work education.

Eunice O. Shatz, PhD
Executive Director
Council on Social Work Education

Acknowledgments

During the fourteen years that I have been Director of Field Instruction at George Mason University, I have had the opportunity to exchange ideas and experiences, to debate and argue and to participate in research efforts with field instructors, colleagues, students and field instruction directors. Our goal, whether we agreed or disagreed was to enhance both individual and collective knowledge about field instruction. The multitude of ideas generated over the years, and the questions left unanswered have helped motivate me to begin and complete this volume.

The members of the Mid-Atlantic Consortium of Directors and Coordinators of Field Instruction (Nancy Bennett, Ada Williams, Nat Branson, Audrey Sheppard, Dick Christie, Mattie Giles, Barbara White, Eva Stewart, Pearl Moulton, Glenda McNeil, Eloise Bridges) have been a support group for me and for this project. I deeply appreciate their tolerance of my many challenges and my usual desire to engage the group in research no matter what project they would embark upon. They have encouraged me in every way possible, especially in reaffirming in my own mind that field instruction is important and deserves attention.

I am especially proud to be able to publish my first volume with The Haworth Press and to have the support of Carlton E. Munson, Editor of *The Clinical Supervisor*. This volume could not have become a reality without his own strong commitment to social work education, supervision and field instruction as well as his understanding of the need, by the profession, for empirical studies in field instruction.

I am sure that Mary Blackwell, Coordinator, Office Support Services, and her staff will be sad not to see me at her door week after week with chapter corrections and more chapter drafts. They have been extremely cooperative and helpful in typing the manuscript and have made meeting my deadlines possible. A special thanks to

© 1989 by The Haworth Press, Inc. All rights reserved.

Susan Pufnock, secretary to the department of Social Work who assisted in the completion of the manuscript, kept track of the many details necessary in an edited volume and who assures me that someday I'll be famous. It won't happen without you, Susan!

In a dual career family, members need to be skilled in cooperation, empathy, patience and negotiation. I am grateful to my family for displaying these skills at their highest level during my work on this project. I especially want to thank my husband, Ira, for his strong personal support, and his expert assistance in the technical preparation of the manuscript. His willingness to discuss stumbling blocks in the project, to provide sound alternatives, and most importantly, his commitment to my professional work was and is most appreciated.

Others have helped me reach the goal of publishing this volume (Jack, Jirina, Robenia, Ralph). I am endebted to those who contributed to my personal and professional growth and who share my vision about field instruction.

Miriam S. Raskin

Introduction

Miriam S. Raskin

Every profession has to step back once in a while to assess its state-of-the-art: where it's been, where it is, and where it is headed in the future. This periodic assessment provides opportunity for the profession to reflect upon its accomplishments, to review its activities and "practice-wisdom," and to open new avenues for refinement and growth. Study of a profession's state-of-the-art tests commonly-held beliefs that previously have not been questioned or challenged.

The first part of this volume looks at the state-of-the-art of one segment of social work education—field instruction. One purpose of this volume is to question some of the professional mythology that exists in field instruction. Much of the activity and thinking in field instruction has withstood the test of time. The thesis of this book, however, is that some field practices may not be able to survive critical and systematic evaluation.

Schools of social work have been placing students in fieldwork agencies for almost a century. Despite great strides made in providing learning experiences for students, relatively little is *empirically* known about placement models, learning outcomes, and the nature of the relationship among school, agency, student, field instructor, field liaison, community, and clients. A profession often builds its knowledge base through trial and error, "think pieces," descriptive and exploratory studies, and carefully designed empirical inquiry. The social work curriculum has evolved through such a process. A sizable literature and a group of recognized "experts" have been produced. The principal exception to this maturation process is field instruction.

The profession can point to "classic" works by Towle (1954), Bisno (1959), Boehm (1959), and Simon (1972). These authors

© 1989 by The Haworth Press, Inc. All rights reserved. *1*

made significant contributions to the understanding of field instruction and the state-of-the-art. Sheafor and Jenkins (1982) develop and build on previous ideas, primarily through narrative and discussion. The profession is not totally devoid of research studies. Few have been published, however, and these often provide findings based on the experience of a single school. Other work has remained in-house, presented at conferences, or comprised of lengthy dissertations.

Some attention in the literature has been given to staff supervision in social work. Major works by Munson (1979) and Kadushin (1976), however, do not deal with student supervision. There are some similar elements in supervising staff and students, but distinctions exist and data about the supervision of students are lacking. Wilson (1981) and Shulman (1983) wrote "how to" books. Since one component of field instruction involves "doing," books that instruct on the "doing" are very useful. These books, however, continue the existing trend of providing the field with "practice-wisdom" and, therefore, remain limited in expanding the knowledge base. How do we know that the techniques or methods and goals suggested in the literature work in practice? There has been no volume to date that sorts and synthesizes empirical research and that attempts to critique tradition in field instruction. This volume will help to address this gap in the literature.

Anderson (1979) and Roberts (1973) note that students view field instruction as the most important course in the curriculum. Yet, it is an area which has received limited attention in the professional journals. Can a profession arrive at judgments about placement decisions, student and field instructor satisfaction, and learning outcomes without the analytical work necessary to proceed beyond intuition? Social work has reached these decisions but primarily through decision rules that, while conceptually appealing, often are without empirical foundation.

If we begin to examine "what is," and to pose relevant questions or hypotheses to test if "what is" "really is," then we can begin to develop empirically-based models of field instruction. Why test something that seems to be working? Students attend school, are assigned a field placement, graduate, and become social workers and field instructors who train new students. This is a familiar scenario. Why disturb the status quo if all seems well? Agencies and university administrators insist that programs utilize time and other resources in a cost-effective manner. Field directors bemoan the high turnover rate for field instructors, generally one-third to one-half each year. This is costly for everyone involved. An enormous amount of time is expended to recruit and train new field instructors. Would analysis of the reasons for turnover/burnout of field instructors, and then taking constructive action, be a more efficient use of resources for all concerned?

In the early days of social work, schools were run primarily by social agencies where emphasis was placed on field experience. "Formal education for social work at first adhered closely to the needs of voluntary agencies and differed little from the concept and content of apprenticeship training" (Rothman, 1966, p. 1). As the number of volunteers used by social agencies grew, it became necessary to train them. An individualized tutorial approach to supervision emerged and has become the predominant model for the profession (Watson, 1973). In his study of this particular phase of social work education, Engle (1977) observes:

> The "master" controlled the activities of the "apprentice" and passed on his practice wisdom. As more volunteers became paid workers and gained experience, they, too, became masters supervising new, less experienced volunteers, thus perpetuating this system of supervision. (p. 3)

As social work became more diversified in practice settings, a different approach to field learning began to evolve. A shift from the apprenticeship model to an educational activity model occurred. This model was based primarily on the work of John Dewey (1938) and his principle of "learning through doing." As the number of undergraduate programs proliferated, field instruction moved beyond the goals of the 1930s. The focus became student-centered and differed from apprenticeship training where the apprentice learned to give specific service in a specific way and in a specific agency (Simon, 1972). Although approaches and emphasis in field instruction changed over time, the importance of the student-supervisor relationship has remained the key element for personal growth and learning.

The need for training of field instructors was recognized by Bertha Reynolds in the 1940s. Training of field instructors seems to be an almost universal practice today by the schools of social work, but the amount and type of training vary widely. The accepted practice of training field instructors, however, has yet to show what relationship training has with student performance, skills, knowledge, or teaching ability. Some schools report that they hold a one-day session, while others require once a week attendance for 10-14 weeks in a training course. Since the training of field instructors is part of a developing field instruction model, the effect of the training (if any) on specified field work outcomes must be demonstrated. Such empirical work has not been reported, although the majority of graduate and undergraduate programs have curriculum to train field instructors.

During the early years of the profession, the majority of schools used concurrent placements. Smith College first offered a block placement to provide opportunity for students who attended a school that was geographically isolated. Block placements are currently used routinely in the majority of both MSW and BSW programs that are not geographically isolated. Questions regarding the utilization of the block versus the concurrent placement have not been empirically resolved. Placements of one type or the other are based on convenience or administrative decree. Ramsey (Part II) presents one of the few studies which indicates that there is a difference in students' practice orientation based on the type of field placement.

Constructive challenges to the present state of affairs will help to develop the knowledge base of field instruction. The objective of this volume is not to develop carbon copies of field instruction programs in each school. It is intended to stimulate dialogue, to encourage further research, and to make changes in the system based on empirical analysis rather than on guesswork. The breadth of the areas to be covered remains relatively narrow. Although this is a shortcoming, it does provide a good illustration of what we know empirically at this point in time. Each of the four major sections of the volume will focus on both primary and secondary "myths."

When some customary practices are in conflict with the results of empirical research, a strong profession encourages the review of the status quo and supports continued knowledge development. This does not imply that all traditions are bad, or that everything that has been accomplished in field instruction must be thrown out or dismissed as irrelevant. Before the profession is ready to exchange or accept new principles in field instruction, some cautions are necessary:

1. Research questions must be well constructed and be grounded in theory;
2. Research designs need to be adequate and capable of being replicated;
3. Results should be carefully drawn to avoid creating a new mythology based on less than scientifically-valid conclusions; and
4. Without internal and external validity, study findings may be no better than mythology based on long-term and untested intuition.

At this juncture in the pursuit of knowledge about field instruction, findings and recommendations can only be tentative.

This volume is intended for undergraduate and graduate classroom instructors, students, faculty field liaison personnel, field instructors, researchers, and directors of field education. Doctoral students interested in field instruction can build on the available research and carry out replication studies. The volume also can be used as a primary or supplemental text in field instruction seminars where field issues such as supervision, satisfaction, stress, and burn-out are areas of exploration.

The volume is divided into four parts and includes a bibliography. Each part is summarized in a separate introduction. Each chapter either was previously published or was selected from papers submitted in response to a "Call for Papers" in the spring of 1984.

Part I, "The State of the Art in Field Instruction: A Century of Progress?" addresses two myths. The first is whether preparing students prior to entering field placement makes a difference in outcome; the second is a broader issue that emerges from three of the papers that assess progress in field instruction. This myth is the belief that there is an agreed upon empirical base for the activities carried out in field instruction. The papers in Part I recognize that allowances must be made for individual school objectives and needs of the community. However, systematic research can help to address many common problems and issues that confront each school.

Part II, "The Field Placement Process: In Search of the Perfect Placement," brings to the forefront questions about "the matching process," the impact of sex-role combinations in field instruction, and the view that the student's practice orientation is influenced by the type of field instruction (block or concurrent, or a combination).

Part III, "Field Instructors: Myths and Challenges," includes papers whose authors begin to question the requirement of the MSW degree for social work field instructors. There also is some focus on the turnover rates and burn-out of field instructors. It is shown that providing fringe benefits such as library privileges or tickets to school athletic events may be a nice gesture, but it has no significant impact on whether a field instructor will continue to participate in a school's field instruction program.

Part IV, "Stress, Satisfaction, and Success in Field Placement," looks at the student as a participant in the field instruction process. What do we know about this group and how important to satisfaction and performance are the field instructor, the student's age, sex, work experience, and grades? Part IV considers the myth that these and other factors make a great deal of difference.

What would happen to student outcome if we changed how we carry out field instruction? If no significant differences are found, traditions can prevail. If empirical research demonstrates that some aspects of the educational process adversely affect outcomes, changes will be needed. It is incumbent upon us as a profession to respond to the pressures for greater economy and performance being imposed on both schools and agencies. The response requires the ability and responsibility to ask difficult questions, and pursuit of the answers requires creative, sound research efforts.

Although my comments and some of the articles may seem critical, it is out of commitment to students, the profession, and to the clients we serve that the various issues are being raised. I view this volume as very positive for the profession because it provides for new possibilities for research endeavors. New field directors who often come to the position with little background or experience can use it as a starting point and for reference. This volume provides a message to other professions and the community at large that we want students to have the best possible field experience, that we are willing to make the necessary changes to train top-rated social workers, and that we are capable of doing cross-cultural and international studies which enhance the knowledge of each country. Other positive aspects of the material in this volume will be gleaned by the individual readers. It is hoped that the collective benefits and strengths of this contribution to the literature on field placement outweigh the deficiencies that merit resolution.

REFERENCES

Anderson, W.A. (February 1979). *Education for employment: BSW graduates' work experience and the undergraduate curriculum*. Paper presented at the annual program meeting, Council on Social Work Education. Boston.

Bisno, H. (1959). *The place of the undergraduate curriculum in social work education*. New York: Council on Social Work Education.

Boehm, W. (1959). *Objectives of the social work curriculum of the future*. New York: Council on Social Work Education.

Dewey, J. (1938). *Experience in education*. New York: MacMillan.

Engle, P.R. (1977). *Supervision of the baccalaureate social worker*. New York: University of Syracuse School of Social Work.

Kadushin, A. (1976). *Supervision in social work*. New York: Columbia University Press.

Munson, C.E. (1979). *Social work supervision, classic statements and critical issues*. New York: Free Press.

Roberts, R.W. (1973). An interim report on the development of an undergraduate, graduate continuum of social work education in a private university. *Journal of Education for Social Work*, 9(3), 58-64.

Rothman, J. (1966). Working paper on field instruction in community organization. *Community organization curriculum development project*. New York: Council on Social Work Education.

Sheafor, B.W., & Jenkins, L.E. (1982). *Quality field instruction in social work program development and maintenance*. New York: Longman.

Shulman, L. (1983). *Teaching the helping skills a field instructors guide*. Illinois: Peacock.

Simon, B.K. (1959). Field instruction as education for practice: Purposes and goals. In K. Wenzel (Ed.). *Undergraduate field instruction programs: current issues and predictions*. New York: Council on Social Work Education.

Towle, C. (1954). *The learner in education for the professions as seen in social work education for social work*. Chicago: University of Chicago Press.

Watson, K.W. (1973). Differential supervision. *Social Work, 18*, 80-88.

Wilson, S.J. (1981). *Field instruction techniques for supervisors*. New York: Free Press.

PART I:
THE STATE OF THE ART
IN FIELD INSTRUCTION:
A CENTURY OF PROGRESS?

Introduction

The four articles in Part I explore the state of the art in field instruction. The research methodologies in these studies include an experimental, single school, study design; the Delphi Technique; a national survey; and a comparative study of the results of U.S. and Canadian national surveys of field instruction.

William E. Gordon and Margaret Schutz Gordon co-authored one of the earliest monographs describing an empirical study of field instruction. The original *Field Instruction Project* was partially funded by the National Institute of Mental Health and conducted at Washington University, St. Louis, Missouri. The authors set up experimental and control groups consisting of students entering field placement. The purpose of the study was to determine if "traditional" field instruction (students begin practicum immediately upon entering graduate school) or "experimental" field instruction (delayed entry into the field for a certain period of time) turned out better products. The results led the authors to a radical recommendation: field instruction should be taken out of the educational institutions and placed in the hands of agency teaching centers, similar to the intern system utilized for physicians.

© 1989 by The Haworth Press, Inc. All rights reserved.

After twenty years of research, teaching, and practice experience, Gordon and Gordon reflect on their original conclusion in their article, "George Warren Brown's Field Instruction Research Project: An Experimental Design Tested by Empirical Data," and reaffirm their position. For the variables used in their study, they found no significant differences in outcome in the control and experimental groups. Although Gordon and Gordon found no significant differences between the two groups, laboratory classes mushroomed in our educational programs and reports of successful laboratory classes appeared in the literature. Generally students were tested at the beginning of the training and again before the training ended. Scores seemed to rise, videotapes seemed much improved, and educators seemed convinced that students acquired the necessary basic skills needed to perform in the field. Intuitively, and based on limited single school studies, something seemed to be changing in students' abilities while in the classroom laboratory.

While more schools developed laboratory training during the 1970s, there was no evidence to show that the skills learned in the classroom were being transferred to, or used in, the field. The quantum leap from the classroom to the field was taken even though there was little or no empirical evidence to support such a notion. The "myth" that students who have the laboratory experience are better prepared for field work became entrenched (contrary to the findings of Gordon and Gordon).

In 1982, Collins and Bogo *(Competency Based Field Instruction: Bridging the Gap Between Laboratory and Field Learning)* began with the premise that laboratory training has been effective in training students in interpersonal interviewing skills. The authors challenge the assumption that once skills were performed in the classroom, they were transferred to the field placement. They specifically looked at empathy, warmth, and genuineness. The results "indicate a lack of support for transfer of skill from the laboratory to the field with an actual client." In fact, students in the first year MSW program that participated in this study seemed to regress to behaviors that were indicative of pre-laboratory training. (This phenomenon also was found by Gordon and Gordon.)

In order to develop a cost- and time-effective field instruction model, the right questions must be asked, adequate research design

used, and studies replicated. Is laboratory training useless for preparation for skill transfer to the field? Should laboratory work be
modified in order to achieve the goals for which such classes are
designed? Should the training in skills be taken out of the classroom
and taught by the practitioners in the field? Collins and Bogo state
that the field instructor plays a key role in enhancing the transfer of
skills from the laboratory to the field. Their recommendations, including a competency-based model of instruction, outlines a mini
laboratory for the field instructor to carry out with the student.

Raskin's article, "A Delphi Study in Field Instruction: Identification of Issues and Research Priorities by Experts," asked "experts" to arrive at a consensus about various ongoing and unresolved field instruction issues, and to develop a prioritized research
agenda for field instruction. The experts were to describe the state
of the art and to suggest new empirical studies in field instruction.

The task of identifying experts through a random sample of undergraduate and graduate field directors was a formidable project. It
was assumed that directors of field instruction would be up-to-date
on the relevant literature and, therefore, be able to identify experts.
The respondents developed a list with a total of 201 names of experts. Experts often were identified by directors of field instruction
as members of their own faculty who were assigned field liaison
duties. Only sixteen (16) of the 201 names on the list received more
than one vote identifying the person as an expert on the subject of
field instruction.

The areas that the experts identified as the most critical in terms
of needed research also were selected by a national sample of
American and Canadian field directors and field instructors in the
studies reported by Skolnik, and by Wayne, Skolnik, and Raskin.
Researchers and educators are able to describe how things are and
what we need to know. The pursuit of this knowledge, however,
requires further motivation.

The third paper focuses on an indepth review of the state of the
art of field instruction within social work education programs. The
review was sponsored by the Council on Social Work Education
(CSWE) and a Technical Assistance Group on Field Instruction.
The high response rate of the study, entitled "Field Instruction in
the 1980s — Realities, Issues and Problem-Solving Strategies,"

sheds light on the realities of field instruction and problem-solving strategies. The readers will not be surprised that the issues, problems, and concerns first identified in the descriptive literature of the 1940s through the 1960s continue to be strongly identified in the present volume as still being unresolved. Louise Skolnik presents extensive results and analysis of this CSWE-sponsored study.

Part I concludes with a study by Wayne, Skolnik, and Raskin, that compares the results of the national study carried out by CSWE with similar research sponsored by the Canadian Association of Schools of Social Work. The results in each country were strikingly similar. The following needs were identified in each country: clearer standards from the national organizations; field instructor training; preparation of students to enter the field; differentiation of tasks of undergraduate and graduate students; and integration of class and field.

The four articles in Part I highlight the urgent need to upgrade the status of those engaged in field education and to encourage the scholarly work of those who want to test the "practice wisdom." The profession needs to become invested in field education research, to encourage inquiry beyond its current emersion in the study of core curriculum such as Social Policy, Human Behavior in the Social Environment, and Methods of Social Work Intervention.

Experts identify the following questions that are worthy of research: How do we know that competencies (objectives) are achieved by students in field instruction? How do we differentiate learning tasks for undergraduates, first year, and second year students? What learning assignments are related to an effective professional learning experience? How does the learning experience in field education contribute to difference in curriculum content and skill level of different students? How does planning for field education fit into the overall education and curriculum planning process?

How can the answers to some of these questions contribute to resolving the concerns of field directors and field instructors surveyed both in the U.S. and Canada? Can a practice laboratory class with early field experience on the undergraduate level, and a 2-3 week intensive field preparation mini course for first year graduate students, address the concern of field instructors that students aren't as prepared for the field as they should be? Further empirical work is needed to aid in curriculum planning.

The articles utilize different research methods to explore the state of the art and the progress made in field instruction. Has it been a century of progress? It has been one of relatively limited sophistication in scientific enquiry. The essays that follow begin the arduous task of confronting long held traditions in field instruction.

George Warren Brown's Field Instruction Research Project: An Experimental Design Tested by Empirical Data

William E. Gordon
Margaret Schutz Gordon

ABSTRACT. An experiment to determine whether two different field instruction arrangements made a difference in student outcomes involved thirty-one matched pairs of students followed through their two years of study leading to the MSW degree. The study required substantial elaborate conceptualizations. The investigators felt that these conceptualizations and the answers to several subsidiary questions were more important than the overall major conclusion that the two forms of field instruction did not seem to make any significant difference in student outcomes. A learning frame of reference, a practice frame of reference, and numerous measurements of student learning in class and field were developed in the study.

INTRODUCTION

The purpose of the Field Instruction Research Project, which took place at the George Warren Brown School of Social Work from 1963-1968, was to determine if two different arrangements of field instruction were associated with differences in outcomes of student learning.[1] The two arrangements were: (1) the *traditional* with early case assignment, full professional responsibility, and individual student-field instructor supervision; and (2) the *experimental* with delayed case assignment while students were taught specific knowledge thought to be needed for application to practice. The experimental plan, which primarily used group supervision,

© 1989 by The Haworth Press, Inc. All rights reserved.

also provided broadened field experiences designed to reflect the whole curriculum. It was assumed that practice guided by knowledge and values was a goal to be sought in all social work education, an assumption probably not uniformly held in the profession.

The results of the study were based on data obtained from a sample of incoming first-year graduate students, starting with fourteen matched pairs each year (about one-fourth of the first-year class). After allowing for withdrawals and delays, the study analyzed a total of thirty-one matched pairs (62 subjects) who received their MSW degrees in 1966, 1967, and 1968. Variables on which students were matched were sex, age, social work experience, undergraduate GPA, and scores on the Terman Concept Mastery Test. All students were placed in one of four faculty field units, with one of each pair of students randomly assigned to one of the two experimental units and the other to the traditional or control units. Project staff included four experienced field instructors, two co-directors, a research associate, a project supervisor for the four field units, and a secretary.

EXPERIMENTAL CONDITIONS

There were six experimental conditions in the Project. First, full service case assignments were delayed anywhere from eight weeks to a full semester after the start of field instruction. This allowed students the time necessary to acquire some specific knowledge and understanding before taking responsibility for professional action — it was intended that expectations for service should not exceed the student's knowledge base at that time. (The maximum prior social work experience of any student in the Project was only six months.) Second, carefully planned field assignments were provided during this delay. These assignments helped to make very explicit the social work practice frame of reference developed in the Project. Most of these early assignments were in written form and required the specification of learning objectives.

Third, the breadth of field situations and learning experiences was stressed, ensuring the students' exposure to people of many different ages and living situations, various coping capacities and patterns, and being impinged upon by many different kinds of environmental outputs. Students had extensive opportunity to learn about the community and environment in which their clients lived and worked. In the two experimental units, students operated out of a homebase agency from which most of their later case assignments were made, but they had a great number of early assignments in other agencies and in the community at large. In this early period, much use was made of focused observation and contrast. For example, students in the experimental units had one assignment to observe and to interact (in a limited manner) with mothers in two newborn nurseries that were located, respectively, at a public hospital which served low-income patients and a large private medical center. The stated learning objectives were to understand the influence of developmental levels on coping capacities and behaviors; to recognize the need for a very structured environment to protect newborns; to note beginning differentiation of coping patterns; and to observe environmental impact even at this early age. Another example involved observation at both a suburban and inner-city day nursery. The objective was to gain further understanding of the effect on coping behaviors of the various age levels, in different types of nurseries, including the impact of the teachers' coping and the kind of feedback to the children this entailed.

Fourth, the peer group seminar with field instructor remained the major teaching and learning tool throughout, although individual conferences with students also were used once full case assignments were made, and prior to that, if a student or field instructor felt the need. There was generally a seminar after each of the early assignments, and at least a weekly group meeting was held throughout the year.

Fifth, evaluation of each assignment, except cases, was required from each student and instructor. A written report was made by the instructor, but often the student evaluation was done in the group seminar.

The sixth experimental condition required emphasis on student acquisition of some fundamental knowledge about people and how they behave. This included explanations of behavior, knowledge about the environment in which people were expected to develop, and the difficulties of that development. There was less emphasis on enhancing the specific skills of the student or imparting any particular intervention techniques. Some of these, however, were taught and learned.

Although the control units were always operating from the same practice frame of reference as the experimental units, no special assignments were given to the control units to *seat in* any aspects of it. Instead, the practice frame of reference was taught as appropriate in the unfolding of regular case assignments. While some group supervisory sessions were held in all control units, the major teaching and learning tool remained the weekly student and field instructor conference. Work with groups was introduced to all Project students in the last year of the Project, at the same time all second-year students in the School of Social Work were expected to begin group work activity.

THEORETICAL CONSIDERATIONS

Emphasis in the Project was on outcomes for students, not on the almost innumerable explanatory variables thought to influence the outcomes. Empirical analysis of outcomes required the development of measurement instruments. This, in turn, necessitated a great deal of conceptualization about such measurement and led to a number of subsidiary formulations which, in some instances, seemed more important than the overall conclusions about the effect of the two arrangements of field instruction on outcome.

In order to be relevant to the purpose of the study, empirical studies must not only clearly identify the purpose, but must be cast in a conceptual framework that guides the selection of the data and gives a rationale for interpreting them. It became clear very early in the Project that, in order to test for what students know and can do, it was essential to have some formulation of how students learn and of the practice toward which the learning was directed.

In the formulation developed in the Project for how students learn, the use of conceptual knowledge was thought of as involving three related steps in learning that would require data in order to be tested. These three steps were: *knowing, understanding,* and *doing.* The first step, *knowing,* referred to the cognitive grasp of knowledge revealed by the student's ability to discriminate and manipulate concepts and generalizations, the units of knowledge. Similarly, *understanding* was thought of as the application of a cognitive mapping system (knowing) to instances where reality is confronted, to make sense of that confronting reality, and, thus, to provide a basis for action or *doing*. The final stage, *doing*, was thought of as the stage in which the behaviors of the students were guided by the end-product of knowing and understanding. It should be noted that these three steps involved three different neurological bases (i.e., knowing involved the cognitive, understanding involved the cognitive and the perceptual, and doing involved the motor system which was then correlated or guided by the understanding). Each of these three steps required the development of instruments to collect data and the actual collection of data in order to make empirical comparisons that were relevant to the study's purpose.[2]

The practice formulation developed for the Project is briefly stated as follows in the original Report:

> The frame (of reference for practice) was centered and primarily focused where person and environment make direct and active contact, at the interface between people and whatever they confront in living their lives moment by moment, hour by hour, and day by day. This was called the *transaction* field through which people obtain what they need from their surrounding environment and make their contribution to that environment. The action field is created by the individual's *coping* activity on the one hand, and the activity of the *impinging environment* on the other. The resulting mix of activity in the transaction field varies with the *coping patterns* of the people and the *qualities of the impinging environment*. Where the coping patterns and the qualities of the impinging environment do not match, the transfer between person and environment is impeded or is inimical to both in terms of the environment being rendered more recalcitrant to yielding what that or other individuals need. Where the match is *adequate*, there is the necessary transfer, resulting in a *growth-enhancing outcome* for the individuals and an *amelioration of the environment*. (Gordon & Schutz, 1969, p. 32)

DATA COLLECTION INSTRUMENTS
AND RELATED CONCLUSIONS

With the development of these formulations, the staff was then ready to consider ways of making the measurements necessary for an empirical approach to the study. Knowing Test I, designed to test the students' mastery of specific knowledge, was based on concepts and generalizations which the Research Associate selected.[3] Since it was believed that the major pieces of knowledge used in the field were presented in the classroom, the Research Associate selected these by attending first-year classes, reading many of the books and articles on the reading lists, keeping a log, and then verifying his selection of major concepts with the classroom instructors. After the identification of a sample of concepts and generalizations that were thought to be stressed in the classroom and important for use in the field, and representative of essential *knowing*, the task was then to measure the extent to which students actually knew these concepts. This was the basis for collecting empirical data.

The Research Associate selected the mastery of the concepts and generalizations, including the students' ability to see the essential relationships between the component attributes of these concepts and generalizations, as the underlying principle for measurement. The test took the form of True-False or matching questions with which students were familiar. He also added the variable of *certainty* in their knowledge — the extent to which students were confident about the answers they were making, whether they were guessing, or did not know the answer. Other variations were tried to measure the extent to which the students knew the concepts that had been identified. The process proved to be very formidable because of the difficulty in identifying the significant concepts and generalizations with a minimum of overlapping.

Despite all the effort, the conclusions from Knowing Test I proved disappointing. The Research Associate concluded that an "overall test of relationship between the different field groups and changes in students' mastery of classroom knowledge proved not to be significant" (Gordon & Schutz, 1969, p. 87). He further observed that, "Within the limits and the scope and method of this study, the general hypothesis of concern that variations in the structure of field learning differentially affect changes in the students' mastery of classroom knowledge *(knowing)* has received relatively little support'' (Gordon & Schutz, 1969, p. 88).

With respect to the degree of certainty with which students knew, there were two conclusions to be drawn from the data: students developed their own sense of certainty about what they knew more rapidly than their actual mastery of concepts, and there was very little relationship between correctness of the answer and the certainty of the students' knowledge — both conclusions that were neither expected nor desired![4]

For a number of reasons, Knowing Test I proved inadequate. These reasons were: that much uncertainty developed about whether the concepts and generalizations selected from classes for Knowing Test I were those most needed for students to practice in the field; rapid changes in classroom content reduced the hoped-for connection to the field; and, most importantly, it became clear that the most necessary knowledge to be taught students for use in the field would have to be taught by the field instructors, and not by classroom instructors as had been originally thought. Knowing Test II was therefore developed to supplement Knowing Test I.

Knowing Test II attempted to get at the students' grasp of words, the medium in which knowledge is couched, both for communication and use in thinking. How precise was their grasp of the meaning of words, to what extent did students get beyond the word to what it substantively denoted, and to what extent were students able to develop a sense that what was denoted by the word was out there (reified)? It was assumed that unless students could develop a sense that what they were dealing with was *reality-based*, they could not very well base their thinking and their actions on the concepts and generalizations being taught since one behaves toward reality in the way that is consistent with what one thinks reality is. Precision of meaning was tested by having students select matched pairs of words (e.g., was *coping* more clearly associated with *struggle* than with *success?*). Extension beyond the word to what it denoted was similarly tested by word matching, the correct word being one that reflected a quality of what was denoted, not just a synonym for the word. For example, when presented with the word, *transacting,* and asked to choose the one word that best captured the core idea, students were expected to select *exchanging* over *behaving* or *interacting*. Reification was measured by the students' judgment about the extent of their *feeling* that what was denoted was really out there.

After many statistical comparisons on Knowing Test II as a whole and its various parts, the following conclusions emerged:

> As far as detecting any differences between experimental and control we did not. Since the samples were small and the reliability of the tests limited, there is nothing more to be said than that the effect of experimental field instruction on these variables was non-existent or relatively small. (Gordon & Schutz, 1969, p. 106)

Despite this overall conclusion, the Knowing Test II approach considerably sharpened concern about some important questions which the Project, up to this point, had only impressions to go on. While all of the Knowing Test II variables may need more development, even their original form suggested limited learning at the concept level during the first year of graduate social work education, and little development of, and sometimes even regression in, practice learning. This leads to a larger question — are we bringing about any substantial learning of ideas during the first year of graduate social work education, or is it more a loose and imprecise sort of *word learning* that can enlarge students' ways of talking about what they are doing but scarcely serve to guide what they are doing? Are we initially getting students who are more responsive to words than to meanings and ideas, and practically not helping them at all to distinguish between words, ideas, and the instances of reality to which they might be applied? Is this related to the offering of such a volume of lightly and imprecisely developed concepts that students are encouraged to engage in superficial and imprecise thinking, and generally have little respect for knowledge as a factor in professional practice?

It was not possible to develop a test to measure extent of *understanding* because both class and field instructors could not clearly separate understanding from knowing and doing. Understanding seemed to them to be a part of both, but not distinct. Thus, it would be expected that instructors would pay less attention to helping students make a distinction between rationalization after taking action from rationale prior to the action. Since instructors did not see understanding as a separate entity from knowing and doing, it would also be expected that they could not teach the application of concepts which they did not themselves know.

Since *doing* was one of the three steps in learning originally identified in the Project's framework, and it is the essence of field instruction, it was necessary to develop an instrument to measure and compare how well the students were doing in the two field instruction arrangements. The test was based on behaviors that field instructors considered essential for students to master in practice and to qualify for the second year of graduate education. Each behavior encompassed a number of actions. Doing was measured by grading student performance in field instruction, judged by field instructors on a list of thirty-three behaviors encompassed in facilitating transactions between client and environment. Examples of the behaviors were: initiating, involving, explaining, and differentiating. Each behavior was related to the transactional-coping frame of reference for practice which was developed in the Project and stressed heavily in the teaching of all Project field units. Each behavior was defined by actions of the student that explained the behavior. A sample of two items from the Doing Test (see Table 1) may help to clarify (Gordon & Schutz, 1969, App. D, pp. 1 & 3).

The test results were extensively analyzed and failed to show definitively that there was any statistically significant difference in the average Doing scores obtained by the experimental and control groups — the effects of the experimental field instruction on the variables measured in the Doing Test were essentially nonexistent. However, some secondary findings seemed to be more definitive and, perhaps, more valuable. Factor analysis of the data revealed two major variables, one associated with the student and the other with the combination of student and field instructor. With respect to the student variable, it would appear that field instructors made one overall judgment of a student's field performance and all individual items of Doing were judged accordingly, as revealed by their high intercorrelation. An attempt to build up a single judgment of a student's performance by combining scores on individual items would appear to be nonproductive.

TABLE 1

RESPONSIVE BEHAVIOR	TRANSACTIONAL-COPING FRAME OF REFERENCE IN A NUTSHELL	ACTIONS	RATING	COMMENTS
Preparing	Behavior directed toward increasing readiness to meet with expected or assumed coping demands through anticipatory action	reading about, studying for, reviewing, discussing beforehand, thinking about		
Focusing	Within the differentiated transactional field, behavior that selects out and centers upon particular aspects of the field as the object(s) of coping efforts	narrowing down, converging upon, limiting to, bounding		

The strength of the student-field instructor combination is revealed by the relatively high correlation between the assessment of student performance for the first and second semesters, when the same field instructor is usually involved, and between assessment of performance for the third and fourth semesters, when again the same field instructor is usually involved. But the correlation is greatly diminished between the second and third semesters, when there is almost always a change in field instructor. The data strongly suggest that the two most important variables in how field performance is judged are (1) a pervasive variable in the student which seems to make all of his/her field behavior equally good or not so good, and (2) the field instructor to whom a student happened to be assigned.

Students continuing in school and entering the profession are dependent upon these judgments by the instructor. The school takes responsibility for these judgments but has relatively little control over them once a field instructor has been accepted. Students have apparently been aware for some time of their vulnerability, indicated by their only half-facetious remarks about their being *right* with their field instructors, and their more serious demands for a procedure to appeal an adverse field grade.

The solution to both the educational and research problems is a standardized evaluation procedure that is more objectively administered. It cannot be predicted at this time whether the definition of social work practice will ever stabilize enough in the profession to warrant the considerable investment required to develop such an instrument. In the absence of some progress in this direction, there is danger of students tending to treat social work education more and more as an initiation rite into the profession, subject to negotiation and adversary proceedings rather than as educational preparation for practice.

FINAL CONCLUSIONS AND RECOMMENDATIONS

This study began with a focus on what at first appeared to be a simple question, namely, what are the educational merits of one arrangement of field instruction compared to another? The study revealed that this apparently simple question could not be answered simply. In general, there seemed to be no essential difference in educational outcomes related to these two different field arrangements. But, in arriving at this answer, a number of significant subsidiary questions arose that were probably more important than the original question. Answers to these subsidiary questions lead to what may seem to many like a rather startling overall conclusion, as presented in the following statement from the original Report:

> We complete . . . our experiment with the conclusion that field instruction, while an essential component of graduate education for social work, should be focused completely and explicitly on solidly building in the *fundamentals for practice*, and that field experience directed toward actually *practicing* the student should be removed from the schools and placed under an instrumentality of the practicing profession. We are not unmindful of the unwelcome demands this proposal places on schools and the practicing profession. Schools would need to come to real grips with what they regard as the essential fundamentals for practice, how best to teach them, and more reliably and responsibly certify the level of the student's educational preparation. Schools might also have to face the fact that they may well be able to teach all they have to teach well in less than two years. The practicing profession must develop some means of picking up its proper responsibility to accredit agencies and training centers as suitable places for internship and in developing the means and the safeguards for final certification of level of competence justifying full entry into the profession.
>
> The net effect, we believe, may well retrieve social work education from its present tendency to abdicate its responsibility to educate for an identifiable profession, and the practicing profession's tendency to abdicate to the schools total responsibility for educating and certifying incoming members. Beyond this, we believe our proposal will result in a salutary redistribution of power over entry into the profession that will spur schools to teach better, agencies to practice better, and students to study better. Students now clamoring for a greater voice in where they will be placed in field instruction can be freed completely to negotiate with agencies for their internship

and will compete with each other in terms of the academic credentials they earn in preparation for practice. Agencies wishing a larger voice in what students are assigned to them by the schools will be freed to compete for interns on the basis of the level of practice they maintain and the quality of the internship they offer. The school, no longer the sole certifier of the quality of its own educational preparation, would become properly accountable to both students and profession in having the efficacy of its educational program evaluated where it should be — how well it has prepared a student in the fundamentals required to become a professional practitioner. This, we submit, is the pattern of the future. Who moves in this direction and how fast, we must leave to those with the wisdom and the privilege to effect the changes we envision. (Gordon & Schutz, 1969, p. 155[5])

In this proposed plan, there would definitely be field instruction, but it would be planned totally to help the students learn what they needed *for* practice. The design and structure of the learning experiences would be very much tailored to enhance the knowledge, the understanding, and the essential, fundamental *doing* dictated by the major concepts and generalizations arising from the social work practice frame of reference and utilized by the profession as a whole (if ever such agreement is reached!).

Some might ask, do the authors still believe, nearly twenty years after the study ended, that the above conclusion is reasonable and one they would come to today? The answer is a qualified yes. Schools, agencies, and students still seem to be struggling with some of the same concerns. This plan seems well worth a try as a means of developing more knowledge-guided practitioners, development essential to strengthen the profession. Will it ever happen?

NOTES

1. This paper is based on a 240-page monograph (155 pages plus appendices) entitled *Final Report: Field Instruction Research Project*, published by the George Warren Brown School of Social Work, Washington University, St. Louis in 1969, and authored by William E. Gordon and Margaret L. Schutz (now Gordon), Co-Directors of the Project.

2. For further discussion of both the learning frame of reference and the practice frame of references described herein, see Chapter 2, The Role of Frames of Reference in Field Instruction. In Sheafor & Jenkins, (Eds.). (1982). 21-36.

3. Richard Sterne, Research Associate for the Project from 1963-67, carried major responsibility for designing, implementing, and analyzing Knowing Test I. His doctoral dissertation (Sterne, 1967) contributed additional data and analysis on this aspect of the Project.

4. The volume of statistics and their analyses contained in the original Final Report precluded any meaningful summarization in the space available in this paper. Reference, therefore, is limited to the results of some of the important analyses.

5. For further development of this idea, see Schutz and Gordon (1977).

REFERENCES

Gordon, W. E., & Schutz, M.L. (1969). *Final report: Field instruction research project*. St. Louis: George Warren Brown School of Social Work, Washington University.

Schutz, M. L., & Gordon, W. E. (1977). Reallocation of educational responsibility among student, school, agency and NASW. *Journal of Social Work Education, 13*(12), 99-106.

Sheafor, B. W., & Jenkins, L. E. (Eds.). (1982). *Quality field instruction in social work: Program development and maintenance*. New York: Longman.

Sterne, R. (1967). The initial influence of structural variations in casework field instruction upon students' mastery of classroom knowledge (Doctoral dissertation, Washington University, 1967). *Dissertation Abstracts International, 28*, 3268-A.

A Delphi Study in Field Instruction: Identification of Issues and Research Priorities by Experts

ABSTRACT. The Delphi Technique was used in a three-phase national study on field instruction in an attempt to identify the research needs or issues in field instruction. A panel of fifteen experts participated. The top five research issues identified were: (1) How does one test for the attainment of the specific skills established as objectives to be achieved in field instruction? (2) What are appropriate learning objectives and related tasks for undergraduates, first year, and second year graduate students? (3) What makes for an effective professional experience in terms of field instruction learning assignments and characteristics of field teachers? (4) What types of learning experiences contribute most effectively to the achievement of different content and skill by different students? and (5) How does planning for field instruction fit into the overall educational and curriculum planning process?

Prior to a weekly faculty meeting, something rather curious occurred. Social work faculty were left speechless when confronted with the following rather simple question: Can you name an *expert* in the area of social work field instruction? With paper and pen in hand, the author was ready to tackle the onslaught of names. What? Not a sound from knowledgeable, experienced professors? When the group was queried regarding *experts* in social work policy, research, human behavior in the social environment, and methods, names as well as titles of books were suggested.

For several months, the author repeated this "experiment" at

Reprinted by permission from the College of Social Work, University of South Carolina from *Arete*, Vol. 8, No. 2, Fall 1983, pages 38-48.

professional meetings and with agency personnel. The results were almost identical. (Occasionally someone would say, "What is her name . . . the one who wrote that book about ten years ago?") This situation raised several questions for the author:

1. If experts cannot readily be identified, how have educational programs developed the theoretical base (knowledge, values, and skills) for field instruction?
2. Are there experts in field instruction, and, if so, who are they?
3. Can research priorities in field instruction be developed and agreed upon by experts?
4. Could identified experts reach consensus about issues of field instruction (or is everyone out there doing his or her own thing)?

PURPOSE OF THE STUDY

Although field instruction is seen as an important component of the social work curriculum (BSW and MSW), it is an area which has been subjected to minimal *empirical* research and has received even less attention in the professional journals (Anderson, 1979; Roberts, 1973). In the past sixteen years (1965-1981), only 6 percent (44) of the 688 articles published in the *Journal of Education for Social Work* focused on field instruction, and only one book on field instruction was reviewed. During the same years, six articles on this subject appeared in the journal of *Social Work*.

The purpose of this paper is to report on a three-phase national study on field instruction which used the Delphi Technique. Dalkey and Helmer (1963) report that the Delphi Technique began as a study sponsored by the Air Force in the use of expert opinions. "Project Delphi" had as its objective the attainment of the most reliable consensus of a group of experts. This technique is a systematic procedure which elicits and collates judgments on a particular topic. For example, the Delphi concept has been used to reach consensus on continuing education needs in social work and to identify research and development objectives for the mental health needs of children (Faherty, 1979; Bregman & Salasin, 1977). An advantage of the Delphi Technique is that it provides a means for people who are geographically separated to carry on a dialogue and to strive for consensus in an area of shared expertise. However, this technique has not been previously used with field instruction experts.

In the present study, twenty field instruction experts were identified, and the consensus or lack of consensus among these experts with respect to twenty-eight statements on field instruction recorded. Field instruction statements were taken from the available literature and from questions repeatedly raised at national social work conferences which did not seem to be resolved or have some degree of agreement. Examples of issues used in this study that have been discussed in the literature include: (1) the role of the faculty field liaison (Rosenblum & Raphael, 1983; Gordon & Gordon, 1982; Wilson, 1981; Gitterman, 1975); (2) the incorporation of the concept of adult learning in field instruction (Wilson, 1981); (3) training for the role of field instructor by agency workers (Austin, 1979); (4) the competency-based model for field instruction (Larsen, 1980; Pettes, 1979); (5) opportunities available for students to observe their supervisors (Raskin, 1982); (6) field instruction literature generally lacking empirically-based studies (Sheafor & Jenkins, 1982; Brownstein, 1981); (7) to a large extent the cooperative relationships between school and field have been explicated better in theory than in practice (Fellin, 1982); and (8) the relationship between the quality of supervision and learning (Shubert, 1983). Five priority research needs for field instruction were also developed by this national group of experts. Significant questions were raised and divergent viewpoints were expressed.

CHARACTERISTICS
OF THE DELPHI TECHNIQUE

There are several methods of collecting expert opinion. These include face-to-face conferences, workshops, polling, literature reviews, and committee meetings. The Delphi method has two major characteristics that distinguish it from other methods. These characteristics are *feedback* and *anonymity*, designed to minimize the effects of dominant individuals and group pressure to conform during the communication process, since there is no one-to-one exchange between individual experts.

All communication is through written group summaries. The judgments of the panel members are collected by the researcher and then aggregated to summarize the group's position. The experts are provided with a statistical summary (medians and lower and upper quartile range) of the group's responses in order to review their own positions and written comments/reactions to each statement. On subsequent rounds, each expert can decide to take a different position (based on the feedback) or to respond in the same manner as the previous round. Evaluation and re-evaluation in order to reach consensus generally continues for three to five rounds.

The use of feedback and anonymity is seen as advantageous by Turoff (1971) in the following circumstances:

1. Where the individuals who need to contribute their expertise to a complex problem have no history of adequate communication, and the communication process needs structure in order to be understood.
2. Where there are large geographical distances and/or time is scarce, factors which deter the individuals from frequent group meetings.
3. Where a group communication process would be beneficial to subsequent face-to-face meetings.

METHODOLOGY

To determine who is viewed as an expert in field instruction by social work educators, a letter was sent to the directors of field instruction of all eighty-eight graduate schools of social work in the United States and to a random sample of sixty-eight directors of field instruction of accredited undergraduate programs in March of 1981. The letter (1) explained the author's interest in identifying experts in field instruction; (2) asked each director to list individuals whom they considered to be experts; (3) asked that each expert be ranked according to expertise (e.g., #1 having the most expertise, #2 next, etc.); and (4) encouraged respondents to include themselves on the list if they considered themselves to be experts.

Two follow-up letters were sent to nonrespondents in May 1981 and July 1981. A total of sixty-nine useable responses were received (thirty-one from graduate schools and twenty-eight from undergraduate programs). Two hundred and one (201) names of experts were generated by the sixty-nine respondents. If a nominee received two or more votes (regardless of rank) by at least one graduate level and one undergraduate level respondent, he or she was placed on the *expert* list. Only sixteen of the 201 names received two or more votes by graduate and undergraduate educators. This may be partly explained by the fact the eighteen (18) directors of field instruction identified only individuals in their own schools as experts in field instruction. In addition, four (4) directors (all of undergraduate programs) wrote that they did not know of *any* experts in field instruction. Perhaps expertise in field instruction is measured or recognized in some manner other than the sharing of research with the professional community, research that leads to the building of knowledge, a theoretical base, and a stronger foundation for field instruction.

In February 1982 the twenty panelists received a letter confirming their participation as well as detailed instructions and procedures to be followed in the three Delphi rounds.[1] All responses were returned to the researcher. No panel member knew who else was participating and extensive feedback was provided after each round. In March 1982 the first round was sent to the panel, and the study was completed in December 1982. (See Figure 1 for chronological summary of steps in the Delphi Study.) As Figure 1 shows, during Round III panel members voted for the last time on each of the twenty-eight items after reading all new comments made by all experts. They were now also asked to narrow the top ten research priorities submitted by the panel to the five areas they felt needed most attention. Two supplemental questionnaires were included during the last round. The first had four questions which ascertained panelists' views on the effectiveness of the Delphi Technique. The second asked for demographic, employment, and publication data of panel members. Participants were asked to give written permission to use their names if the study were ever to be published or presented at a conference.[2] Consensus was achieved for thirteen of the twenty-eight statements and was derived by computing the Quartile Deviation for each item.[3]

This approach to research demands much time and commitment

Figure 1: Summary of the Delphi Approach

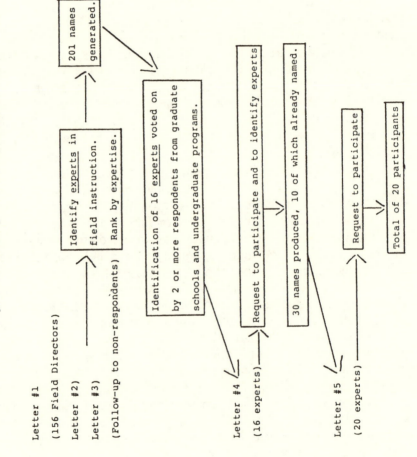

Letter #1
(156 Field Directors)

Letter #2)
Letter #3)
(Follow-up to non-respondents)

Identify experts in
field instruction.
Rank by expertise.

201 names
generated.

Identification of 16 experts voted on
by 2 or more respondents from graduate
schools and undergraduate programs.

Letter #4
(16 experts)

Request to participate and to identify experts

30 names produced, 10 of which already named.

Letter #5
(20 experts)

Request to participate

Total of 20 participants

Round I (March 1982)

Round II (June 1982)

Round III (September 1982)

Feedback provided including medians, upper and lower quartile range, and aggregated summary of comments on 28 statements; list of research priorities generated.

Final Summary (December 1982)

A. Results of medians and consensus reached for the 28 statements of Round III; B. Comments by participants for Round III; C. Top 5 research priorities selected by panel members; D. Panel members' views of effectiveness of Delphi Technique; E. Demographic data of study participants; F. Names of participants who gave permission to use their name; and G. Percent of response rate by rounds.

on the part of both the panelists and the researcher. Panel members must read all comments, respond to each question, and grapple with their own past experiences, values, judgments, knowledge, and the challenge of their position by peers.

RESULTS

Of the twenty individuals who agreed to participate, three never responded to Rounds I and II and were, therefore, eliminated from the last round. In Round I (N = 20), seventeen people responded, a response rate of 85 percent. For Round II, fourteen of seventeen people responded, an 82 percent rate; for the last round fifteen people responded (88 percent). Although the response rate remained consistently high, it must be remembered that the study involved a small group of people.

The panel of experts consisted of twelve females and three males. Of the three people who never responded, all were male. This brings the ratio of females to males closer to the ratio in the profession as a whole. The majority (eleven) of the respondents were over fifty years old and all fifteen had the MSW degree. In addition, four had PhDs, one had the DSW and one was an EdD candidate. No panelist had less than five years of experience in student supervision in an agency or as a faculty field liaison. Nine panelists had over twenty years of social work practice experience. Twelve respondents had published from zero to four articles, books, and monographs specifically in the area of field instruction. The majority (twelve) had ten or more years of college teaching experience. Two interesting findings about the panel were that less than half (seven) had served as director or coordinator of field instruction and ten were presently not engaged in research in the area of field instruction. Of the fifteen experts, seven had been reviewers for a social work professional journal, while only two had reviewed papers for CSWE annual program meetings.

Table 1 summarizes how the panel viewed the effectiveness of the Delphi Technique. According to the participants in this study, the Delphi Technique seems to have strengths in its ability to allow dialogue between geographically separated experts and as a means of learning for panel members.

The panel voted on the following items as the top five research needs in field instruction.

1. How does one test for the attainment of the specific skills (competencies) established as objectives to be achieved in field instruction? Is there evidence that this knowledge is being consciously applied in field instruction?
2. What are appropriate learning objectives and related tasks for undergraduates, first year, and second year graduate students?
3. What makes for an effective professional experience in terms of field instruction learning assignments and characteristics of field teachers?
4. What types of learning experiences contribute most effectively to the achievement of different content and skill by different students?
5. How does planning for field instruction fit into the overall educational and curriculum planning process?

The need for the five priority areas of research is supported by the thirteen statements which reached consensus at the end of the third round. When the quartile deviation was calculated for the first round, only four statements reached consensus; in Round II, nine statements reached consensus; and by the third round, thirteen statements. The process of dialogue, feedback, and anonymity provided a means for considering and reconsidering issues and priorities while moving toward mutual understanding by panel members. The following six statements reached consensus and the panel was in agreement with the statement:

Statement 1   The concept that "adults learn differently than children" must be incorporated in the planning for, and implementation of, field experience.

Statement 3   Schools distinguish between first and second year placements, yet criteria for each are not clearly spelled out.

Statement 7   The profession has been unable to make a commitment to a specific set of objectives in field education.

TABLE 1. Effectiveness of Delphi Technique

	Level of Agreement					
Questions	Strongly Agree	Agree	Undecided	Disagree	Strongly Disagree	No Response
1. Do you agree it is effective as a means of gaining consensus?	3	8	5	1		1
2. Do you agree it is effective as a means of dialogue around an issue with others whom you are geographically separated from?	3	8	3	1		

3. Do you agree it is effective
   as a means of learning for the
   panelists, i.e., it can communi-
   cate knowledge on the subject
   under discussion as the panelists
   reconsider their answers and
   receive feedback from the
   entire panel.

   3   9   2   1

4. Would you like a summary
   of the final report?

   Yes 15   No ___

Statement 12   The literature on field instruction is generally lacking empirically-based studies.

Statement 14   Field instruction programs have not specified precisely what it is that students should be learning in the field and how well they should learn it.

Statement 17   Training to take on the role of field instructor by agency workers has not received adequate professional attention.

Consensus and agreement with statements 1, 3, 7, 12 and 14 support the importance of the five top priority research needs voted on by the panel.

In the following statements, the panel reached consensus that they disagreed with the statement:

Statement 5   Theoretical content taught in the field is differentiated by field instructors for the first year graduate students and senior undergraduates.

Statement 6   The social work profession has been able to successfully articulate and transmit the appropriate field learning (tasks) for graduate as well as undergraduate students.

Statement 9   We have research-based knowledge as to how field work decisions are made (e.g., process of choosing practicum settings or which students are placed in which agency and why).

Statement 10   Practitioners who become field instructors are sufficiently versed in theories of learning and can easily apply educational principles to student learning needs.

Statement 11   Students in field work are generally dissatisfied with the opportunities available to observe their supervisor (or other professionals) work with clients (individuals, groups, and community).

Statement 26   Simulation and gaming techniques are effective methods of learning and should be used in field instruction.

Statement 27   Ethical issues are adequately covered in field instruction.

Consensus and disagreement with statements 5, 6, and 10 also seem to support the list of research priorities chosen by the panel. No consensus was reached on the following fifteen statements:

Statement 2   Field instruction manuals are frequently developed separately from classroom teaching and lack guidelines that provide systematic and operationally developed field learning objectives.

Statement 4   To a large extent, the cooperative relationships between school and field have been explicated better in theory than in practice.

Statement 8   The literature has shown that there is an association between the quality of supervision and the learning that takes place.

Statement 13   The role of the faculty field liaison is well defined.

Statement 15   When you come right down to it, we know very little about field instruction.

Statement 16   Although we have accreditation standards for social work programs, the variety of settings, learning opportunities, level of supervision, and evaluation instruments don't really allow us to know how well prepared our students are.

Statement 18   There is insufficient literature to guide faculty in structuring the content of integrative seminars.

Statement 19   The ultimate success of field work is dependent upon the convergence of the school's educational objectives, the teaching resources available within the agency, and needs of each student.

Statement 20   The curriculum objectives of the school are of primary importance in determining student learning tasks in the field.

Statement 21   Field instruction should follow a competency-based model.

Statement 22   Professional journals place too little emphasis on field instruction when selecting articles for publication.

Statement 23   We can justify having individuals with other than social work degrees supervise students in the field.

Statement 24   Field instruction is a generic term and actually includes many forms of learning experiences.

Statement 25   No field instruction program should be offered without provision for immediate as well as long term evaluation of its effectiveness.

Statement 28   Students learn better in a block rather than concurrent placement.

DISCUSSION

Although at times it was difficult for panel members to take a position of agreement or disagreement to a free standing statement, the results of the study seem to suggest that answers are being sought to some very basic field instruction questions.

Eighty percent of the participants in the Delphi Study had published from zero to four articles, books, or monographs during careers that spanned almost twenty years of practice and teaching experience. During their dialogue, the panelists wondered if lack of attention by professional journals to articles in field instruction was due to selection bias or to the quality and quantity of material actually submitted. The panelists strongly argued (in response to Statement 15) that we do know much about field instruction, but what we know "is rooted in myth and tradition rather than solid knowledge"; "even the practice wisdom is not published"; "we have not systematically shared what we know nor researched field instruction as we should." Can we, therefore, conclude that we do have experts and we have knowledge about field instruction but have not published, shared, or systematically researched it?

Can a profession and its educators afford to remain in this posture? Can we be satisfied with practice wisdom, or should that form the basis for systematic exploration? Could "yes" be the answer to the question, "Is everyone out there doing his or her own thing?" If we do know much about field instruction, as argued by the experts, should more statements have reached consensus? Or, is it that we just can't agree about what we know?

The needed areas of research identified by the experts have not been totally ignored in the literature. However, panelist feedback indicated that the majority of the present writings are descriptive in nature and provide individual schools' experiences or the author's opinion. Some schools have adopted exit interviews, videotapes, and credit for field work in order to obtain evidence that knowledge is being consciously applied in field instruction (priority 1). These empirically tested methods are not widely used, since the testing for the attainment of specific skills was ranked number one over twenty-nine other research priorities.

Appropriate learning experiences for different levels of student, effective learning assignments, and the fit of field instruction in the overall educational planning process have received attention but have not resulted in data which are systematically used.

The statements which reached consensus (and agreement) can be summarized as those which point to things we have not done or accomplished in field instruction. That is, we have a lack of empirical work, a lack of specificity of what is to be learned, a lack of clearly defined criteria for first and second year placements, and inadequate attention to training for the field instructor role. Adding to a composite picture of expert opinion is panelist disagreement with statements in areas which indicated adequacy or success, for example, that ethical issues are adequately covered, that practitioners who are field instructors are versed in theories of learning, that theoretical content is differentiated for different levels of students, or that we make field work decisions based on research.

It is difficult to generalize from the statements in which consensus was not reached. What the lack of consensus might imply is that there is much empirical research needed especially when agreement is lacking in regard to the role of the field liaison, the educational credentials of supervisors, and the provision for evaluation of effectiveness of field instruction programs.

The implications of this study may begin to sound like gloom and doom, but, in fact, they provide positive challenges for those who have knowledge to share it; for journals and CSWE to encourage and provide the opportunities for professional dialogue; for those interested in specific issues which were raised to do further in-depth studies through empirical work. One respondent summed things up by saying, "The fact that all our knowledge has not been published does not deny what we do know. More should be written, but it's tough stuff to write!"

CONCLUSIONS

This study indicates that we have traveled many miles in field instruction, gathering information, trying new ideas, and refining our techniques. We are not at point zero, although sometimes it may feel that way. The miles ahead can and must build on what we have if we are to survive the difficult technical and economic challenges of the 80s and beyond.

Aase George (1982) has written an excellent history of social work field instruction. An extension and further contribution to the "state of the art" could be undertaken through a replication of the present Delphi Study with other identified experts. It is clear that rigorous and systematic research needs to be carried out and the results shared with the professional community. The five research priorities previously identified provide a beginning with many potential spin-offs.

Expert opinion must be turned around toward consensus of the accomplishments of field instruction and the knowledge, values and skills that could be attained by every student in field placement. Individuals involved in field instruction must begin to have dialogues on a regional and, hopefully, national level. If field education is to be successfully integrated into the curriculum, it must develop along with other educational components and not be left to haphazard and untested methods.

NOTES

1. The original 16 experts were asked to identify experts. Additional individuals were contacted with four agreeing to participate. This brought the final participant total to 20.

2. Betty Baer, Norma Berkowitz, Sheldon Gelman, Margaret Schutz Gordon,

Philip Hovda, Nancy Johnston, Francis Manis, Margaret Matson, Aleanor Merrifield, Rhoda Sarnat, Bernice Simon, Elaine Switzer, Dorothy Turner, Julianne Wayne and Suanna Wilson.

3. The quartile deviation is arrived at by determining the quartile range, subtracting the lowest number and dividing it by two (2). A quartile deviation of 1.00 or less indicates consensus by the group.

REFERENCES

Anderson, W.A. (February 1979). *Education for employment: BSW graduates' work experience and the undergraduate curriculum.* Paper presented at the annual program meeting, Council on Social Work Education. Boston.

Austin L.N. (1979). Basic principles of supervision. In C.E. Munson (Ed.). *Social work supervision classic statements and critical issues* (pp. 56-69). New York: Free Press.

Bregman, H., & Salasin, J. (1977). *The Delphi technique: Analysis of responses to a survey of children's mental health services development.* McLean, Virginia: Mitre Corp.

Brownstein, C. (1981). Practicum issues: A placement planning model. *Journal of Education for Social Work, 17*(3), 52-58.

Dalkey, N., & Helmer, O. (1963). An experimental application of the Delphi method to the use of experts. *Management Science, (3).*

Faherty, V. (1979). Continuing social work education: Results of a Delphi survey. *Journal of Education for Social Work, 15,* 12-19.

Fellin, P.A. (1982). Responsibilities of the school: Administrative support of field instruction. In B.W. Sheafor & L.E. Jenkins (Eds.). *Quality field instruction in Social Work* (pp. 101-115). New York: Longman.

George, A. (1982). A history of social work field instruction. In B.W. Sheafor & L.E. Jenkins (Eds.). *Quality field instruction in social work* (pp. 37-47). New York: Longman.

Gitterman, A. (1975). The faculty field instructor in social work education. In *Dynamics of field instruction: Learning through doing.* New York: Council on Social Work Education.

Gordon, W.E., & Gordon, M.S. (1982). The role of frames of reference in field instruction. In B.W. Sheafor & L.E. Jenkins (Eds.). *Quality field instruction in social work* (pp. 21-36). New York: Longman.

Larsen, J. (1980). Competency-based and task-centered practicum instruction. *Journal of Education for Social Work, 16*(1), 87-94.

Pettes, D.E. (1979). *Staff and student supervision.* London: George Allen & Unwin.

Raskin, M.S. (1982). Factors associated with student satisfaction in undergraduate social work field placements. *Arete, 7*(1), 44-54.

Roberts, R.W. (1973). An interim report on the development of an undergraduate, graduate continuum of social work education in a private university. *Journal of Education for Social Work, 9*(3), 58-64.

Rosenblum, A.F., & Raphael, F.B. (1983). The role and function of the faculty field liaison. *Journal of Education for Social Work*, *19*(1), 67-73.

Sheafor, B.W., & Jenkins, L.E. (1982). *Quality field instruction in social work*. New York: Longman.

Shubert, M. (1983). *Field instruction in social casework*. Chicago: University of Chicago.

Turoff, M. (1971). Delphi and its potential impact on information systems. *AFIPS conference proceedings*, *39*, 317-326.

Wilson, S.J. (1981). *Field instruction techniques for supervisors*. New York: Free Press.

Field Instruction in the 1980s — Realities, Issues, and Problem-Solving Strategies

Louise Skolnik

ABSTRACT. In 1984, the Council on Social Work Education sponsored a one year Project on Field Instruction to explore current challenges to quality in field education. Under the auspices of a Technical Assistance Group, two surveys of field education were conducted. The first was a national study of all BSW and MSW field education departments; the second, a selected sample of field agencies. Findings indicated striking agreement between field educators and agency personnel about problematic areas: the integration of academic content and field experience; conflicting demands of job and field instruction responsibilities; need for standards for the evaluation of students; training for new and experienced field instructors; communication between schools and agencies; and the qualification and needs of students. Both educators and practitioners identified standard-setting, ongoing training, and recognition of field education and field instructors as key problem-solving strategies.

INTRODUCTION

Maintaining and supporting the quality of the social work field practicum is a critical contemporary issue facing social work education, and one that greatly impacts on the practice-education relationship. Field education provides an arena for skill development, knowledge integration, and affective learning; as such, it is a pivotal core component in the professional education process.

The current challenges to the social work profession and the related demands on educational institutions make it even more imperative that quality in field education be examined and buttressed. Obstacles to the maintenance of excellence in this arena include diminishing resources for faculty field instruction, increased de-

© 1989 by The Haworth Press, Inc. All rights reserved.

47

mands on experienced agency personnel, and increasing numbers of students with special field placement needs.

The Council on Social Work Education (CSWE) initiated in 1984 a special one year Project on Field Instruction to explore issues and needs, and to identify problem-solving mechanisms to support and enhance field instruction. The project was stimulated by the Council's perception that the development of special programs to meet the needs of field educators, and to further field education and the practice-education relationship, would constitute an important and appropriate goal.

The project's activities were guided by a Technical Assistance Group comprised of 21 BSW and MSW field educators and agency personnel.[1] The group focused its efforts on developing recommendations in the following areas: introducing a more formalized Council structure (e.g., a formal Committee on Field Education); providing an arena for problem-solving and policy formation on field education; enhancing opportunities for information sharing and problem-solving among field educators (e.g., a clearinghouse for materials on field instruction to be developed by and located at the Council); and designing and implementing mechanisms to recognize field instructors and encourage their identification as educators (e.g., the development of a National Academy for Field Instructors). As part of these initiatives, the group recognized the need to gather data on the current state of field instruction. To this end, a national study of field education was undertaken. In addition, there was a more limited effort to obtain the perspectives of field agencies. In the following pages, the project's findings will be presented in two parts:

1. An exploration of the position of field education in the social work curriculum and in curriculum policy; and
2. Results of the field instruction surveys.

FIELD EDUCATION IN THE SOCIAL WORK CURRICULUM AND IN CURRICULUM POLICY

Field Education in the Social Work Curriculum

The educational process for any profession involves learning by doing and opportunities to engage in practice so as to learn. Katherine Kendall (1959, p. 1) notes: "All professions, therefore, provide students, at one point in their educational program, with experience in working with the clientele served by the profession." Social work, however, unlike most other professions, traditionally incorporates practice into every phase of the learning process. Educational policies guiding professional preparation have stressed the integration of the academic and practicum realms, and some form of practicum is introduced with, or not long after, the beginning of formal academic learning (Schutz-Gordon, 1975). As Richard Lodge (1975) stated, "Unquestionably, much of the genius of social work education has been, through the years, an intermingling of conceptual and experiential learning. Other professional disciplines have looked to social work as a model in the use of the practicum."

Social work education's approach to the practice component recognizes the potential for a vital, ongoing interchange. Theory taught in the classroom informs practice, bringing it from the realm of the particular to a more generalizable experience, and the practice experience in turn influences and modifies theoretical constructs. Within the framework of social work field education, experiences in the field serve as the primary arena for integrating knowledge and values with skills—the professional person takes shape and is shaped.

Many factors have influenced the prominent position assigned by field education in the development of the social work professional. Certainly the historical origins of professional education within the purview of social agencies must be considered. Formal social work education has its roots in apprenticeship training programs (Kendall, 1953). Supervised practice, rather than the acquisition of a specified body of theory, was perceived as the primary element in the development of a social worker (George, 1982).

A significant role for the practicum persisted even when, in the 1920s, the focus of control for the educational process shifted to the university. Over time, within traditional academic settings which so highly value research and publication, issues regarding the relative status of those involved with field education have emerged (Turner, 1984). The field component, however, has to this day been purposefully retained as part of the educational curriculum, and programs continue to exercise the legitimate authority to develop, control, and "provide a structure in which an educational process takes place" (Bloom, 1963, p. 3). As in the earliest days of social work training, the arena for this process has, with few exceptions, remained not in a school-based setting, but in community-based agencies.

Another element, also closely related to the historic emphasis of education within the agency context, is the profession's belief in the tutorial relationship between student and field instructor as a key facilitative factor in the learning process (Dana & Sikkema, 1964). This perspective was supported by the profession's stance that interpersonal relationships function as a primary growth-producing factor. The positive aspects of a close tie between student and agency employee were recognized almost from the inception of social work education. Jeffrey Brackett, in 1933, noted the benefits of "constant guidance in details of the person of experience who knows of, and thinks constantly of, and believes in, the little things as well as the larger issues of philanthropic work. . . ." Students should be "under the guidance of persons of experience, who have learned how to focus with reasonable accuracy the objects before them, who really know somewhat of the needs and resources of the needy, or ill, or delinquent, or defective individuals for whom they care" (p. 6). Forty years later, Bertha Reynolds (1965) stated:

> Their (students') relation to the supervisor is their most reliable help in learning to do the things they can really accomplish. . . . The supervisor needs to be a person big enough to take from school and agency and society the best to be gained from each, and blend them all for the students' use. Perhaps someone in the school setting does this, but not with as intimate a touch with the social realities which the student is meeting as the supervisor has who goes with him through his individual struggle. (p. 229)

Other elements contributing to the salient role of the field component include the profession's domain and societal function (i.e., its position in regard to the psycho-social interface of the individual, family, group, and community with social institutions, and its related obligation to contemplate and intervene in any and all spheres impacting on these entities). Such a multiplicity of responsibilities and forces demands an individualized approach to each problematic situation and the exercise of keen judgment guided in part by a professional value base. Without such aids as specific legal rules, treatment protocols, and medical prescriptions, decision-making predicated on experience becomes a critical dimension in developing practice knowledge and skill. Another salient factor is that theory-building in social work has largely evolved out of practice imperatives — theory has been adapted and developed in relationship to its potential or actual application to practice. Indeed, the search for practice theory rather than for a grand theory of practice has been said to dominate social work's epistemological quest (Vigilante et al., 1981).

Doing does not await knowledge — it can lead to and stimulate the growth of knowledge. As a consequence, field experience is not conceptualized as alien to the execution of an academically rigorous search for knowledge. Instead, a close integration of the cognitive and the experiential becomes a scholarly imperative.

In summary, the roots of professional education in social agencies, the belief in the efficacy of the tutorial relationship in the teaching and learning of practice, the nature of professional practice, and the pattern of theory development have all contributed to the relatively prominent position of the practicum in social work education. This position becomes apparent when one reviews the guidelines for professional education which have emerged over the past fifty years.

Curriculum Policy Statements and the Field Component, 1932-1982

The field component has been formally recognized as a basic element in social work education since 1932, at which time the first standards of curriculum were issued by the then existing professional education association, the American Association of Schools of Social Work (AASW). Over the ensuing fifty years, five modified curriculum policy statements have been adopted, each reflecting the perception of field as the educational component which implements and integrates the academic curriculum. The relative degree of attention paid to the field and the specificity of guidelines and standards have varied, as indicated in the following summary of each policy statement.

1. *1932*—Under the auspices of the American Association of Schools of Social Work, a minimum one-year curriculum consisting of field work and four core course groupings was prescribed. The 1943 *Accreditation Manual*, designed to implement the 1932 standards, reflects the then dominant position of the field component, in that:

> where class work and field work are concerned, it is essential that schools realize that while the two should be well-correlated, class work should not be regarded as of value as it relates to field work. . . . Class work is more than a mere aid to field work; it is a supplementation of it. (AASW, 1943, p. 37)

The manual suggests guidelines regarding "qualifications of field work instructors and the agencies selected as field work centers, general practices of these agencies, placements of students in the agency, content and method instruction, integration of class room and field work content" (AASW, 1943, p. 38). Specific elements are offered "not as requirements, but as objectives to be strived for" (AASW, 1943). Field work instructors, for example, should "have a certificate or degree from an accredited two year school of social work, a minimum of one year's supervisory experience, and eligibility for membership in the American Association of Social Workers or other appropriate professional organization" (AASW, 1943, p. 39). Agencies, among other recommendations, should have the majority of their professional personnel eligible for membership in the AASW or other appropriate professional organization. Assignments should include "one rather long experience, and provision for progressive educational content and sequences" (AASW, 1943, p. 41).

2. *1944*—Under the AASW, minimum course expectations were incorporated into eight basic subject areas: social case work, social group work, community organization, public welfare, social administration, social research, medical information, and psychiatric information. Field work was not seen as one of the basic eight— "an approved program of field work shall be integrated with and

implement the above course of study" (AASW, 1932). The 1950 *Accreditation Manual* implementing this policy repeats the detailed guidelines regarding the filed component which were offered in relationship to the 1932 Curriculum Policy Statement (see the preceeding).

3. *1952* — The First Curriculum Policy Statement of the newly formed Council on Social Work Education referred to field education under its section on social work practice. Emphasis was on generic skill development; field and class faculty should "be prepared to identify the professional skills that are common to all social work practice and to assist the student to develop an awareness of how these common skills are utilized in social work practice" (CSWE, 1953, p. 3). Field education was to be integrated with the classroom curricula, and was to provide for practice experiences with individuals and groups prior to any practice in the area of community work, administration, or research (CSWE, 1953).

4. *1962* — The Curriculum Policy Statement for 1962 does not make many references to field education. Objectives regarding classroom and field activities in practice are linked together. In discussing field learning experiences, reference is made to the need for clarity regarding educational objectives, for two years of field practice, and for a diverse as well as in-depth experience. However, much greater specificity is achieved in a twelve item statement issued in March 1962 as an addendum to the standards for the 1962 Curriculum Policy Statement. Among major points made in this "General Basic Standards for Field Instruction Agencies" are the following:

- The agency, the staff, and Board should be committed to social work values and education.
- The staff size should be large enough to sustain an appropriate level of service without the use of students.
- Student assignments should offer a diverse experience, one which includes group as well as individual practice.
- Field instructors should have, among other criteria, an MSW and several years of post-MSW experience.

In 1965, the criteria were modified, beginning with a statement that each school is responsible for establishing its own specific standards. Also incorporated was the specific guideline that an agency should provide placements for both first and second year students and be willing to accept a minimum of two students. Omitted were the specific professional criteria for acceptance as field instructor.

5. *1969* — This statement reaffirms the central position of field education, the need to include direct practice in service delivery, and the need for educational objectives to be integrated with all other aspects of the curriculum. A school's right to determine the specifics of its practicum program, alluded to in some previous statements, is underscored: "Subject to these general principles, each school shall have freedom to determine the particular nature of its practicum, including the degree of variation for groups of students and the instructional experience to be provided through the practicum" (CSWE, 1969).

Appendix II of the *Manual of Accrediting Standards*, published in 1971, discusses "Criteria for Learning Experiences Provided through the Practicum." While similar to the 1962 and 1965 criteria, a major difference is that there is recognition that the field teacher may *not* be a social worker under certain circumstances. When this occurs, "the school has the obligation to insure the basic planning and evaluation of the practicum experience and the organization of the teaching contribution of non-social workers are carried out by a social work teacher through (additional) specific staff or faculty arrangements" (CSWE, 1971, p. 61). In addition, it was acknowledged that, although students should not be the basic service providers for a program, "an exception may be made when it is necessary to create a setting in which students, on a planned and time-limited basis, provide basic services not currently offered by an established social agency" (CSWE, 1971, p. 62).

6. *1982* — The most recent Curriculum Policy Statement again reaffirms that "the field practicum is an integral part of the curriculum in social work education" (CSWE, 1982). The direction of each school regarding the organization of the field practicum and the development of standards for selection of setting, field instructors, and assignment are recognized. There are several specific new policies: undergraduate programs must provide a minimum of 400

instruction hours and MSW programs 900 hours, and the practicum at the advanced social work level (2nd year Masters) must include instruction in the areas of the students' concentration (CSWE, 1982). Moreover, the *Manual of Accreditation Standards* acknowledges that a field instructor may not have a social work degree. It states that if the field instructor does not hold a social work degree, "the social work program faculty should assume an additional responsibility to assure that a social work focus is maintained. . . ." (CSWE, 1984, p. 3). This is the first statement to specifically address BSW education, and specifies that one BSW faculty member be assigned "responsibility for the practicum's educational direction" (CSWE, 1984, p. 3).

RESULTS OF SURVEYS OF FIELD INSTRUCTION DEPARTMENTS AND FIELD AGENCIES

Two surveys were conducted under the project's auspices, one of all CSWE-accredited BSW and MSW programs, and one of a sample of field agencies. Selected survey findings are presented in the following.[2]

A. Surveys of Field Instruction Departments

To explore the needs of field educators and to determine the present "state of the art," a questionnaire was developed and distributed to the field instruction offices of all BSW and MSW programs. The questionnaire consisted of 21 items and was designed to obtain base-line data on field education structures, administration, and practices, and to gather information on the perspective of field educators regarding major problems, issues, and suggested means to address these concerns. The survey was distributed in Spring/Summer of 1984, and results are based on data available at that time. Three hundred forms were returned by Fall 1984, representing a response rate of 75 percent of BSW programs (261 of 349) and 98 percent of MSW programs (89 of 91).

B. Results — Respondents

Of the 300 returned forms, 70 percent (211) were from BSW-only programs, 17 percent (50) from combined BSW-MSW programs, and 13 percent (39) from MSW-only programs. Twenty-six percent of the respondents returning questionnaires held the position of dean or program director; 61 percent held the position of field instruction director or coordinator; and 13 percent were other members of the school's staff.

Structure and Personnel of the Field Education Unit

In 50 percent (164) of responding programs, there is a separate department of field education; in 45 percent (134), field education is not administered through a separate division. In the 164 schools with a separate department of field education, the units were headed by persons with the following credentials: 66 percent (104) MSW degree; 7 percent (11) DSW degree, and 27 percent (43) PhD or other degree.

In the 161 reporting programs, the respondents had been field educators for an average of 5 years (median of 4 years). Their experience/time as faculty members averaged 9 years (median of 4 years). The faculty rank of field education directors was as follows (147 reporting): 9.7 percent (11) Professor; 29 percent (42) Associate Professor; 58 percent (42) Assistant Professor; 0.5 percent (7) Instructor-Lecturer; 0.7 percent (1) Adjunct or Clinical; and 0.7 percent (1) Other.

Liaison with Field Agencies

The field liaison role was assumed by full-time teaching faculty in 92 percent of the 275 responding programs; by part-time teaching faculty in 15 percent of the programs; by full-time faculty on staff whose major responsibility is field liaison work in 7 percent of the programs; by part-time nonteaching faculty in 4 percent of the programs; and by administrative staff in 10 percent (29) of the programs.

Fifty-two percent (143) of 277 reporting programs provided for annual evaluations of field liaison personnel; 48 percent (234) did not conduct an evaluation on an annual basis. Of 111 of these programs, 47 percent (53) conducted some other form of evaluation; 52 percent (58) did not. In 81 of the 277 programs reporting in 1984 (29 percent), therefore, field liaison personnel were never evaluated.

The Field Instructors

The median number of field instructors utilized by a program during the 1983-84 academic year was 18 (293 reporting). The percentage of first-time field instructors used in 1983-84 was 11 percent (274 reporting). Eighty-nine percent of 294 reporting programs required field instructors to have the MSW degree; 11 percent did not. Fifty percent also accepted a BSW degree as a credential for field instruction; 50 percent would not. Fifty-six percent of these programs stated that they would accept a field instructor with a degree other than MSW, BSW, or DSW, while 64 percent would not use anyone with a non-social work degree.

In 107 programs where a BSW person is used, the median number of post-BSW years of experience required was 2.3. In 176 programs where MSW persons are used, the post-MSW years of experience required was reported as a median of 2 years. In 70 instances where persons other than a BSW, MSW or DSW were used as field instructors, the required post-degree years of experience were reported as a median of 2.3 years. Other requirements were cited by 273 programs. Of these programs, letters of recommendation were required by 12 percent, in-person interviews were required by 88 percent, and curriculum vita were required by 62 percent.

Training for field instructors was institutionally sponsored by 73 percent of the 296 responding programs; 27 percent of these programs did not sponsor training. Ninety-nine percent of 212 programs providing training did so for new field instructors; 71 percent provided it for advanced field instructors. In 31 percent of 212 programs, the training provided was required for new field instructors; in 61 percent, it was recommended. In 20 percent of 154 reporting programs, training is required for advanced instructors; in 71 percent, it is recommended. The median hours of training provided was 10 hours as reported by 186 respondents. A median of twelve weeks of training was given (179 respondents).

A written evaluation of field instructors was conducted by 58 percent of 297 responding programs. Field instructor evaluations, when done, were completed by students (95 percent), program liaison personnel (40 percent), the field education director (29 percent), the field agency (9 percent), and "other" (5 percent).

Use of Full-time Faculty as Field Instructors

Full-time faculty were used as field instructors in 30 percent of 296 responding programs. The faculty serving as field instructors did so in the following settings (N = 84): 27 in a program's own service site; 45 in a field unit in another agency; 10 in a field unit separate from an agency; and 29 in "other" sites.

Identified Problems

Out of the 300 surveys returned, approximately 267 respondents completed the question on identifying the "five major problem areas of concern affecting field instruction." Of those responding, the majority cited the following areas of concern in order of frequency:

1. *Qualifications of Field Instructors* (Total N = 241) — How to find and keep persons able and willing to provide field instruction to students was a major problem. The following were perceived as contributing elements: lack of time for field instruction because of increased agency responsibilities and demands (N = 61); lack of compensation, recognition, and incentives for field instruction (N = 36); lack of appropriately credentialed persons willing to do field instruction, particularly in rural areas, BSW programs, and nontraditional settings (N = 34); lack of comprehension of the teaching aspects of field instruction (N = 24); and turnover (N = 19).

2. *Field Placements* (Total N = 173) — A second major problem was how to locate and work with those agencies which are appropriate for, and committed to, educating students. The following were perceived as contributing elements: locating agencies that can provide a generic experience for students (N = 24); cutbacks in funding and the impact on agency commitment to field instruction (N = 21);

nontraditional settings which may have no MSW staff onsite (N = 14); and the availability of placements for BSW students (N = 11).

3. *The Lack of University Support and Appropriate Administration for Field Education* (N = 92) — The perceived lack of support for field education colleagues in social work academic departments and the general university community was of particular concern (N = 47). Problems also were identified (N = 22) regarding minimal concrete supports for field education (e.g., too few staff, time pressures, faculty field workloads, lack of secretarial support, and limited funds for travel to agencies).

4. *Student-Related Issues* (N = 89) — These included the need for special field work arrangements because of work and family responsibilities (N = 35); lack of funds for transportation especially in rural areas (N = 22); writing skills (N = 10); and issues concerning liability and licensing (N = 9).

5. *Training of New and Experienced Field Instructors* (N = 81) — Of particular concern were finding resources to support training; time for field instructors to attend; and distance to travel to training in rural settings.

6. *Evaluation of Students* (N = 77) — The predominant problem cited was the lack of consistent, objective criteria for evaluating field performance (N = 24), for detecting and dealing with problem students (N = 10), and for grading (N = 9).

7. *The Integration of Classroom Curricula with the Field Experience* (N = 65) — The focus of these concerns largely centered on the perceived need to insure consonance between the model of practice taught in the classroom and the actualization of practice skills and concepts in the field.

8. *Development of Field Curriculum* (N = 56) — The most frequently noted need in this category was to formulate measurable objectives and guidelines for expected skill attainment of the BSW, and the first and second year MSW (N = 33). Respondents emphasized the need for more empirical research on curriculum objectives and assignments, skill development, and student learning styles.

9. *Faculty Liaison* (N = 50) — The need to support more structured, effective ties between the school and agencies and to develop more specific, consistent expectations for the faculty liaison role

were stressed. Receiving adequate financial support to obtain appropriate coverage was of primary concern.

10. *Suggested Area of Activity and Change* (N = 300) — Several suggestions were made with respect to the future of field education:

a. *Training* (N = 88) — Both national and regional training programs were requested. Sixteen suggestions pertained to activities related to the Annual Program Meeting (APM), including the need for an organized segment for field work presentations. Respondents emphasized the importance of regional workshops for field directors. Several asked for training of those who teach field instructors.

b. *Standards* (N = 54) — Most frequently cited was the need to develop standards and guidelines with respect to the field instructors' role and training. Also cited were standard setting for the faculty liaison role, field directors' time and credentials, number of field hours, curriculum, and outcome goals for student performance.

c. *Publications* (N = 45) — Twenty-five suggestions pertained to the development and/or dissemination of materials for use in the training of field instructors and for the development of policies and procedures regarding field education. For example, there were several requests for written and audio-visual case materials, model evaluation tools, learning modules, and a training manual for use in seminars for field instructors.

d. *Recognition of Field Education* (N = 17) — Respondents emphasized the importance of, and need for, greater acknowledgment of the role of field education in professional social work education by CSWE and others within social work education and practice. In addition to this broad request, there were some specific suggestions: promote awareness by the university and the public regarding the role of field education; assign a CSWE staff person to help convene a Committee on Field Instruction; and increase pressure for release time for field instructors.

e. *Field Instructors' Organization* (N = 16) — In addition to several suggestions for the CSWE field education committee and an Association for Directors of Field Education, there were requests for regional consortia of field educators for purposes of mutual problem-solving and collaborative activities.

f. *Recognition and Involvement of Field Instructors* (N = 11) —

Several suggestions pertained to an Academy for Field Instructors; certifying field instructors; rewarding field instructors (e.g., release time); raising the status of field instructors by granting them adjunct faculty status; and enhancing communication among CSWE, field instructors, and agency executives.

g. *Clearinghouse for Field Education Resource Materials* (N = 13) — Suggestions in relation to a clearinghouse focused on the development of a resource center for field instruction to systematically collect, compile, develop, and distribute materials such as lists of publications, current research, samples of evaluation forms, and model curricula.

h. *Miscellaneous* (N = 25) — Other suggestions, not subject to categorization because of the small number of responses and the diversity of the subject areas, included developing policies on liability; a reduced CSWE membership fee for field instructors; lobbying for funds for student field stipends; and investigation of the use of high-technology in field education.

FIELD AGENCY SURVEY

The survey of field agencies was distributed to a nonrandom sample of agencies identified by members of the Technical Assistance Group. The sample is highly selective. The purpose was to obtain preliminary data from agency-based personnel regarding: problems concerning field instruction, possible solutions, the concept of an Academy for Field Instructors, and the current source of training for agency field instructors. There were 183 responses to the survey.

Survey Results

Of 181 respondents, 45 percent were agency directors, 4 percent supervisors, and 54 percent "other." A median of 3.3 professional staff per agency served as field instructors. In 169 cases, the agency had served as a social work field instruction site for an average of 8 years (median). Agencies (N = 178) were affiliated with a median of 2.4 schools. Although the most common affiliation was with one school, 44 agencies reported affiliation with two programs, and another 44 reported ties with 3 programs.

Training was received by 90 percent of the field instructors in 180 agencies. Ninety-five percent of the training is provided by a college or university (N = 167). Forty-six percent of these agencies provide their own training for field instructors. Training is mandatory in 63 percent of the agencies (N = 171). The median number of training hours provided was 12.4 (N = 120).

Eighty-seven percent of the agency respondents (N = 155) supported the establishment of a system for certifying the credentials of a field instruction program.

Identified Problems

Respondents were asked to identify problems and issues in field education. Responses were clustered in several key areas:

- *The level of compatibility between field and classroom curricula* (N = 48). There were two clusters of responses in this area: (1) the school's lack of specific information about the realities of agency practice and, concomitantly, the agency's lack of knowledge and communication about the nature of practice taught in educational programs; and (2) an emphasis by schools on clinical practice and a loss of interest in, and emphasis on, generic practice.
- *Communication between the agency and educational program and the lack of availability of a faculty liaison person* (N = 33).
- *The experience and qualifications of students* (N = 32). Specifics included a lack of basic clinical knowledge prior to placement, level of maturity, work responsibilities, writing skills, and the need for classroom preparation prior to entry into the field.
- *Standards for field instruction and for the evaluation of student progress* (N = 31). Specifically cited were a need for more explicit guidelines regarding orientation of students, curriculum content, and goals; the development of assignments beneficial to student and agency; the assessment of student learning style; the evaluation of students' work; and differential assignments for BSW/MSW students.
- *Dealing with the demands of the job and the demands of field*

instruction; lack of agency supports for the field instruction role (N = 21). Respondents reported the difficulty of finding time to supervise and suggested that field instructors be reimbursed by the educational program.

- *The need for standards for selecting and evaluating the work of field instructors* (N = 15). Some respondents addressed the lack of uniform criteria for field instructors; others expressed the feeling that programs are not selective enough, and that field instructors are not trained as educators.
- *Loss of income to agencies when students are the service providers* (N = 6). Issues cited were that third-party payments are not applicable when students are used to provide services, and the challenge to agencies to locate noninsured clients for students (leaving the reimbursable client services to professional staff).

Suggested Areas for Activity and Change

- *Standard Setting* (N = 40). Respondents suggested that the CSWE set minimum standards for, and take action related to, field instruction in such areas as: required number of school visits; faculty review of process records; training of field educators; standards for student caseloads; continuing education requirements for experienced field instructors; guidelines for evaluating student performance; the integrating of field and classroom curriculum; and enhancing field-school communications.
- *Ongoing Training for New and Experienced Field Instructors* (N = 28). Suggestions included day-long and regional conferences; the development of working papers on the integration of the academic and field curricula; and the creation of support groups for field instructors and a newsletter for field instructors.
- *Enhancing Interaction Between Programs and Agencies* (N = 12). Suggestions from the respondents included: involvement of field faculty in classroom teaching; increasing the field faculty's knowledge of the academic curriculum; developing educational contracts containing detailed expectations for both faculty liaisons and agency field instructors; and providing

more opportunities for discussion of curriculum between field instructors and academic faculty.

- *Recognition of the Field Instructor's Role in Social Work Education* (N = 11). Suggestions included a national organization for field instructors; certification of field instructors; recognition of years of service by field instructors; and payment of field instructors.
- *Reviewing and Redirecting the Emphasis in Students' Orientation to the Profession* (N = 9). Respondents emphasized the need to provide students with a more complete picture of the breadth of the profession; to introduce them to a generic orientation, including community organization practice and policy development; and to consider the implications of psychotherapy being taught as the primary professional function.

Discussion

As the following tables indicate, there is striking agreement between field educators and field agency personnel about current challenges, needs, and directions for change in social work field instruction. Table 1 shows the common perceptions about many problematic areas: the integration of academic content and field experience; conflicting demands of job and field instruction responsibilities; need for standards for the evaluation of students; training for new and experienced field instructors; communication between schools and agencies; and the qualifications and needs of students. Indeed, with a few exceptions of items specifically linked to the schools (e.g., recognition by the university) or the agency (e.g., loss of income when students deliver services), the lists of identified issues and problems were closely parallel. Moreover, in offering problem-solving mechanisms, both agency and school respondents suggested similar strategies. Both, for example, included standard-setting, ongoing training, and recognition of field education among their top priorities (see Table 2).

The identified issues and strategies for change represent recurrent themes. The review of previous Curriculum Policy Statements highlighted historical efforts to set some standards. MacDonald's

(1961) comments on the 1952 document are equally pertinent today:

> Are we now prepared to adopt curriculum policy that will incorporate more definite requirements? First, should specific objectives for field work be stated? Second, should learning experiences be specified? Third, should the objectives provide for learning in other methods as well as the principal one? Fourth, should the policy remain silent on the proportion of time to be spent in the field? Fifth, should there be a provision on orientation or preparation for assuming direct service responsibilities in the field? Finally, should the Curriculum Policy Statement have anything to say about field work agencies, the vehicle for so much of the curriculum? A proposal to accredit field agencies has been made. Should the Curriculum Committee legislate on any or all of these questions relating to field instruction? (p. 10)

Raskin's (1983) Delphi study in field instruction identified consensus statements which are identical to issues raised in both the field education and agency studies, i.e., "a lack of specificity of what is to be learned, a lack of clearly defined criteria for first and second year placements, and inadequate attention to training for the field instructor role" (p. 12). The 1985 Canadian study (Wayne, Skolnik & Raskin) of field instruction found issues of concern which are similar to those found in this study—lack of communication between school and agency, the relationship of the academic curriculum and agency practice, and the agency and instructional demands on field instructors.

Moreover, both the practice community and field educators are looking to the Council on Social Work Education for guidance and leadership in similar areas:

- Setting guidelines and/or providing models for assignments, evaluations, and curriculum objectives
- Assistance with training (e.g., replicable modules); regional training; a forum at national conferences; and a clearinghouse on field instruction

Table 1

Identified Problems by Field Education Administrators and Agencies

Field Education

Administrators-(N=300)   Agencies-(N=81)

a) The integration and compatibility   a) The integration and
of classroom curricula with the   compatibility of
field experience - N=65   of classroom curricula with the
                                          field experience - N=48

b) Effectiveness of faculty liaison;   b) Communication between the agency
support for school- agency linkages -   and educational program; the avail-
N=50   ability of a faculty liaison person
                                          N=33

c) Student-related issues (e.g., working students; qualifications) - N=89

c) Student-related issues (e.g., working students; qualifications) N=32

d) Lack of standardized criteria for the evaluation of students - N=77

d) Standards for different aspects of field instruction and for student evaluation - N=31

TABLE 1 (continued)

Field Education	Agencies-(N=81)
Administrators-(N=300)	
e) Lack of university support and adequate administrative structures for field education - N=92	e) Lack of agency supports for field instruction role; dealing with the demands of job and educational responsibilities - N=21
f) The recruitment and retention of qualified field instructors - N=241	f) Need for standards for selecting and evaluating the work of field instructors - N=15
g) Development of field curriculum with measurable objectives for the BSW and MSW levels - N=56	g) Inadequate agency and professional recognition for the role of field instruction - N=7

h) Training for new and experienced
field instructors - N=87

h) Training for field instructors,
particularly for the advanced instructor - N=7

i) The recruitment and retention of
appropriate placements - N=73

i) Loss of income to agencies when
students are the service providers -
N=6

Table 2

Suggested Activity and Change

Field Education Administrators –
(N=300)

a) Standard-setting – CSWE guidelines (e.g., for the training of
field instructors and the faculty
liaison role) – N=45

b) Training – national/regional –
N=88

Field Agencies – (N=181)

a) Standard-setting – (e.g., required number of agency visits;
standards for student assignments) –
N=40

b) Training – for new and experienced
regional; a newsletter for field
instructors – N=23

c) <u>Publications</u> - training
modules for field instructors,
model evaluation forms, and
learning modules - N=45

d) <u>Recognition and Involvement of
Field Instructors</u> (e.g., an Academy
for Field Instructors; raise status
via adjunct faculty status and release
time; certification) - N=17

c) <u>Enhancing Interaction Between
School & Agencies</u> - (e.g., use of
field faculty for classroom teaching;
formal structures for ongoing communication; increase field faculty's
knowledge of classroom curricula) -
N=12

d) <u>Recognition of the Field Instructor's Role in Social Work
Education</u> - (e.g., a national organization for field instructors;
certification of field instructors;
recognition for years of service;
adjunct academic status; payment) -
N=11

TABLE 2 (continued)

Field Education Administrators -
(N=300)

Field Agencies - (N=181)

e) Establishment of a Field Instructors' Organization including
regional consortia and an Association
for Directors of Field Education -

N=16

e) Reviewing Students' Pre
paration for Field Practice -
need for generic orientation and
more intensive clinical know-

ledge - N=9

f) Clearinghouse for Field Education
Resource Materials - to compile,
develop, and distribute lists of publications, current research, samples of
evaluation forms, and model curricula -

N=13

g) Recognition of Field Instruction -
greater acknowledgment by CSWE and
others within social work education
and practice of the role of field
education in professional social
work education - N=11

• Mechanisms for recognizing field instructors and for helping them feel that they are part of the educational community.

The outcomes of the Field Education Project's surveys appear to offer an optimistic perspective for future problem solving. For identified problematic issues, some popular pessimistic views appear to be mitigated by the survey results — for example, most field education directors are *not* new to the job, and turnover in this position is *less* than commonly perceived. The thoughtful and high rate of survey responses and the extent of agreement on needs and strategies, suggest that change emanating from cooperative efforts among field educators, agencies, and CSWE may be possible.

Indeed, it appears that the contemporary issues confronting field education may be providing the stimulus needed to move beyond problem recognition to an active process of creative problem-solving. In order to utilize this opportunity for growth, we need to consider the development of mechanisms for insuring ongoing dialogue and continued acquisition of data on the state of the art. The CSWE project strongly suggests that both will be necessary guides as we move forward.

NOTES

1. The following individuals were the original members of the Technical Assistance Group on Field Instruction: Diane Elias Alpern; Nancy H. Bennett; Harry Blumenfeld; Esther Chachkes; Jack Conklin; Helene Fishbein; Helen Graber; Margaret Schutz-Gordon; Bart Grossman; Reva Fine Holtzman; Lowell Jenkins; Dorothy Jones; Allie C. Kilpatrick; Eve Lodge; Deena Mersky; William Perry; Miriam S. Raskin; Priscella Riley; Dean Schneck; Martin Schwartz; Beatrice Seitzman; and Julianne Wayne. Staff comprised Louise Skolnik and Margaret Gibbleman.

2. Complete findings can be obtained from the author.

REFERENCES

American Association of Schools of Social Work. (1943). *Accreditation Manual*. New York: Author.

Bloom, T. (1963). Untitled Paper, In *The future for field instruction: Agency-School commitment and communication*. New York: Council on Social Work Education.

Brackett, J. (1983). Training for work. In C. E. Munson, (Ed.). *Social work supervision, classic statements and critical issues* (pp. 6-17). New York: Free Press.

Council on Social Work Education. (1974). *Accreditation manual*. New York: Author.

Council on Social Work Education. (1953). *Curriculum Policy Statement*. New York: Author.

Council on Social Work Education. (1969). *Curriculum Policy Statement*. New York: Author.

Council on Social Work Education. (1982). *Curriculum Policy Statement*. New York: Author.

Council on Social Work Education. (1984). *Handbook of accreditation standards and procedures*. New York: Author.

Council on Social Work Education. (1971). *Manual of accrediting standards for graduate professional schools of social work*. New York: Author.

Dana, B. S., & Sikkema, M. (1964). Field instruction, fact and fancy. In *Education for social work, proceedings, twelfth annual program meeting*. New York: Council on Social Work Education.

George, A. (1982). A history of social work field instruction: Apprenticeship to instruction. In B. W. Sheafor & L. E. Jenkins (Eds.). *Quality field instruction in social work: Program development & maintenance* (pp. 37-59). New York: Longman.

Kendall, K. A. (1953). A conceptual framework for the social work curriculum of tomorrow. *Social Service Review, 28*, 15-26.

Kendall, K. A. (1959). Selected issues in field instruction. *Social Service Review, 33*, 1-9.

Lodge, R. (1975). Foreword. *The dynamics of field instruction: Learning through doing*. New York: Council on Social Work Education.

MacDonald, M. E. (1961). Major current issues in curriculum policy. In *Major issues in curriculum policy and current practices in accreditation*. New York: Council on Social Work Education.

Raskin, M. (1983). A Delphi study in field instruction: Identification of issues and research priorities by experts. *Arete, 8*(2), 38-48.

Reynolds, B. C. (1965). *Learning and teaching in the practice of social work*. New York: Russell.

Schutz-Gordon, M. (1975). *Current issues in field instruction*. Paper presented at the Annual Program Meeting of the Council on Social Work Education. New York.

Turner, J. B. (June, 1984). *Excellence in field education*. Paper presented at the New England Conference on Field Education. West Hartford, Connecticut.

Vigilante, J. L., Lodge, R., Lukton, R., Kaplan, S., & Mason, R. (1980). *Searching for theory: Following Hearn*. Unpublished Manuscript, Adelphi University School of Social Work, Garden City.

Wayne, J., Skolnik, L., & Raskin, M. S. (1988). Field instruction in the United States and Canada: A comparison of studies. In M. S. Raskin (Ed.). *Empirical studies in field instruction* (77-87). New York: The Haworth Press, Inc.

Field Instruction
in the United States and Canada:
A Comparison of Studies

Julianne Wayne
Louise Skolnik
Miriam S. Raskin

ABSTRACT. This paper reports the results of a national study of field educators and field agencies in the U.S. and Canada. Mutually recognized dilemmas and gaps in field education are identified and suggested changes are offered. Recommendations for policy and standards in this critically important, though currently undervalued, educational arena are presented.

INTRODUCTION

Tensions have always existed in the university setting between the academic and practical segments of the social work educational process. Within the university environment, research, publications and theory building are more valued and rewarded than excellence in teaching the necessary skills for professional practice. Within such an educational context, Sheafor and Jenkins (1982) argue that "field instruction programs of good quality have not typically developed" (p. ix) and that "field instruction is too often relegated to a second-class citizenship" (p. x).

It is the belief of many social work educators that current conditions further threaten the commitment of energy and resources to the practicum component. These conditions include the increasingly difficult standards for promotion and tenure. For the most part, these standards do not include field-related activities. As a result, many faculty members are less committed to field education than to academic achievement. At the same time, practitioners con-

© 1989 by The Haworth Press, Inc. All rights reserved.

cerned with fee-for-service-arrangements face increased pressure to spend more time in direct client care and less in activities such as supervising students. Thus, field instruction appears to be under stress from both directions.

Yet, the mission of the Bachelor's (BSW) and the Master's degree (MSW) in social work is to prepare graduates for different levels of practice. To devalue field instruction is to threaten an effective means of fostering the integration of theory and practice, and incorporating a strong sense of social responsibility by the student. Moreover, current concerns could herald the diminution of what has long been viewed as a primary strength of social work educators. "Unquestionably," the educator Richard Lodge noted, "much of the genius of social work education has been, through the years, an intermingling of conceptual and experiential learning. Other professional disciplines have looked to social work as a model in the use of the practicum."

Educators and practitioners already operate in different arenas and frequently speak a different professional language (Bartlett, 1950). The weakening of the classroom-agency partnership would widen this gap. Frumkin (1980) developed a framework for analyzing school-agency relationships. He states:

> Because the total needs of both agencies and schools are not taken into account, neither is satisfied with the other's performance. Schools begin to question the competence and professional commitment of agencies, agencies react to this questioning with hostility toward the school, and the traditional battle lines are drawn. (pp. 91-92)

This situation does not appear to be idiosyncratic to one region of the world. Ada A. Mere (1981), writing about university and agency perspectives regarding field education in Nigeria, notes that, "one of the major challenges facing the field work training programme is the implementation of field work goals in agencies with different aims and objectives" (p. 42).

PURPOSE OF THE STUDY

In recognition of these and other concerns about field instruction in social work education, the Canadian Association of Schools of Social Work and the American Council on Social Work Education independently engaged in national surveys to study various aspects of field instruction in their respective countries. The purpose of these studies was to learn more about various dimensions of field instruction such as the preparation of field teachers, the structural aspects of student supervision, quality control of field experiences, and the agency as an educational context.

This paper compares the two studies. The Unites States and Canada provide similar cultural contexts within which to study common problems, while providing somewhat different perspectives to help shed new light on shared concerns. As part of this comparison, gaps in each study are identified, and suggested directions for continued research are offered.

The United States and Canada enjoy a frequent exchange of students, teachers, and practitioners. These studies provide the opportunity for the exchange of ideas and the merging of problem-solving skills, and will encourage the development of policy and standards for this critically important educational arena.

DESCRIPTION OF THE UNITED STATES AND CANADIAN FIELD INSTRUCTION STUDIES

U.S. Study

Rationale and Purpose

The study was conducted under the auspices of the Council on Social Work Education (CSWE) during 1984-1985. The Council's Technical Assistance Group on Field Education initiated and guided the research. The study was stimulated by a perceived need to gather data on contemporary realities of field education as a means to develop problem-solving strategies. The study was predicated on a recognition of the primacy of the field component in professional education and of the contemporary challenges to maintaining quality in this sphere (e.g., diminishing resources, increasing demands on agency personnel, and students with special placement needs). The purposes of the investigation were as follows:

1. To explore the current state-of-the-art by obtaining baseline data on field education structures, administration, and practices.
2. To gather information on needs, problems, and issues facing field directors and agency field instructors.
3. To develop strategies for addressing identified needs and concerns, including means for supporting the role of agency-based field instructors as social work educators.

Study Design

The study utilized a two-part, exploratory-descriptive design. Data was collected through two mailed questionnaires. Both instruments were developed by CSWE (Skolnik, 1985).

The first survey was designed for school-based, field education personnel in both BSW and MSW degree programs. It requested information on demographic data for the field unit's administrator; baseline data on administrative structures, requirements for students, and credentials for training for field instructors; training needs and problem areas affecting field instruction; and comments or suggestions on how identified issues might be addressed. This questionnaire was distributed to each CSWE-accredited educational program in the spring/summer 1984. Three hundred forms were returned, representing a response rate of 75 percent for BSW programs (261 of 349) and 98 percent for MSW programs (89 of 91). Of these, 70 percent (271) were from BSW programs only, 17 percent (150) from combined BSW-MSW programs, and 13 percent (39) from MSW programs only.

The second survey was developed to gather descriptive data regarding the field agencies' involvement in field education; the training of agency personnel in their field instruction role; and the identification of problems and problem-solving strategies, including means to more formally recognize field instructors as educators. The survey was distributed to a nonrandom sample of agencies identified by the CSWE Technical Assistance Group. Each member of the group utilized field instructors at their own school as the sample population. Members agreed to distribute the questionnaires at the end of the academic year, and respondents returned questionnaires directly to CSWE. There were 183 respondents, of whom 45 percent identified themselves as agency directors, 4 percent as supervisors, and 54 percent as "other."

Canadian Study

Rationale and Purpose

In 1979, the Commission on Services of the Canadian Association of Schools of Social Work, responding to requests by practice teachers, field instructors, students, deans, and agency directors, initiated a tri-phase study of field education. (The Canadian study refers to the field practicum as field preparation, and the U.S. study uses the term field education. For purposes of uniformity, we are utilizing the term field education or instruction throughout the paper.) The findings reported are the outcome of Phase I (November 1979-March 1980) and the beginning of Phase II (through March 1982) (Thomlison, Watt & Kimberley, 1980).

The rationale for this study refers to the field component as a core element in social work education. Quality in field education is considered essential for quality in the social service delivery system. In order to investigate and act on the issue of insuring quality in field education, the study was designed to gather data regarding the status of field education and related trends, issues, and recommendations for change.

Specific questions addressed by the Canadian study centered on the costs and benefits of field education programs; remuneration for field educators; difficulties faced by schools in their efforts to develop and maintain quality field placements; integration of host-agency and school-based instructors into agency programs and services; trends in the operationalization of field education; and alternative methods of field education (e.g., laboratories and simulations).

Study Design

The study consisted of three components: a mailed questionnaire for field instructors; an interview schedule to be used with individual faculty field coordinators; and an interview schedule for use with groups of agency representatives and field instructors. The written questionnaires and the interview schedules were printed in both French and English. Each component is described in the following.

1. *Interview Schedule for Field Instructors.* The questionnaire for field instructors was ten pages in length. It was comprised of open and closed Likert scale questions. It was developed to obtain the following: descriptive data on the agencies used as field placement sites; demographic data regarding field instructors; knowledge about current practices; and information about instructors' concerns and issues.

   All Canadian schools (n = 24) submitted lists of current field instructors for BSW and MSW students. Systematic, random sampling procedures were applied to each list. From 1500 names of instructors, 682 names were selected. There were 428 responses, or a 63 percent return rate.

2. *Interview schedule for faculty/field coordinators.* Twenty-eight, open-ended questions were designed to gather data regarding the planning, development, maintenance, evaluation, and administration of field placements; the nature of the field coordinator's position; and the costs and benefits of field education to the University. Interviews involving two to three hours were conducted with 46 persons who were identified by their respective schools as occupying positions of field coordinator and/or faculty with responsibility for the planning of field education. The study report does not state whether every school participated, but the high number of respondents suggests a universal sample was desired, if not achieved. The interviews were conducted at each school.

3. *Group Interview Schedule.* Group interviews with field instructors were held at each school with a sample of 5 to 10 field instructors randomly selected from the school's current

list. The total number of interviewees was 142. The purpose of these meetings was to get further in-depth data on instructors' perceptions of trends, concerns, costs, and benefits. Emphasis was on regional and local issues.

Limitations of Both Studies

The U.S. and Canadian field education questionnaires did not correspond on every item. However, the common elements and unique features of the findings can be compared in order to begin the development of an international perspective on the state-of-the-art in field instruction.

In the U.S. study, the principal respondents were directors of field instruction of MSW and BSW programs (a total of 440). Members of the Ad Hoc Technical Assistance Committee were primarily directors of field instruction, and their individual orientation may partially explain this focus. A subsample of 183 nonrandom field instructors also were asked to respond to a questionnaire. Of the 1500 field instructors in Canada during 1979-1980, a systematic random sampling procedure was utilized to get a sample of 682 field instructor respondents. Forty-six (46) field instruction directors were interviewed. Although the same groups were seen as important in terms of input, the reverse strategy was used by the two countries. The U.S. study focused more on field directors, while Canada focused more on field instructors.

Three of the primary reasons for carrying out national field instruction studies were the same for both countries. These included: (1) to determine the status of field preparation or the state-of-the-art; (2) to gather information and describe issues and problems in field instruction; and (3) to obtain base-line data on field education structures, administration, and practice. Two additional purposes emphasized in the U.S. study were to explore the needs of the field educators and to develop means to recognize individuals in those roles. The Canadian study also wanted to identify trends. Both countries were motivated to initiate their studies because of impressions that the field component was getting short-changed in the educational process. The underlying purpose was to find ways to strengthen and improve field instruction.

The response rate for both studies to the mailed questionnaire was very similar. In Canada, 63 percent of the respondents returned usable questionnaires, compared to a 61 percent response rate for the U.S. study. These return rates were more than adequate for national studies.

The Canadian study recognizes at least four limitations. Although not explicitly stated, the U.S. study suffers from the same limitations of the Canadian research. Both studies are descriptive of many issues and concerns, but no one issue is looked at in depth; there is no way to know whether the responding sample of field directors or field instructors varied from those that did not respond; generalizations are necessarily limited; and many other relevant questions about field education are not addressed.

FINDINGS

Eleven percent of the field instructors in the U.S. and 47 percent of those in Canada were first-time field instructors. The number of students in the field was relatively stable. Therefore, unless first-time field instructors are under- and over-represented in the American and Canadian samples, respectively, Canadian field instructors seemed to have experienced a much higher turnover rate. Thirty-two references were made about the lack of preparation by students entering placement in the U.S. In Canada, 25 percent of the field instructors agreed that students were adequately prepared overall to begin practice before entering placement. Ten percent were unsure, and 65 percent did not feel students were adequately prepared. The required hours for field work are within comparable ranges in the two countries. For a BSW (in the U.S., junior and senior level), the median total hours were 500; in Canada, BSW programs reported a range of 400 to 992 hours. First and second year MSW programs ranged from 400 hours (median, U.S.) to 600 (2nd year U.S.); in Canada, the range was 256 to 546 hours (first year), and 945 to 1120 hours in the second year.

In both countries, field instructors felt that there was a lack of communication between the school and the agency; more effective ties were needed. There seemed to be great disparity between the countries in the training of field instructors. In the U.S., 73 percent of the responding schools had training for field instructors, 10 hours being the mean number of hours provided. In 58 percent of the programs, the field instructors are evaluated. In Canada, only two schools (about 10 percent) had a formalized program that focused on teaching skills. The majority of schools do not formally evaluate the field placements or the field instructor on a regular basis. Respondents in both countries perceived that the schools failed to reward the efforts of field instructors. In both countries, a reduction of support for nontraditional services and agencies has led to a decrease in nontraditional field placements.

Three other areas of ongoing concern in the U.S. also were issues that were raised in the 1980 Canadian Study. First, there is a need for clear differentiation of expectations by the schools for the BSW and MSW levels of students. Second, the concern was expressed that academic input received by students was irrelevant to direct practice. Students often had a lack of specific information about the realities of agency practice. Third, field instructors feel a conflict in demands between their role as an instructor and the expectations and demands of their role in the agency.

SUMMARY AND CONCLUSION

The United States and Canadian studies reveal, as expected, similar concerns related to field instruction. There are certain areas, however, in which the situation in the U.S. appears less problematic than the Canadian. Schools in the U.S. had significantly fewer new field instructors during the time period of this study, and more schools provided some training of field instructors. In addition, more field instructors in the U.S. felt that students were prepared for the field practicum experience. Both countries reported the need to deal with the different expectations held for the BSW and the MSW students, the important interrelationships of class and field experiences, and the conflict of field instructors with respect to their accountability to agency, student, and school.

These findings raise many new research questions. Why do the two countries experience a different rate of first-time field instructors? Is it because of the turnover of field instructors or the development of new and different practicum settings? Rapid faculty turnover is a negative factor in the educational process because experience is a key component in the development of expertise. What is the average number of years field instructors in each country remain in that role? What factors contribute to the stability of field instructors? Schools in the U.S. provide significantly more field instructor training to new supervisors. Is this a factor in the presumed lower turnover rate? Are there supports that the U.S. and Canadian schools offer new field instructors in addition to a seminar on supervision?

Fewer Canadian than U.S. field instructors find students adequately prepared to begin field placement. If so, could this perception be based on the actual preparation that students receive or on the different expectations that instructors have for the two groups? Faculty members who teach seminars on supervision to new field instructors frequently report that much of the focus of the sessions is on helping new field instructors learn what to expect from students. Without opportunities for learning how to judge students, the novice field instructor may use the performance of seasoned staff members as the standard.

These two descriptive studies document the need for further research about field instruction. Neither study explored the perceptions and attitudes toward field instructors of top level decision makers, Deans of Schools of Social Work, and high level agency administrators. Field instruction cannot flourish in a vacuum, but must be supported by universities and field settings. How strongly committed to field instruction are the social work educators and practitioners who do not have direct responsibility for its success? What do these professionals believe about how people learn? Are they distracted from the questions by the practical considerations of their daily professional lives?

The answers to these and other questions must be sought as we attempt to improve the effectiveness of the social work education process. Going beyond our boundaries contributes to "enlarging our sphere of awareness," Kimberley (1984) stated. "A practice and a scholarship of international social work and social welfare may be established that transcends not only national boundaries, but also the restrictive bounds of academic norms that impede the arrival at new understandings" (p. 2).

REFERENCES

Bartlett, H. (1950). Responsibilities of social work practitioners and educators toward building a strong profession. *Social Service Review, 24,* 379-391.

Frumkin, M.L. (1980). Social work education and the professional commitment fallacy: A practical guide to field-school relations. *Journal of Education for Social Work, 16*(2), 91-99.

Kimberley, M.D. (Ed.) (1984). *Beyond national boundaries: Canadian contributions to international social work and social welfare.* Ottawa: Canadian Association of Schools of Social Work.

Lodge, R. (1975). Foreword. *The dynamics of field instruction: Learning through doing.* New York: Council on Social Work Education.

Mere, A. (1981). Field work instruction in Nigerian schools of social work. *International Social Work, XXIV*(3), 41-45.

Sheafer, B.W., & Jenkins, L.E. (Eds.) (1982). *Quality field instruction in social work.* New York: Longman.

Skolnik, L. (1985). *National study of field instruction.* New York: Council on Social Work Education.

Thomlison, B., Watt, S., & Kimberley, D. (1980). *Trends and issues in the field preparation of social work manpower.* Ottawa: Canadian Association of Schools of Social Work.

PART II:
THE FIELD PLACEMENT PROCESS:
IN SEARCH
OF THE PERFECT PLACEMENT

Introduction

Part II takes us from the state of the art to a more specific area of field instruction—The Field Placement Process: In Search of the Perfect Placement. This section includes six articles, four of these previously published. The placement of students in the field is probably one of the most complicated, yet least understood, aspects of field instruction. There is wide variability in placement procedures with little attempt to examine their professional value. Are some placement methods more efficient or cost effective? Do different placement methods affect replacements, learning, and professional practice orientation after a student graduates? The six articles focus on decision-making with a view toward clarifying some of these questions.

Brownstein's paper, "Practicum Issues: A Placement Planning Model," presents one of the first studies that surveys agencies, field instructors, and students in one graduate school in order to determine the variables considered important in matching a student with both agency and field instructor. Brownstein found that, as enrollments increased, the placement decisions for 328 students (who were placed in a total of 124 agencies) took 400 hours. The

© 1989 by The Haworth Press, Inc. All rights reserved.

author developed a model for standardizing the variables thought relevant to practicum placement decisions. The use of a computer program reduced to one-third the necessary hours to place students (140 hours versus 400 hours). Computers were used to assist in the administrative aspects of the placement process. An addendum to this previously published article has been written specifically for this volume in order to bring the reader up-to-date on the author's experience with computer utilization in field placement.

Some of Brownstein's findings are challenged by Raskin in the paper entitled, "Field Placement Decisions: Art, Science or Guesswork?" This study utilized a purposive sample of field directors who were asked to rank, in order of importance, variables that related to making placement decisions. Respondents also were asked to indicate how often each variable is used (ranging from "always" to "never"). Fourteen (14) of the eighty-one (81) variables studied showed an association between the rank or importance of the variable and its actual use in making placement decisions. The only statistically significant association (between rank and use) with respect to the *Student* variables was "Placement Preference."

Not all schools request the same information from students in order to place them in a field agency. Do we need all the data that are asked, or are we in information overload? According to Raskin's study, only a limited number of variables considered important are actually used in making a decision. For example, although it is "commonly accepted" that the learning needs of the student are important in relation to selecting a field placement, this variable was ranked 13th in importance by field directors when first year and senior undergraduates were considered.

Field directors find that they need to replace students each year. On rare occasions, a student may even require a third placement. In their article, "Why Field Placements Fail: Study Results," Holtzman and Raskin explore the reasons students are replaced. The pilot study identifies the factors that contribute to placement disruption, the number of students that are affected, and the time involved in replacing students. "Critical cases" or examples of students who were in need of more than one placement are presented. Some factors that were cited more often as reasons given for replacement included the unavailability of both learning opportunities and a supervisor at the agency, and unethical practices at the agency.

Some schools do not replace students if there are "personality conflicts." Others may spend two to three weeks looking for a new placement. At some schools students are allowed to interview with an agency prior to finalizing a placement. Studies which focus on the placement process, compiling new insights drawn from empirical results and practical realities, will begin to assist both new and seasoned field directors in decision-making.

In "Practice Orientation of Students in Field Instruction," Patricia Campbell Ramsey suggests that the type of placement (concurrent, block, or a combination of these) influences a worker's practice orientation to be either classroom/theoretical or agency/practice. The study utilizes a quasi-experimental, static-group comparison design. The practice orientation of 150 graduates was tested by means of the Practice Orientation Scale.

According to Ramsey, students who are in a block placement adopt an agency/practice orientation. That is, the orientation is practical and accomplishment-oriented, and learning by doing is the primary frame of reference. Students in concurrent placements adopt a classroom/theoretical orientation. This orientation is deliberate and long-range, and utilization of theory is the primary frame of reference. The author believes that a worker needs to utilize both orientations. A combination of a concurrent (one semester) and block (summer) placement will provide graduates this dual orientation.

The last two articles try to determine if different gender combinations between student and field instructor have an impact on the evaluation of students' field placement experiences and student satisfaction with field instruction. Behling, Curtis, and Foster recommend that "the field placement of students and instructors must be matched carefully and thoughtfully." The match they recommend in their paper, "The Impact of Sex-Role Combination on Student Performance in Field Instruction," is female student/female field instructor or male student/male field instructor.

Thyer, Sowers-Hoag, and Love found that their initial research results seemed congruent with Behling et al., but further statistical tests showed that student gender and field instructor gender accounted for only five percent of the variance of students' evaluation of their field instructors. Contrary to the recommendation of Behling et al., these researchers suggest a gender-neutral policy with respect to the field placement process. It is interesting to note that in Raskin's study ("Field Placement Decisions: Art, Science or Guesswork?"), field directors ranked the sex and race of the student and field instructor as least important in placement decision-making. However, when indicating the actual use of this variable (sex), the range was "sometimes" and "occasionally" rather than "never" used. To date, the literature and actual placement behavior by directors of field instruction indicate inconsistency as to the importance of student-field instructor gender combinations.

What can be gleaned about the placement process from the empirical research that is available? Much data are collected but not necessarily used in the field placement decision. It is not known whether the data make a difference in performance or outcome. The process could be more efficient (and more time made available to pursue research) if some of the information currently "needed" by the decision-maker(s) is scaled down, and more emphasis is placed on up-to-date information about the agency. The evidence is not consistent in support of prespecifying gender combinations of student and field instructor. Also, further study of the relationship between practice orientation of students and the type of placement (concurrent, block, or a combination of both) is merited. Finally, replication of studies of the placement process should allow our knowledge to move beyond results that are based on a single school to findings derived from samples that allow greater generalizability.

Practicum Issues:
A Placement Planning Model

Cynthia Brownstein

ABSTRACT. The significance of the practicum's role in the professional education of social workers is discussed. A model is proposed for matching student with practicum settings, to be used as a tool to facilitate the administrative work of the practicum. Major variables inherent in the placement decisional process are highlighted and codified into a standardized format. The results of a pilot test utilizing an earlier draft of the model are reviewed.

THE PROBLEM

Most professional education includes an "on the job" training sequence along with the formal or academic classroom experience. Medicine has internships, education requires student teaching, and social work has the practicum or field placement.

In order to discuss the "becoming" of a social worker, the functions of social workers and the tasks they perform need to be identified clearly. The practicum is the primary place where much of this role definition occurs. When the student is in the practicum, teachers are concerned with both the individual student and the specific setting. What are the practice behaviors the student needs to learn? How is the student's performance evaluated? Does the setting offer the appropriate learning opportunities so that the student can acquire the knowledge, values, and skills requisite for professional social work practice? This paper attempts to provide greater specificity about practicum learning opportunities as they relate to professional social work educational objectives.

Reprinted by permission, Council on Social Work Education, from the *Journal of Education for Social Work*. Fall 1981, Vol. 17, No. 3, pages 52-58.

In this paper a model is suggested for standardization of the variables relevant to practicum placement decisions. It attempts to fill a conceptual and practical gap in our knowledge about the practicum. Organization of the data in the proposed model is a management tool that is to be used to facilitate student placement in practicum settings. Specification of the features considered in using agencies as placements may help establish better means for evaluating those agencies on their performance as placement settings.

THE SOCIAL WORK PRACTICUM

Heavy emphasis is placed on the practicum in social work. In some schools fully half the social work students' time is spent in practicum settings. This emphasis can be traced to the strong practice roots of the profession. Social work began on a "doing" base. Providing charity relief to paupers and assisting in the settlement of immigrants were the initial tasks of the profession. Though practice is an aspect of all professions, the theoretical base played a stronger role earlier in the beginnings of the traditional professions (that is, the ministry, law, and medicine). As social work has developed as a profession, its theoretical base has become more important.

To date, research exploring the practicum has been minimal. There are well-established practice modes and beliefs that have not been examined for their current professional value. One of these traditions is that the relationship between student and practicum instructor is a critical element in the education experience. The belief has been that:

> Through association with and supervision by the supervisor, the students are to be purged of feelings, attitudes, biases, and prejudices inappropriate to the social work profession . . . social work education is seen as precipitating changes in personality and attitudes. The supervisor performs casework functions vis à vis the trainees . . . enabling them to develop skills, but more importantly, to influence attitudes, affect philosophies, and develop maturity. (Gartner, 1976)

The intensity of this personal relationship is unique to social work training, where the emphasis is as much on the practicum teacher as on the setting. That individual, however, is not responsible to the sponsoring school of social work. Some schools do have faculty-based practicum instructors, but for the most part practitioners provide practicum instruction in addition to their agency responsibilities. This results in a lack of clarity about who is actually responsible for the outcomes of the practicum instruction — the schools or the agencies.

Some schools have attempted to match the learning styles of the students with the teaching styles of the practicum instructors. However, the little that we actually know about the teaching and learning process, when added to the issue of accountability, raises doubts about the value of such an effort. Schubert (1963), who has written extensively on the practicum, commented: "No light has been thrown on the association — if there is any — between the quality of field work instruction and the learning that takes place." Other schools don't attempt to match students and placement instructors at all, but actually allow students to develop their own placements.

Factors such as the cost of actual time, credit hours, and personal investment spent by students in the practicum, the time spent by agencies, and the critical role of the practicum in social work education force schools to pay careful attention to placement decisions.

The literature does not reveal any discussion of the decisional processes inherent in placement decisions. Finestone (1967) discussed the physical and social environment of the agency as it impacts on clients, but he did not deal with the relationship of that environment to teaching and learning. Blackey (1967) raised questions about the process of choosing practicum settings, acknowledging that it is an issue with which the profession must deal.

INFORMATION SYSTEMS IN SOCIAL WORK

The organization and standardization of data have not been attempted often in the social work profession. Boyd, Hylton, and Price (1978) offered an extensive bibliographic review of the use of computers in social work practice between 1970 and 1976. They found only 15 articles detailing actual computer systems, and 12 of those were for administrative tasks of accounting and statistical compilation. Very few dealt with planning and programming. They concluded: "there appears to be little interest in examining how computer technology can be applied to professional tasks that involve discretionary decision-making" (p. 370).

Scheoch and Arangio (1979) found the same lack of use of computers in the field of human services. Reid (1974) discussed the complexities of working with qualitative analyses of data, and also offered optimism about future methods of inquiry and analyses.

RATIONALE

The wide variability of placement procedures and processes is generally acknowledged. A review of the Council on Social Work Education's accreditation standards (1971) reflects this lack of specificity. How much time should an MSW student spend in the practicum? How does the school provide linkage to the field setting? What are the specific factors to consider in using a setting as a practicum placement? These questions are answered differently by each school of social work. Documentation of each school's unique set of answers is not readily available.

This paper assumes that it is possible to identify the specific agency features to be considered in deciding on the use of a setting as a practicum placement. It is further hypothesized that these variables can be identified and codified into a standardized form that can be used to "match" students and settings. A simulation of matching students and settings is attempted. The objective for the matching is to make placement decisions that are as individual as in the more traditional model and to achieve a significant reduction in the time used for the decision making.

THE MODEL

Background

This proposal for practicum placements was developed at the University of Kansas School of Social Welfare, which offers BSW,

MSW, and PhD degrees. A base or general curriculum and practicum experience is required for both BSW and MSW students. The BSW students engage in this base training in their senior year. They spend a minimum of 480 hours in a practicum setting. The first year of the 2-year MSW program provides students with their general or base social work practice. At the end of the first year, MSW students choose a specialization or concentration in either clinical work, community intervention, or administration-management-evaluation. The objective of the base or general experience is to expose the students to a broad range of case situations, including work with individuals, small groups, organizations, and communities. The focus is that the *process* of intervening with these different types of "clients" is the same, though the specific interventive *strategies* may be different.

During the 1970-71 year there were 65 students receiving base-level placements. When second-year students were included, a total of 121 students were in practicum settings. Thirty agencies were utilized as settings. For 1978-79, 177 students received base practice placements — 129 first-year MSW students and 53 BSW students. There was a total of 328 students in 124 settings. This large growth in the school over a relatively short period changed a formidable task into one that was inherently unmanageable. For example, during the 1978-79 year over 400 person hours were spent making placement decisions. Considering that the data matrix numbered in the millions, the 400 hours does not seem excessive.

Placement decisions were made on the basis of information provided by students and agencies. Students were asked to provide lengthy autobiographical statements, including their views about social work, short- and long-range career interests, general knowledge gaps, learning styles, and so on. Agencies provided such information as the philosophy of the setting, theoretical approaches used, and the major purpose or function of the setting.

The information was not organized in a way that allowed easy access. It was a highly complex and overwhelming effort to analyze and assess the information in order to use it for decision making. This is not an uncommon problem: over-information is defined as a situation where "too much information is made available to the decision-maker. Detailed or refined data are supplied when summary or gross data would suffice" (Davidson & Trueblood, 1970, p.20). Holloway (undated) addressed this issue as well: "large quantities of information often hamper the planning decision process rather than improve it."

The term "management information system" is usually used to refer to a system based on computer technology. The critical issue is not the use of computers, but whether or not the information is organized in a manner that will enable the user to extract what is important. This first attempt at standardizing the practicum information will focus solely on base-practice placements. The base experience, whether for undergraduates or first-year MSW students, is designed to offer an opportunity to develop base social work skills. Placement decisions for students in the second year of the MSW program are related to the concentration choices of clinical, community, or administration-management-evaluation areas. Once a placement-decision model is developed, it might be possible to modify it for use with second-year placement decisions.

Procedures, Samplings, Data Collection

All student and agency forms then in use for placement decisions were thoroughly reviewed and dissected. The following major dimensions or variables that were being considered in the decision-making process were initially identified: level of experience, geographic location, hours of setting, population group, service areas, attributes of the student and related special needs of the setting, work style, cultural diversity, level of structure, style of supervision, and current crisis that might affect work in the practicum.

After these major dimensions were identified, they were listed and submitted for review to a panel composed of five faculty-based practicum instructors, and five base-practice classroom faculty, all on the school's faculty. They, in turn, developed two questionnaires — one to obtain agency information and one for students.

A pilot test was run on a sample of students and agencies chosen on a random basis. A total of 35 agencies were included — about one-third of the total number of agencies used by the school. A sample of 25 base-level students was used.

A cover letter was sent to the students explaining the purpose of the study and asking them to complete the questionnaire as if they were providing the information for their practicum placement. The concern here was not necessarily for reliable information on each student, but rather to obtain information on the set of identified dimensions to see if "matches" could be made. The students were given a date for completion, told where to return the completed form, and were given a name and number to call if they had any questions. Follow-up letters were sent to nonrespondents. Twenty-two students completed the pilot questionnaire, an 88 percent response rate.

A cover letter also was sent to each agency explaining the purpose of the study. They were advised that they would be called after a week by the student research assistant to obtain the information and answer any questions they might have. This procedure was followed in order to maximize feedback from the agencies on questionnaires. A 100 percent agency response rate was achieved.

A code plan was designed and the information from the questionnaires was then transferred to key punch cards. A card sorting machine was used to sort the cards into piles for each dimension. An ordering of priorities was established for each dimension so that a decision could be made at each stage of the sorting process.

Analysis

The card sorting procedure proved to be inadequate for this complex task, which was much more than a shuffle and sort procedure. It quickly became evident that space for piling the cards in the computer center was a problem, just as space for piling and sorting the paper forms we had used in the past had been a problem. Therefore, it was necessary to eliminate the simulation match from this project. Emphasis was placed on the development of a questionnaire that could then be utilized to assist with placement decisions for the 1980-81 school year.

The responses to the survey were received and a completely revised form was developed, in close collaboration with the director of field practicum. Questions were rewritten with greater specific focus and clarity of purpose. Questions resulting in a lack of discriminatory responses were eliminated. Information was included about the school's base practice program and curriculum objectives to provide the agencies with a framework to guide them in answering some of the questions. The newly revised dimensions were included in both the agency and the student forms.

The students were asked to provide information about their BSW placements and social work related employment experience on this same set of dimensions. These four dimensions were:

1. Service Areas: Women's issues, chemical and alcohol abuse, child protective services, adoption and foster care, aging, corrections, schools, health and illness, adult protective services, financial assistance, mental health, handicaps and disabilities, mental retardation, other and explain.

2. Population Groups: Children, adolescents, young adults, middle-aged, older adults, women, men, no primary group and explain.

3. Provision of Services: Direct work with individual clients in facilitating their use of community resources, work with community resources in direct provision of services, work with community resources in developing and improving the service rather than direct service provision, work directly with clients focusing on personal growth and development, direct work with clients on utilizing peer support systems and developing interpersonal skills (such as residents in a half-way house or adolescents in a school setting), providing and helping clients obtain concrete services, planning for service provision, program development, program evaluation, research consultation to persons or organizations outside the setting, fund raising, staff development, training of professionals or paraprofessionals, continuing education, other and explain.

4. Features of the Setting: This was broken down into the following sections:
   a. whether the staff worked with individuals, families, or small or large groups.
   b. whether the staff spent its time making home visits, seeing clients in agency settings or other relevant settings; writing reports; or other and explain.
   c. whether the planning of the intervention involved work as a

member of a multidiscipline team or jointly with other relevant persons or working singly.

d. the kinds of opportunities for learning about agency policy, including whether staff meetings dealt with client interventions or agency and work issues, board meetings or committee work, other and explain.

e. the composition of the social work versus the nonsocial work staff.

f. the percentage of the service to ethnic minorities of color.

g. the opportunity for exposure to urban versus rural problems.

h. the opportunity for exposure to diversity of cultural and economic backgrounds.

i. the work-time arrangements, including the need for evening or weekend hours.

For most of the questions, agencies and students were asked to number in order starting with "1" the item that best described their setting or preference. For example, under the category "provision of services," the agency was asked to check *all* the services that described how the social work staff spent its time, with "1" assigned to the service on which they spent most of their time. They were to check only those items that applied. The students were asked to check all the services they provided when they were in placement as BSWs or for their past employment experiences.

Several additional questions covered basic areas such as transportation and geographic location. The agencies were asked if student attributes of gender and ethnicity, or their ability to speak a foreign language would be relevant to the placement. They also were asked to indicate the number and level of students they could accommodate.

In addition to a description of their past opportunities to engage in social work practice, the students were asked to provide a profile of themselves with an indication of their preferences for practicum placements. They indicated their preferences on the entire set of dimensions except for the category "features of the setting." The items from this dimension were covered in a different way. The students were asked to check the choice which best described them:

1. Whether they viewed themselves as self-starters or in need of structured situations.
2. Whether or not their life experiences had provided them with exposure to cultural, racial, economic, and religious diversity.
3. Whether they would do best in a team or solo-oriented setting.
4. Their interest in urban or rural issues.

Hours of work and unique factors such as handicaps, single parent, or parent of young children also were included. A final question asked the students to indicate whether they were facing personal stress in their lives that might affect their practicum work. This was a voluntary question.

All of this resulted in a standard set of information on the students' previous practicum placements and job experiences. The students had indicated their preferences for practicum placements and the agencies had described themselves on the same set of dimensions. Thus a composite picture of the agencies and students emerged. The student preferences would be considered in the context of their past experiences, taking into account the school objectives for base-level training.

CONCLUSION

The research reported in this paper resulted in the development of a standardized practicum placement questionnaire.[1] This questionnaire provides access to the information relevant to practicum placement decisions, allowing for decision making on an equitable and efficient basis. Without the simulation it is not possible to document either the extent of individualization possible with this format or the amount of time saved. What can be documented is that once the coding system was known (remembering to which questions the punched card holes were corresponding), it took less than a minute to review each card. This can be compared to the expenditure of minimally a half hour devoted to reading each student's autobiography and other relevant forms.

It can be concluded that the potential for time saving is enormous. This format provides a systematic method of detailing and organizing the information needed for placement decisions. The questionnaire was completed by agencies and students and used as the basis for placement decisions for 1980-81. A next step may be the utilization of computer assistance with a program for sorting. A listing of potentially appropriate agencies for each student can be printed. This listing then can be narrowed and refined by practicum administration to result in the final "matching" decisions.

ADDENDUM

The next step was taken the following academic year, 1981-82.[2] Information obtained from both questionnaires was programmed resulting in a computer-assisted placement procedure. This produced printouts on each agency and student, providing a highly succinct format and the information most relevant to the placement decisions. A choice of several potential placement sites was listed for each student, along with a placement score which indicated how closely the match met student preferences and needs around transportation, hours, etc.

The printouts were used by Practicum Administration to *assist* with placement decisions. The computer "matches" ended up becoming the actual placements in some cases. Most of the time, *one* of the agencies listed as a potential placement on the printout was used as the placement setting. The printouts greatly facilitated the entire process by transforming data into usable information. The number of hours spent on placement decisions was down to 140, about one-third the amount of time spent by Practicum Administration without the computer assistance.[3]

NOTES

1. Copies of the questionnaire are available on request from the author, Bryn Mawr College, The Graduate School of Social Work and Social Research, 300 Airdale Road, Bryn Mawr, PA 19010.

2. The Addendum was written specifically for this volume.

3. The computer program was written for Ratfor, uses Fortran extensions specific to Honeywell level 66 computers. More information may be obtained from the author.

REFERENCES

Blackey, E. (1967). *Field learning and teaching*. New Orleans: Tulane University School of Social Work.

Boyd, L. H., Jr., Hylton, J., & Price, S. (1978). Computers in social work practice: A review. *Social Work, 23*, 368-371.

Council on Social Work Education. (1971). *Manual of accrediting standards*. New York: Author.

Davidson, J. H., & Trueblood, R. (1970). Accounting for decision-making. In A. Rappoport (Ed.). *Information for decision-making: Quantitative and behavioral dimensions*. New Jersey: Prentice-Hall.

Finestone, S. (1967). Selected features of professional field instruction. *Journal of Education for Social Work, 3*(2), 14-26.

Gartner, A. (1976). *The preparation of human service professionals*. New York: Human Sciences Press.

Holloway, W. (no date). The underlying information system. (Available from Cynthia Brownstein, Bryn Mawr College, The Graduate School of Social Work and Social Research, 300 Andale Road, Bryn Mawr, Pennsylvania, 19010).

Reid, W. J. (1974). Developments in the use of organized data. *Social Work, 19*, 585-593.

Schoech, R., & Arangio, T. (1979). Computers in the human services. *Social Work, 24*, 96-102.

Schubert, M. (1963). *Field instruction in social casework*. Chicago: University of Chicago Press.

Field Placement Decisions: Art, Science or Guesswork?

Miriam S. Raskin

ABSTRACT. This article reviews the literature related to the decision-making process in field placement for social work students. The results of a pilot study conducted by the author shows that the most important variables utilized in decision-making are related to the field instructor, the agency, the school, and environmental factors. The least important variables were related to the student. Implications of "matching" student to field instructor and agency are also discussed.

INTRODUCTION

Schools of social work have been placing students in field work agencies for almost 100 years. Despite great strides in providing learning experiences for students, procedures, rationales and guidelines have not been developed in order to optimally execute this educational (and administrative) activity. The "how" and the "why" of placement decisions remain unknown. How does a new director of field instruction know which student to place in which agency? How does a seasoned field director know which agency will provide the best learning experience for one of the two hundred students he/she needs to place? Is the process of field placement an art, a science, or purely guesswork? The present state of the art, coupled with the lack of empirical literature related to field placement decision, leaves the educational community with an unfinished jigsaw puzzle.

Field work directors have been operating without research-based

This paper originally appeared in *The Clinical Supervisor*, Vol. 3, No. 3, Fall 1985, pages 55-67, published by The Haworth Press, Inc.

© 1989 by The Haworth Press, Inc. All rights reserved.

data. This suggests the following questions: (1) What is known about decision-making in social work field placement? (2) Can a comprehensive list of variables be identified which field directors utilize in making decisions in field placement? (3) Which variables are ranked as the most important? Which ones tend to "always" be used when making a decision, which ones are "sometimes" used, and which are "never" used? (4) What role do subjective factors play in the decision-making process? and (5) Is "matching" of student, agency, and field instructor a general practice by Directors of Field Instruction and, if so, how significant is that process for field work outcomes?

The social work literature primarily contains descriptions of field work and its various components. A recent study (Raskin, 1983), however, showed that consensus exists among field work experts that we do not have empirically-based research knowledge about how field work decisions are made (e.g., which student is placed in which agency and why).

PURPOSE OF THE PAPER

The purpose of this paper is twofold. First, the literature pertaining to placement decisions for the adoption of children and field placement decision-making is reviewed. The literature on adoption illustrates the relatedness of child welfare and field placement decision-making issues. For example, studies of the characteristics of families, thought to be important for the future adjustment of children and parents, found no significant relationships (Kostin, 1972; McGowan & Meezan, 1983). As more empirical studies in child welfare were carried out, previously untested selection criteria of suitable parents changed. Are variables (or factors) also being employed in field placement decisions which are not significantly related to field work outcomes?

The second purpose of this paper is to report the findings of a pilot study. The study begins to address the five questions posed earlier in the paper. Before it can be determined if variables utilized in field placement decisions are significantly related to outcome, we need to establish which variables are actually used by field directors, how often they are used, and if there is a relationship between their rank (importance) and their use.

THE STATE OF THE ART

Adoption Decision-Making

Adoption screening requires predicting the applicant's capacity for parenthood. There is sufficient documentation to show that the relative number of available children affects the selection process, with selection becoming more problematic as the number of applicants exceeds the number of children (primarily white, healthy infants). The criteria considered important in evaluating couples who wish to adopt have shifted due to supply and demand. When criteria used in the selection of adoptive parents for normal white infants (age; physical and emotional health; marital status; infertility; religion; financial stability; capacity for parenthood; adjustment to sterility; motives for adoption; attitude toward illegitimacy, etc.) were closely scrutinized with adoption outcomes, Kadushin (1980) reports that "in general, background factors of both the child and the parents appear to have little relation to adoptive outcome" (p. 530). In addition, such factors as number of placements experienced by the child, his/her history of institutional placement, socioeconomic background, and history of pre-adoption deprivation, do not appear to be related to adoptive outcome. Although age at placement is a factor found to be negatively related to outcome, a high percentage of older children are successfully adopted.

A much used practice, despite its lack of relationship to adoptive outcome, is "matching" between adoptive parents and children. The use of this practice is supported in the literature, but its unrelatedness is shown via reports of successful interracial placements. The general factors found to be related to adoption success are attitude of parents toward the child and the nature of their relationships. Acceptance of, and satisfaction in, adoptive parenthood and acceptance of the child are also associated with adoption success. The child's sex is clearly related to outcome according to research. Adopted boys seem more likely to be maladjusted than either adopted girls or non-adopted peers (Kadushin, 1980).

Kadushin stated that "various factors interact with each other so as to modify the effects of the contribution of any one factor to the overall results. Ultimately, it is the configuration of factors that determines outcomes" (p. 531). He also found (p. 517) that 66% of agency-placed adoptions were judged successful; 18% were fair, moderate, or average. Only 16% were judged to be failures. For independent adoption, the failure rate (based on two available studies) is slightly higher at 25%. However, when we look at "hard to place" adoptions, where criteria are often relaxed, the failure rate was 12%. The conclusion, then, is that adoptions tend to be overwhelmingly successful even if minimal criteria (as in independent adoptions) or relaxed criteria are utilized in selecting adoptive parents.

In addition to studies that have assessed adoption success, research has been carried out which looked at the reliability of adoption workers' decision-making. Brieland (1959) taped intake interviews which one worker conducted with five different adoptive couples. He asked 182 caseworkers in 28 different agencies (in 13 states) to decide whether or not the agency should continue contact or reject the couple for adoption. The overall agreement was 73.6% which led Brieland to conclude that although there is some general tendency toward agreement, there is also a considerable percentage of disagreement.

Brown (1970) replicated Brieland's work using videotaped interviews. Eighty-four adoption workers participated in the study. The overall agreement was 72%, again with a substantial deviation from consensus. In a 1968 follow-up study of adoption, Ripple stated that there is "little evidence that potential for good parenting can be assessed with confidence" (p. 494).

Questions similar to those relevant to field placement have been addressed in the child welfare literature. For example, Rosenblatt and Mayer (1970) explain that the Child Welfare League of America has developed standards and even codified the information that a worker is to collect, in order to assist them in decision-making. The manual recommends the collection of data including personality of each family member, their functioning at work or in school, their relationship with others in the community, etc. However, Rosenblatt and Mayer stress that the manual fails to indicate how the information that is gathered is to be used. What bearing does all this information have on the dependent variable, the welfare of the child? What relevance do these data have for the social and psychological functioning of those involved? The amassing of information which plays no role in the decision-making process can be looked on as nonproductive activity. "The effectiveness of placement decisions can only be improved through empirical study" (Rosenblatt & Mayer, 1970 p. 59).

Field Instruction Placement Decisions

The field instruction literature, comparable to the earlier adoption literature, stresses the importance of matching students with agency and field instructors. Suanna Wilson (1981) describes the role of students and directors of field instruction in the placement of students. The field director reviews files regarding the experiences offered by the agencies, reviews student's files and feedback from classroom instructors, and begins the process of matching student to agency. Students express their preference for a type of placement and participate in interviews for preliminary screenings or matching with agency.

Wilson feels that an effective field placement program matches students' personalities, educational requirements, and learning styles with field instruction settings and individual supervisors who can provide what the student needs. Although she admits this is not an easy task, there is no empirical basis for matching or for the variables that are recommended for matching. She notes that a student must provide other basic information before a placement is made: availability of a car, where the student lives, age, level of training, previous courses, grades, previous work and volunteer experience, previous field placement, strengths, limitations, life experiences, and student preference for placement. The literature, however, indicates that many of these variables (information) are not related to student success (outcome) in field placement. Findings are drawn from admissions prediction (Cunningham, 1982; Pfouts & Hinley, Jr., 1977; Dailey, 1970) and field work performance studies (Torre, 1974).

Wilson recognizes the role of intervening variables that may contribute to less than ideal placements — that is, variables that are not considered when making a placement but which may influence placement decisions. For example, sometimes the agency administrator determines who will supervise students. Often this may be someone who has supervised for years, although years of experience are not synonymous with good field instruction. If there are several schools competing for placements, the best agencies will become overloaded. Agencies often request students with specific types of attributes and background experiences. Yet, recognizing the presence of a host of circumstances and their possible configuration and interaction with each student, Wilson maintains that difficulties encountered in the field are frequently due to "poor matching between their (students') expectations, needs, and educational goals and those of the setting" (p. 304).

The importance of matching students was emphasized by the United Nations:

> The choice of a particular agency for a given student will depend on the student's needs and desires, his stage of training, the kind of supervision he needs and a variety of other issues at any given time and place. The careful matching of student, supervisor, and agency is an important element in successful learning. (United Nations, 1958)

In 1972, Manis supported the notion of the ideal placement model. He says that in the industrialized nations, with long established relationships, the schools have the means of matching student, field instructor, and agency. He was contrasting this experience to that of the then lesser developed countries. Manis and the United Nations do not state why matching is important and which variables really make a difference.

One of the few empirical studies that tries to look at factors that affect field work performance was carried out by Behling, Curtis and Foster (1982). These researchers took the variable of sex and tried to determine not only if the sex of the student affects field performance, but whether the sex-role combination of female student and male instructor influences the student-instructor relationship and performance in field instruction.

The premise underlying this study was that research has shown that the sex of the client and the worker is a significant factor which affects the helping relationship. Therefore, the sex-role combination of students and field instructors needs to be considered in the teaching/learning relationship and, subsequently, student performance in field.

Data from the Behling et al. study showed that the same sex-role combination (female-female; male-male) was associated with more positive outcome generally than unlike combinations. The researchers conclude that the most problematic sex-role combination is female student and male instructor. "We suggest that the field placement of students and instructors must be matched carefully and thoughtfully" (p. 97).

A recent article by Brownstein (1981) reports on the first attempt to derive a placement-planning model. This was a beginning attempt to standardize variables relevant to practicum placement decisions. Brownstein reports that some schools don't match students at all and allow (graduate) students to develop their own placement. The lack of guidance in this area points to the absence of much discussion in the literature about the process inherent in placement decisions. Brownstein feels it is possible to identify specific agency factors, codify them into a form, and use this to "match" students and settings. The information was put on computer cards. Although the information could be read off the card in one minute versus the half hour previously needed, storing the cards became cumbersome and a placement decision model was not developed by the time Brownstein's article was published. Moreover, no rationale for any of the items listed on the newly developed forms is given by Brownstein.

In a paper at the Council on Social Work Education Annual Program Meeting in 1977, Cronian describes the George Warren Brown School of Social Work's experience of student-initiated field learning. A five year study led the faculty to the conclusion that field learning should be open to more decision-making on the part of the student and field instructor, rather than limited to the decision of a faculty person. Cronian showed that different styles of learning were not significantly related to a student's development in the field.

THE PILOT STUDY

A list of variables was developed by the author that could be utilized by a field director when making a field placement decision. The original list contained 44 variables which were grouped under five major factors: Student, Agency, Field Instructor, School, and Environmental. Three directors of field instruction were asked to react to the list and were also requested to add any variables which were not included, but which they used in making field placement decisions. The revised list, ultimately used in the pilot study, included a total of 81 variables and an "Other" category. In addition to the pilot study instrument, a questionnaire which asked for demographic information of each field director and questions related to amount of time spent on field work tasks was included. Space was allocated for respondents to determine if the variables which were listed were used by them "always," "very often," "often," "sometimes," "rarely," "hardly ever," or "never" (see Table 1 for sample of study instrument).

A purposive random sample of twenty (20) directors of field instruction from accredited programs was selected for the study—ten from undergraduate programs, and ten from graduate schools. Participants were asked to: (1) rank the variables within each factor from most important to least important as they related to the decision-making in field placement; and (2) indicate how often each variable is used ranging from "always" to "never."

Nonparametric statistics, Frequencies, and Spearman RHO from the SPSS computer package were utilized to analyze the responses. The relationship between the rank of a variable and its corresponding degree of use was also explored.

RESULTS

Of the 20 schools that were surveyed, 12 responded (a 60% response rate). Table 2 illustrates the geographic distribution of the responding schools. Six schools are located in urban areas, four are rural schools, and two are in suburban areas. Six respondents represented undergraduate programs, three MSW programs, and three from both BSW and MSW programs.

The directors of field instruction have an average of 8.1 years of teaching experience. The respondents held their positions as field directors from as little as 2 months to a maximum of 14 years, with the average time being 3.4 years. Five respondents had been directors of field instruction at other universities, but only one individual held this post for 14 years (present and other university). Of the 12 participants in the study, six carried out research in the area of field instruction (not specified) and six had not.

The number of students that were placed by each director per year ranged from a low of 8 to a high of 250. The respondents estimated that it took an average of three (3) hours to place one student. The total estimated time to place all students in a given year ranged from 16 hours to 650 hours (with one response being "endless").

The subprogram, Frequencies, was utilized to determine the mean ranks of the variables. The most important variables in field placement decision-making within the 5 Factors were found to be: quality of agencies and field instructors ($\bar{x} = 1.75$); interest of field instructor in supervising students $\bar{x} = 1.47$); professional support system ($\bar{x} = 1.58$); agency provides social work supervision ($\bar{x} = 3.41$); and placement preference/student interest ($\bar{x} = 4.7$). As decision-making studies have shown, it is rare that one variable contributes a major percentage to a decision. Therefore, 3 top ranked variables for each factor are shown in Table 3 in order to provide the beginning of a streamlined, field placement decision model.

Those variables that were ranked as least important in field placement decision-making include: availability of liaison, number of schools in area competing for placements and type of placement offered — block/concurrent; economic situation and receptivity of community; age, race, and sex of the student; whether the field instructor had published or had research experience and age of the field instructor; and the number of students an agency can accommodate; the type of placement it offers — block/concurrent and who the contact person is at the agency.

The Student factor shows the highest ranks (least important in decision-making). In fact, students' educational needs ranks less important than the 3 top school variables, field instructor variables, environmental variables, and top 2 agency variables. In addition,

Table 1

Sample Variables From Five Factors Utilized in the Study

When you consider the list below, think in terms of senior undergraduate students and first year graduates. (Second year student placements often are heavily weighted toward a specialization).

Field Instructor Variables

Age----------------------------------

Sex----------------------------------

Race/Ethnicity-----------------------

School Variables

Offers block/concurrent or both------

Availability of agencies-------------

Availability of supervision----------

Never

Hardly Ever

Occasion-ally

Some-times

Often

Very Often

RANK

Environmental Variables

Economic situation------------------

Number of agencies available in the
community------------------

Professional support system------------------

Agency Variables

Location of Agency (distance)------------------

Type of services provided------------------

Type of clients served------------------

Student Variables

Age------------------

Sex------------------

Previous Volunteer Experience------------------

Table 2

Geographic Location of Respondents

Region	Number	Percent (%)
Northeast	1	8.3
Northwest	1	8.3
Southeast	1	8.3
Southwest	1	8.3
Midwest	1	8.3
West	2	16.7
East	5	41.7
Total	12	100%

the field directors rated the students' age and sex as one of the least important variables in placement decisions. However, as the literature shows, the age of the student (Cunningham, 1982) and the sex of both student and field instructor (Behling, Curtis, & Foster, 1982) are variables that seem to affect field work outcome.

For six variables, a negative correlation between rank and use of the variable in decision-making were found. Five of the variables are included in the Student factor and one in the Environmental factor. Student age ranked 28th, yet only one respondent checked "never" used and two said "hardly ever." Student race ranked 27th while two people said they use this variable "often" in decision-making and 5 use it "occasionally." "Schedule Requested" by the student ranked 11th, yet two field directors said they "always" use it and 4 "very often." "Type of learner" and "skill level" of student tied for 7th rank, yet in both cases 7 people use these variables "always" and "very often." In the Environmental factor, Economic Situation ranked last out of 5 variables, yet 8 respondents said they use this variable "very often."

Spearman correlation coefficients were determined for the ranking of the 81 variables and their corresponding use. Fourteen associations were found to be significant. In the *School factor*, the following variables' ranks and how often they are used were significant:

- Availability of supervision (.018)
- Availability of agencies (.027)
- Type of placement schools offer — block/concurrent (.013)

In the *Agency factor*, the following variables' rank and use were significantly correlated:

- Number of students agency can accommodate (.012)
- Flexibility of agency (.032)
- Meets school's criteria (.026)
- Place for student to work (.001)

In the *Field Instructor* factor, the significant correlations include:

Table 3

Fifteen Variables Ranked as Most Important by Field Directors

Factor	Variable	Rank Within Factor	Mean	Rank All Variables
School	Quality of agencies and field instructors available	1	1.75	(3)
	Availability of agencies	2	2.33	(5)
	Availability of supervision	3	2.68	(6)
Field Instructor	Interest in supervising	1	1.47	(1)
	Previous supervision	2	3.6	(9)
	Degree	3	4.9	(12)

		Mean	Rank
Environmental			
Professional support system	1	1.58	(2)
Number of agencies available	2	2.08	(4)
Supplemental opportunity available	3	3.00	(7)
Agency			
Provides social work supervision	1	3.41	(10)
Type experience agency provides	2	4.33	(8)
Educational commitment	3	6.0	(14)
Student			
Placement preference	1	4.7	(11)
Educational needs	2	5.7	(13)
Transportation	3	6.6	(15)

—Previous supervision by field instructor (.033)
—Degree of field instructor (.020)
—Personality of field instructor (.025)
—Willingness to take course (.001)
—Post MSW experience (.006)
—Previous teaching experience (.023)

In the *Student factor*, only Placement Preference (.014) was found to be significantly correlated.

Of the top ranked 15 variables (Table 3), only five were found to have significant correlations between rank and use.

DISCUSSION

Although there was a 60% response rate, the study involves only 12 programs. There was sufficient representation of geographic locations, type of programs, teaching experience, and research activity by field directors to have a beginning indication of what may be occurring nationwide. The average time to place a student was estimated to be three hours, but several respondents indicated that the time doesn't take into account problem students, arranging meetings, etc. Probably a more accurate estimate of the time involved would be 5-6 hours per student when all activities are considered.

By returning to the five questions posed earlier in the paper, we can attempt to propose some answers as well as pose some additional questions. The literature about decision-making in field work is almost nonexistent. In the present study, the variables within the Student factor had the highest ranks (least important) among the top 15 variables. In addition, only one variable related to the student ("Placement Preference") had a significant association between rank and use.

A list of decision-making variables has been developed, but it is too early to determine if decisions can actually be made by directors of field instruction if they were given only the top ranked 15 or 20 variables. The variables that showed a negative association between rank and use must be considered. Are they part of the "Subjective" role of decision-making? Five of the six variables that had negative correlations were Student variables. That is, we say that student age, race, schedule, type of learner, and skill level are not very important, but then indicate that in practice we do use them. Suppose this information was not available to the decision-maker, could a successful placement still be made? Are we saying one thing but in practice doing another? Are we collecting too much or irrelevant data?

Some questions that remain unexplored include the following: (1) Do the top ranked variables contribute to field work success? (2) If the same information was presented to a group of field directors, would they be able to make the same placement decisions with a high degree of reliability? (3) If reliability in decision-making cannot be achieved, should the profession press for more standardization (less guesswork and more science) or does the profession need to move toward a modified or completely new method of placing students? (4) Is computerizing placements the answer? What variables would be used as input into the computer? and (5) Since important variables seem to focus on the agencies, field instructors, the community environment, and the school itself, should a formal yearly assessment be made of acceptable agencies and field instructors and allow students more participation into the process as suggested by Cronian (1977) and the experience at the George Warren Brown School of Social Work?

The title of this paper (*Field Placement Decisions: Art, Science or Guesswork?*) points to an ongoing process in social work education. There is no doubt that field placement decisions are partially an art. The science component is just beginning to develop. With increased empirical work, we will be better prepared to say just how much of the jigsaw puzzle is guesswork.

REFERENCES

Behling, J. C., Curtis, C., & Foster, S. A. (1982). Impact of sex-role combinations on student performance in field instruction. *Journal of Social Work Education, 18*(2), 93-97.

Brieland, D. (1959). *An experimental study of the selection of adoptive parents at intake*. New York: Child Welfare League of America.

Brown, E. G. (1970). Selection of adoptive parents — A videotape study, PhD Thesis, School of Social Service Administration, University of Chicago.

Brownstein, C. (1981). Practicum issues: A placement planning model. *Journal of Education for Social Work*, *17*(3), 52-58.

Child Welfare League of America. (1959). *Child welfare league of America standards for foster family care services*. New York: Author.

Cronian, D. L. (March, 1977). *A contractual approach to practicum learning*. Paper presented at the Council on Social Work Education Annual Program Meeting, Phoenix, Arizona.

Cunningham, M. (1982). Admission variables and the prediction of success in an undergraduate field work program. *Journal of Social Work Education*, *18*(2), 27-33.

Dailey, D. (1970). The validity of admissions predictions: Implications for social work education. *Journal of Social Work Education*, *10*(2), 12-19.

Kadushin, A. (1980). *Child welfare*. New York: McMillan.

Kostin, L. B. (1972). *Child welfare: Policies and practice*. New York: McGraw-Hill.

Manis, F. (1972). *Field practice in social work education*. California: Sultan.

McGowan, B. G., & Meezan, W. (1983). *Child welfare current dilemmas, future decisions*. Itasca: Peacock.

Pfouts, J., & Hinley, H. C., Jr., (1977). Admission roulette: Predictive factors for success in practice. *Journal of Social Work Education*, *13*(3), 56-62.

Raskin, M. (1983). A Delphi study in field instruction: Identification of issues and research priorities by experts. *Arete*, *8*(2), 38-48.

Ripple, L. (1968). A follow-up study of adopted children. *Social Service Review*, *42*, 479-497.

Rosenblatt, A., & Mayer, J. (1970). Reduction of uncertainty in child placement decisions. *Social Work*, *15*, 525-529.

Shinn, E. B. (1968). Is placement necessary: An experimental study of agreement among case workers in making foster care decisions, PhD Thesis, New York: Columbia University.

Starr, P., Taylor, D. A., & Taft, R. (1970). Early life experiences and adoptive parenting. *Social Casework*, *51*, 491-500.

Torre, E. (1974). Student performance in solving social work problems and work experience prior to entering the MSW program. *Journal of Social Work Education*, *10*(2), 114-117.

United Nations. (1958). *Training for social work*. New York: Author.

Wilson, S. J. (1981). *Field instruction techniques for supervisors*. New York: Free Press.

Why Field Placements Fail:
Study Results

Reva Fine Holtzman
Miriam S. Raskin

ABSTRACT. This paper explores the field placement process as well as reasons for placement disruption/replacement. The results of a pilot study on the replacement of students in field placement is presented. Key variables that may contribute toward a more educationally effective field placement are identified.

INTRODUCTION

The field placement process is a difficult, complicated, and time consuming task. Part of the difficulty is that the process is somewhat of a mystery. The literature has focused on the participants rather than on the process itself. Some studies have looked at students, others at field instructors, fewer at agencies and faculty field liaisons, and even fewer at the primary decision-maker, the director of field instruction.

Since the field practicum component of the social work curriculum is a major factor in students' learning, more attention needs to be given to the many variables considered in the assignment of a student to a particular agency. To what extent do schools pay attention to these variables, and what are the priority variables that contribute to a positive field placement experience? Systematic study of the *process* of field placement by the authors has uncovered a continuum of differences among schools. It ranges from one extreme that permits students to select their own field assignments, to one where the school faculty carry the major educational decision-making role in conjunction with the agency, resulting in a "match" between student, agency, and assigned field teacher. Some schools

© 1989 by The Haworth Press, Inc. All rights reserved.

also are experimenting with computerization of the placement process as a way to reduce the time involved and to facilitate final decision-making.

Limited systematic attention has been paid to placement and even less to the replacement of students. Our understanding of the field placement process can be developed by examining why certain placements "work" and why some do not. When the subsequent process of student replacement is required, it is important to identify what critical variables exist and the specific process that takes place. Frequently, such relevant replacement information either may not be collected or retained by the schools.

The replacement of a student in field work can be an administrative nightmare if there are many cases, if they occur at mid-semester, and if there are few available alternative agencies. Often, this is a problem, especially if it is assumed that the first placement had taken into account all the important factors believed to be required for a successful placement.

PURPOSE OF THE STUDY

This paper reports the results of a pilot study on the replacement of students in field work, with some focus on the variables used in decision-making in initial placements compared to those used in replacement. A questionnaire was developed which requested data from directors of field instruction in both graduate and undergraduate programs, including demographics about the responding schools; agencies used; students; and field work faculty. Data obtained also included the number of students placed and "replaced" in an academic year, steps used in the placement/replacement process, and the success of second and third placements.

Specific "cases" of replaced students and reason(s) for replacement will be discussed. Study findings and their implications will be presented together with issues and dilemmas which they raise. For example, are students being "matched" on any consistent criteria? Does this process work? (Some believe that matching and/or individualization are not necessary, and other methods of placement are considered equally effective.) Can replacements be decreased and/or prevented?

REVIEW OF THE LITERATURE

Suanna Wilson (1981) accurately describes activity in placing students. The process of "matching" student with agency begins with a review by the field director of students' files, available feedback from classroom instructors, student preference for a type of placement, agency files, and current data about available learning experiences. Variables and variations affecting this process are many: the ability of students to develop and/or select their own placements; students' preferences may or may not be considered (especially in first year MSW); students may or may not have a pre-placement interview; in schools where students interview, two or more agencies may be visited and, by mutual agreement between the agency and student, one of the agencies is selected. Although other nuances exist, these descriptions seem to summarize the overall placement process.

The decision-making process may be shaped by the following preferred practice approaches:

1. The placement planning decision is *left completely to the students* to determine their needs and interests, based on the premise that the graduate student is an adult learner able to assume this responsibility. (In the present study survey, some schools reported that they do permit students to find their own placements.) This approach is also recommended by Suanna Wilson and used in some schools in the mid-West. Focus is on the student's basic "rights."

2. Major attention is given to the *agency's requests/needs*. This approach tends to be more "service/worker" oriented than educational. Agency concern is for a student to "fit" its service orientation (i.e., family therapy, case management, or needs of a particular population) and preference is for students who can "match" these as to language, ethnicity, skill, etc. Emphasis may be on "productivity" and expectations of the staff rather than student learning needs. The agency has the option to approve or disapprove the student. In undergraduate programs, interviews are part of a mutual assessment process between student, agency, and field instructor. Interviews allow all parties to agree to go ahead with a placement, initially selected by the school. The results of this study point to widespread use of such pre-placement interviews. How-

ever, some do not endorse this practice. The Consortium of Schools of Social Work in the Metropolitan New York area, for example, has a position statement noting that such pre-placement interviews are not educationally or administratively functional, and such interviews are not sanctioned (except those on a scholarship basis).

3. *All parties are active participants* in the process, but the school maintains the primary role in making the final decision. This option is predicated on an on-going positive school-agency relationship and a high degree of collaboration and trust among all parties involved. The school carries the "contractual" and educational obligation for the student's learning, reviewing and assessing key variables (educational and reality/administrative) to select and approve a sound educational placement.

The literature emphasizes the importance of "matching" in field placement. Wilson (1981) maintains that difficulties in the field are frequently due to "poor matching between their (students') expectations, needs, and educational goals and those of the setting" (p. 304). Others that stress matching include the United Nations (1958), Manis (1972), Behling et al. (1982), and Orzek (1984). A study by Brownstein (1981) attempts to standardize variables relevant to placement decisions. Information about the students' background, agency settings, and field instructors was gathered and placed on computer cards. This method reduced the time in which the information could be read by the decision-maker, but a conclusive placement model has not been established at this time.

In 1977, Cronian described the student-initiated field learning experience at The George Warren Brown School of Social Work. Results from a five year study led Cronian to conclude that different styles of learning were not significantly related to a student's development in the field. The faculty subsequently decided that field learning should be open to more decision-making on the part of the student and field instructor rather than be limited to the decision of a single faculty person.

Raskin (1984) developed a list of variables for placement decisions. Directors were to rank each variable as to its importance and frequency with which the variable was used in making a placement decision. The variables that ranked as least important related to student variables, with only "Placement Preference" having a significant association between rank (importance) and use. Of the top rated 15 variables, the three that ranked the lowest in importance included: (13th) — educational needs of students; (14th) — educational commitment of the agency; and (15th) — transportation of the student.

In trying to continue to build a knowledge base of the decision-making process of field placement, the present study of field placements that fail, and what can be done to reduce such failures, has been undertaken.

DESCRIPTION OF THE STUDY

In 1984-85, the authors conducted a pilot study (in two phases) which examined the replacement of students in field placement. Directors of field instruction provided information and feedback. This first pilot effort helped refine the questionnaire used in the study. Field directors seemed reluctant to fill out the initial questionnaire, contributing to an initial low response rate. As a result, the length and type of questions were revised. The questionnaire was designed to secure certain demographic information about the respondents and their schools, as well as statistics on numbers of students who were placed, dropped out, or replaced. There is variation in the type of data recorded by schools and, in some instances, it was ascertained that schools did not keep sufficient information about this issue to be able to respond. Several respondents remarked that they need to have this type of information more readily available, especially when assessing and evaluating the field component. Some field directors felt that the questionnaire tended to highlight a review of their problems in placement. That is, if a placement was disrupted, the field director felt they had made a mistake — placement failure was their fault.

Schools were selected randomly from accredited social work programs. Sixteen (16) responses were received. Schools where replacements had occurred were asked to provide "case examples" of five different students needing replacement in 1984-85. These examples were to provide a more "in-depth" individualized picture of each student situation. The study also sought to determine if schools are presently utilizing computers in the placement process or if it was a possibility in the near future.

The data analysis is descriptive and the sample is limited. However, such a study, even with preliminary and tentative findings, can contribute to the state of the art in decision-making in field instruction and provide information on the issue of replacements.

RESULTS

The greatest number of responses were received from the East Coast; of the 16 reponses, 6 were from the Northeast and 4 from the Southeast. The majority of schools are located in an urban community (11); four in rural and one suburban. For all responses, the Director of Field Instruction was the person filling out the questionnaire. In four programs, the Director of Field Instruction is the sole person to arrange field placements. In two programs, 8 or more people, other than, or together with, the Director arranged placements. In 1983-84, there were five programs that had 225 or more students in the field. There were 24 students or *less* in field placement in five other programs. The data show that most of the placements were in urban communities with suburban and rural being almost equal. Only two schools indicated they are using computers in the field placement process, while eleven schools responded "no" to the use of computers.[1] Seven could foresee utilizing computers in the next five years, one said "no," and five were unsure.

In fourteen schools, the students are interviewed for field placement by the agency and only one school does not have student interviews. One indicated that only second year students are interviewed. In eleven schools, students may interview with more than one agency and in five schools they may not. The data show an emerging trend of agencies having only one student. Only one school reported that all field instructors hold the MSW. In terms of selecting an agency, 11 schools indicated that they read written material of the agency and 8 read material as part of an on-site visit. Fifteen schools interview the field instructor and ten interview other agency personnel. Fifteen schools hold seminars for new field instructors; only one respondent indicated that these seminars were not held. Ten schools require the seminars, while 5 do not require them. Twelve schools also hold advanced or continuing seminars for field instructors with six conducting them on a regular basis and eight doing so occasionally. Fourteen schools said that they match students, one said they did not match, and one qualified its answer by saying that the school "matches," but students interview and have a choice. The most frequent criteria utilized in the "matching" process included: *Student* — interest; available transportation/ location; previous work and volunteer experience; educational needs; maturity; agency's willingness to work with faculty and to provide learning opportunities; services provided and type of client population in the agency; availability and quality of supervision; participation and time available for meetings and training; and *Field Instructor* — degree; time and support for student supervision; practice experience; and interest in supervision.

REPLACEMENT

Thirty-nine case examples were provided by the respondents. Of these, 13 males and 26 females were replaced; six (6) were minority and thirty-two (32) were nonminority. Twenty-four (24) of the students replaced were between the ages of 20-34. The largest number of students replaced were first year (24 students); the students who were in generic practice (17) also showed the highest number of replacements. Three students in the advanced standing curriculum had to be replaced.

The agency was dissatisfied with the level of student performance and the student's style in seven (7) and eight (8) cases, respectively. Student dissatisfaction occurred in 4 cases because of agency location; in 15 cases, the type of assignments were not liked; and in 8 cases, the type of agency was not liked. Dissatisfaction with the field instructor occurred in 6 cases. In 11 cases, the students needed to be replaced because assignments were not appropriate. In 7 cases, the field instructor was no longer available and several factors unknown prior to the placement resulted in other disruptions. These included: agency cutbacks in service resulting in inappropriate assignments; field instructor fired unexpectedly; undergraduates not in the setting before and not sure how to use them; lack of administrative support; a field instructor who was unwilling to comply with school requirements; lack of social work degree; behavior of other staff; no minority clients; and internal conflicts regarding the responsibilities of the student.

Schools required from one week to three months to find new

placements; most, however, occurred within 4 weeks. For 17 students, replacement occurred during the beginning of placement (first month), but for almost an equal number (18 students) replacement occurred in the middle of placement (end of first quarter/semester). Replacement was seen as successful for 31 students; in 4 cases it was not. For unsuccessful replacements, another placement was made in one case, and no further replacements were made in two other cases. In the schools where replacements took place and where students were permitted to make requests for a type of agency, 25 students requested a particular type of agency; 24 of those received the type of agency requested while only one did not. Receiving one's choice of agency does not seem to be a strong indicator of completion of a placement.

The Directors of Field Instruction reported that the replacement process can be initiated by the field instructor, faculty, field liaison, student, and field director. There was consensus that there is discussion of the problems between the student and field instructor, field instructor and faculty liaison, and generally, a joint meeting between the three parties. In some cases, the agency director is consulted. In the school, the field director is then notified of the problems and further discussion takes place. The decision for replacement seems to come primarily from the faculty field liaison and/or the Director of Field Instruction. In the majority of cases, the field director recruits a different field setting. In a minority of cases, the student also looks for a new placement. At times, the student interviews with the new field instructor. The student is replaced and a second placement begins.

No respondent indicated what factors were considered in making a replacement. It is unknown which, if any, factors relevant to the student are utilized. Only one respondent indicated that the files are searched for a field agency vacancy and the liaison to that agency is then contacted.

Implications

Field placement assignments can involve many complicated judgment-making decisions, particularly if educational guidelines are followed and if there is the goal of "matching" or "harmonizing" the various parties involved. With regard to *students*, there is consideration for their preferences and interests, possible career expectations, and their level of education, needs, and abilities. With regard to the *agency*, consideration needs to be given to the variety, type, quality, adequacy, level, and appropriateness of learning experiences offered. The selection and assignment of the field instructors takes into account their possible preference as to the types of students and educational level, their unique teaching style, availability, and flexibility in the use of different teaching modes. The *school's* stance in regard to placement planning also is essential and is based on its educational objectives for the placement, whether a given agency's focus is congruent with the school's educational emphases and philosophy, and the school's recommendations based on the student's learning style and need for particular learning opportunities (usually made through the Field Work Office faculty and/or faculty advisor).

As described, the placement assignment process in social work education ideally contains a high level of individualization, and the essential focus is on the educational components and the harmonization of the interests of all concerned constituents. However, some suggest the placement process may, or could, be done "as successfully" on a more random ("hit or miss") basis, primarily considering "external" factors such as geography, transportation, and student preference.

The placement and replacement process is primarily administrative and sometimes can be political rather than educational in nature. Based on the replacement results, some of the identified problems stem from inappropriate and inadequate assignments resulting possibly from limited exploration and monitoring by the school of the learning opportunities in different agencies. The need to place large numbers of students may force the school's educational rationale and priorities to take a back seat to political and administrative pressures, and limited school resources. At any given point in time, one or another set of factors may be given priority with different individual students. It also is assumed that there is a set of variables that should be thoughtfully reviewed and weighed in placement planning. However, it is important that a student not be "just placed" but that consideration be given to individual differences — individualized placement planning versus a more "random" approach. Even with use of computerized placements, one needs to be aware of all the elements to be "fed" into the computer and which elements should receive differential priority.

A major premise is that learning be individualized and the field placement process be focused on the varying needs, patterns, and styles of student learning. Yet, despite attention to these given learning differences, each student needs to meet end-of-year norms and expectations. One also has to consider whether there is a relationship between the learning/teaching "environment" that may influence the successful outcome of given placement assignments. For example, Margaret Schubert (1963) questioned if there is any association between the quality of field instruction and the level of learning that takes place.

In placement planning, it is assumed that the schools and their respective faculty involved in placement decisions need to be knowledgeable about a given agency's practice and what the agency offers for student learning opportunities and experiences. Changes in agency functions due to budgetary constraints require constant reviews and reassessment of field centers. Field Work Office faculty must be "on top" of current agency operation and the quality and quantity of available student assignments. Ongoing "monitoring" by the school of student learning during and throughout the student's field practicum is critical (i.e., systematic faculty advising combined with active collaboration between agency and school).

Replacements/Reassignments in the Field Practicum

Replacements occur when the student's initial field assignment is changed or interrupted. This may be based on a variety of conditions including student or agency dissatisfaction and the faculty advisor's opinion that the learning experiences are not satisfactory (due either to level or adequacy or nature of assignments; the quality or availability of field instructor's teaching; or extenuating administrative factors). Factors about a student's progress and level of performance also can be an important element in consideration of replacement (i.e., if a student is not meeting expectations). The recommendation by faculty liaison or review committee may be to replace the student in order to offer an opportunity to test further the student's ability, as well as the causes for poor student performance. Awareness of these conditions requires constant, selective monitoring by the school of the practicum assignment. Careful exploration, planning, and selection of placements (with all parties and with key variables and relevant information assessed), together with ongoing collaboration between agency and school regarding the student's assignments and progress, may reduce the need for replacements or reassignments.

Agencies also may request replacement, either because of inadequate student performance (some agencies cannot tolerate the educational demands of the placement) or because their expectations of "worker" level performance do not match the reality of the student's "learning performance." Frequently, agencies may question a student's capacity to "fit into" its program and staff (especially if interdisciplinary). In addition, there may be situations where a student may have been "over or under placed" due to limited information which inaccurately assessed the student's learning needs and level of performance.

The "match" between student and field instructor also may become a factor for replacement. Frequently a student's learning style may not be compatible with a field instructor's teaching style or vice versa. Gender, racial/ethnic, age, and personality differences also may intervene. However, as the survey findings demonstrate, these more "subtle" issues frequently are not directly reported or mentioned.

SUMMARY: ISSUES AND DILEMMAS

The findings from the pilot study raise several issues and dilemmas for consideration:

1. Is it valid to assume that the field placement assignment and replacement process is individualized, taking into account a special set of educationally-focused variables to more effectively "match" student with the field placement experience of the agency?
2. To what extent do educational factors (e.g., learning style and teaching style; demographic and personality variables) influence effective placement assignments and "matching?"
3. Is "random" selection as effective when only certain limited

factors such as student preference, geographic, and transportation variables are considered?

4. Are "pre-placement" interviews by agencies more useful than a school's careful engagement of all parties involved for placement planning, or (as held by a Consortium of Schools of Social Work in the East) are these interviews educationally and administratively dysfunctional?

5. Who bears primary educational responsibility for field placement and replacement assignments, and what is the rationale underlying such decisions?

6. What are the major factors to consider in placement planning or reassignments, and how does a school's process for the exploration and assessment of field training influence satisfactory placement outcomes?

7. Does the degree and level of the school's "monitoring" of quality of field placements and evaluation of student's field performance to meet criteria influence the quality of the placement and replacement process?

8. For more effective research and evaluation, what relevant information needs to be maintained by field work faculty?

9. Is there a difference in replacement rates between schools who match and schools that allow students to develop their own placements?

10. What effect will societal issues have on placement decisions? For example, some (health) agencies require the testing of students for substance abuse and AIDS. What are the ethical implications of this requirement?

11. What are the implications of "computerizing" field placement assignments for the placement and replacement process? How widespread is this practice?

12. What is the effect on the student of interrupted time without placement and what influence does it have on replacement?

13. How do current constraints on agency and school together with changes in the educational environment affect placement and replacement?

While this pilot study on placement/replacement presents only some initial limited findings, it opens up larger issues about aspects of social work education and the practicum that merit serious future review.

For field instruction to exist as a critical vital component of the social work curriculum and to be responsive to the demands and challenges of the next century, the above questions need to be addressed by schools, agencies, and through additional empirical study. Special attention should be directed toward: (1) ascertaining the criteria and variables that are key for an efficient, functional placement/replacement process; (2) the need to implement the value of effective collaboration between all the principle agents involved — faculty, agency, field instructor, and student; and (3) the quality, quantity, and appropriateness of learning experiences, including their sequence/progression in the field, and relatedness to the school curriculum.

These comments underscore an underlying principle that field/practice and school/theory are interacting dynamics of social work education. This study was an attempt to focus on factors that may help to ensure quality field education.

NOTE

1. Since this 1984 study, there may be an increase in use of available technologies for this process.

REFERENCES

Behling, J., Curtis, C., & Foster, S. (1982). Impact of sex-role combinations on student performance in field instruction. *Journal of Social Work Education, 18*(2), 93-97.

Brownstein, C. (1981). Practicum issues: A placement planning model. *Journal of Education for Social Work, 17*(3), 52-58.

Clincht, B. M., Belenky, M. F., Goldberger, N., & Tarule, J. M. (1985). Connected education for women. *Journal of Education, 167*(3).

Cronian, D. L. (1977). *A contractual approach to practicum learning.* Paper presented at the annual program meeting of the Council on Social Work Eduction. Pheonix, Arizona.

Kadushin, A. (1985). *Social work supervision.* New York: Columbia University Press.

Manis, F. (1972). *Field practice in social work education.* California: Sultan Press.

Orzek, A. M. (1984). Mentor-mentee match in training programs based on Chick-ering's vectors of development. In C. E. Munson (Ed.). *Supervising student internships* (pp. 71-77). New York: The Haworth Press, Inc.

Raskin, M. S. (1984). Field placement decisions: Art, science or guesswork? *The Clinical Supervisor, 3*(3), 55-67.

Ryan, A. S. (1981). Asian-American students. *Social Casework, 62,* 95-105.

Schubert, M. (1963). Admissions decisions. *Social Service Review, 37,* 154-165.

Wilson, S. (1981). *Field instruction techniques for supervisors.* New York: Free Press.

Practice Orientation of Students in Field Instruction

Patricia Campbell Ramsey

ABSTRACT. This article presents the results of an investigation of the impact of modes of field instruction on students' practice orientation. Students completing three models of field instruction were administered the Practice Orientation Scale (POS) composed of cognitive activities — conceptual, operational, and affective. The dependent variable, operationalized through this scale, measures the two types of practice orientations: (1) classroom/theoretical and (2) agency/practice. The independent variable, models of field instruction, consists of: (1) summer block, (2) two-semester concurrent, and (3) concurrent semester block. The results showed: model one — more operational orientation (agency/practice), model two — more conceptual (classroom/theoretical), and model three — blending of the two orientations.

INTRODUCTION

Within the last few years, social work literature has paid little attention to the effect of models of field instruction on practice orientation. The literature, however, has consistently identified three models of field instruction (Gilpin, 1963; Manis, 1972; Matson, 1967; Simon, 1972; Schutz, 1969). These are: (1) block, (2) concurrent, and (3) an amalgamation of the two.[1] Inherent in each model is a value base which strongly influences the nature of the field instruction of the particular approach and guides the students' experiences and learning opportunities. This study examines the impact of the three models of field instruction on students' practice orientation.

© 1989 by The Haworth Press, Inc. All rights reserved.

Field Instruction Modes and Practice Outcomes

Relatively little research has been conducted on the strengths and limitations of different field instruction models on practice outcomes. Practice orientation enables the practitioner to engage in the performance or application of social work knowledge, values, and skills to actual practice situations. For the purpose of this study, practice orientation is defined as the student's manifestation of an inner-directed frame of reference that guides practice.[2] This inner-directed practice orientation includes consciousness or recognition of the professional environmental situation in such a way that social work knowledge, values, and skills become operational through application to field experience (Black, 1979; Dorland, 1974; Good, 1973; Lowy, Blackberg & Walbert, 1971; Thomas, 1977).

A practice orientation enables the practitioner to structure conceptual, affective, and operational problem-solving approaches according to the norms, values, standards, and expectations of the profession. By exercising knowledge of the recognition and treatment of social problems and human distress, the student's practice orientation gives expression to the performance of professional duties and responsibilities. This study evaluates three models of field instruction for their consistency in learning opportunities and the effect the associated learning experiences have on practice orientation.

The three models of field instruction are (Meredith College Self-Study and Application for Reaccreditation, 1981):[3]

A. *Summer Block Model.* This option is taken either during the summer between the junior and senior year or after the senior year. Students receive eleven weeks of field instruction full time (five days per week) in a social agency which may be local or in their hometown, providing they are able to travel to the College for the *Seminar in Social Work.* This seminar meets on five days dispersed throughout May, June, and July. *Social Work Practice II* is taken during the semester either preceding or following the summer placement. Individual consultation, other than midterm and final evaluation conferences, is available through long distance communication or, if time permits, on the five seminar days. Consultation may be available at other times if requested by students who are placed locally.

B. *Two Semester Concurrent Model*. Students engage in field instruction in a social agency two days per week for the entire academic year (Fall and Spring terms), while taking *Social Work Practice II* one semester and the *Seminar in Social Work* the other semester. Consultation with the field work faculty advisor is available both terms.

C. *Concurrent Semester Block Model*. Students participate in field instruction in a social agency four times per week for fifteen weeks. A fifth day is reserved for taking courses, *Social Work Practice II* and the *Seminar in Social Work*, and for individual and/or group consultation with the field work faculty advisor. (See Figure 1 for further illustration of the differences in the models.)

If there are inconsistencies in learning opportunities in field education, this would affect the competence and practice orientation for beginning professional practice of the student intern. The graduates of this program will rely heavily on professional orientations predominantly acquired, reinforced, or honed during field experience. Consequently, any critical differences in the effects of each model of field instruction on practice orientation need to be identified.

Operational Definition of Two Types of Practice Orientation: Classroom/Theoretical and Agency/Practice

The particular type of student practice orientation, classroom/theoretical, or agency/practice, depends on the model of field instruction (concurrent or block) used. The model influences practice orientation to the extent that the model of instruction influences the interaction of three major cognitive learning activities — conceptual, affective, and operational.

Each model of field instruction has a different mixture of these major cognitive learning activities. The elements that predominate in any particular model create a learning environment that tends to

Figure 1

School-Agency Influence Over the Field Placement

Agency Dominated	School Dominated	Shared Responsibility
(Agency Dominates with Minimal School Input)	(Shared but School Dominates)	Agency Dominates with moderate School Input)
A. Summer Block Model	B. Two-Semester Concurrent Model	C. Concurrent Semester Block Model (A Concentrated Program)
Field experience concentrated in summer for 11 weeks, full time, five days per week. School input limited to five Seminar days, and mid-term and final evaluation conferences.	Field experience spread over an academic year (two terms) concurrently with two days in field and three days in classes.	Field experience concentrated in one semester, four days per week for 15 weeks, with one day on campus (two courses)

a. low faculty input

b. no other reference groups available

c. agency dominant force in defining reality of experience

d. pace of learning highest

e. adjustment process fastest

f. continuity of field personnel low due to increased staff vacations

a. faculty input highest

b. reference groups readily available

c. direct impact of field placement on other academic courses (and vice versa) highest

d. supplement of class learning with field learning greatest

e. pace of adjustment to agency can be slower

f. seminar taken concurrently one term

a. faculty has moderate input

b. moderate to high availability of other reference groups

c. instructive for sharing and checking out precepts

d. pace of learning fast

e. adjustment to agency fast

f. one day per week set aside for class instruction and seminars

FIGURE 1 (continued)

Agency Dominated	School Dominated	Shared Responsibility
g. field instructor turnover highest due to increase in job changing (more social workers change jobs during summer)	g. advanced practice course taken concurrently the other term	g. tensions between demands of field placement and those of school – high
h. approximation of true work experience higher	h. longer duration of time for student to find self as a helping person	h. allows for intensive service delivery over a short period of time
i. more relaxed experiences in field placement	i. tension between agency needs and school needs highest	i. anxiety of students highest

generate a particular practice orientation. The following describes the relationship between practice orientation and practice behavior.

Classroom/Theoretical Orientation

The learning environment emphasizes utilization of knowledge and theories from the literature in the classroom/theoretical orientation. Theories are readily learned even if it is difficult for the student to connect them with the client situation. That is, client situations tend to have real meaning for the student's learning when there is a conceptual referent already available. This orientation gives the student opportunity to prepare for a new problem-solving situation by learning practically all that is available about the particular social and individual problem. The student feels best prepared to meet the client since there is opportunity to master information prior to the meeting.

In this learning environment, the student's relationship with the field instructor involves theoretical discussion of the problem rather than suggestions of action to take. The student's learning is based on an adequate grasp of available knowledge. Within this model, *canned* cases (hypothetical or actual tapes, or other recorded materials) are important for conceptualization. The student is able to connect practice experience with concepts and theories when completing written assignments. The student usually feels comfortable if unable to make this valued connection when doing written exercises.

When doing process recordings, it is easy for the student to record what is taking place within a conceptual framework. It is sometimes difficult for the student to move beyond the conceptual and theoretical parameters to further recognize and interpret what has happened. The student's practice analogue is a deductive, abstract one. The learning environment allows the student to set deliberate, long-range goals.

Agency/Practice Orientation

In this learning environment, *learning by doing* constitutes the student's major conceptual frame of reference. Experience that occurs repetitively is a significant component of the student's learning. The student is frequently placed in the act of confronting or evaluating a client. But it is usually *after* the interaction that the student finds that learning has occurred, that the student now knows what confronting and evaluating mean as practice concepts. Concepts that have been read or discussed become real in the mind of the student because they have been experienced. When faced with a new problem-solving situation, the student generally prefers to get started and feels most comfortable when doing something. The student in this model appreciates specific suggestions from the field instructor and finds these helpful as guides in a practice situation. "Canned" or hypothetical cases also are useful as guides for intervention within this learning environment, if the action is well-described.

The student may find it difficult to describe what happened in practice situations. In process recording, the recording is either too detailed or not specific enough; the student may find it easy to be specific but difficult to generalize. The professional literature that makes most sense to the students in this orientation discusses concepts in terms of specific suggestions for practice. Concepts and theory are necessary but less instrusive as a guide to action than the student's own personal momentum, judgment, and evaluation. The student's practice analogue is practical and accomplishment-oriented. The learning environment allows the student the opportunity to set concrete and pragmatic goals (Papell, 1978).

These two distinct types of practice orientation and the three models of field instruction constitute the dependent and primary independent variables of this study, respectively. The major hypothesis of the study is that there is no difference in the post-graduate practice orientation of students among the three models of field instruction. The following section describes the methods used to test this hypothesis.

METHODOLOGY

This study uses a quasi-experimental, static-group comparison design. The sample population consists of 166 female, postgraduate students who completed the field instruction component of the undergraduate social work program at Meredith College between May 1976 and May 1983. (Meredith College is a small, church-related liberal arts college for women in Raleigh, North Carolina.) The majority of the subjects are white females between the ages of 22 and 29 years and from upper-middle class families. The principal independent variable, the types of field instruction, includes: (A) Summer Block—a distinct learning environment which is operational in nature and has the agency as the locus of control, and the students tend to adopt an agency/practice orientation, synonymous with Papell's "operational" model for learning social work practice; (B) Two-semester Concurrent—a learning environment which is conceptual in nature, has the school as the locus of control, and the students tend to adopt a classroom/theoretical orientation, synonymous with Papell's "conceptual" model for learning social work practice; (C) Concurrent Semester Block—a learning environment which is an integration of the two orientations with both agency and school sharing the locus of control. (See Figure 2 for distinctions of the three typologies of field instruction.)

The dependent variable, practice orientation, is measured by a Practice Orientation Scale (POS). This scale, a modification of Papell's "Self-Profile of Learning Style," consists of three subscales reflecting cognitive activities—conceptual, operational, and affective. It is designed to measure two distinct types of practice orientations operationally defined as (1) classroom/theoretical; and (2) agency/practice. The POS was mailed to all 166 subjects. Sixteen questionnaires were returned because of incorrect mailing addresses; 104 of the other 150 questionnaires were completed, a 69 percent response rate. (See Table 1 for number of subjects in the study by Field Placement Option.)

The Delphi technique, factor analysis, and Cronbach's Alpha (1951) were used to test the instrument's construct validity and reliability. Factor analysis was employed to determine which factors (measured by scale items) related to a particular type of practice orientation. The following statistical procedures were applied to the data analysis: frequency distributions, cross-tabulations, analysis of variance, covariance of analysis, multiple classification analysis,

Figure 2

Dimensions of Three Typologies of Field Instruction

Factors	A. Summer Block Option	B. Two-Semester Concurrent Option	C. Concurrent Semester Block Option
1. Faculty input	Lowest	Highest	Moderate
2. Availability of other social work reference groups	Not really	Very available	There, but in a smaller quantity
3. Pace of learning	Fastest	Slow	Concentrated
4. Adjustment to agency regime	Fastest	Slow	Concentrated

5. Agency role in defining the learning experience and its particular needs	Dominant, field instructor is the main teacher (agency needs dominate)	Weakest, field instructor works together with faculty in theory (school has most educational control)	Agency role is strong, but school impact is still present
6. Types of services delivered by student	Short term intensive	Long term, less intensive	Longer term, fairly intensive
7. Type of role student will be called on to play	Employee	Student in training	Intern (student worker)
8. Indentification with agency	Strongest	Weakest	Strong

147

FIGURE 2 (continued)

Factors	A. Summer Block Option	B. Two-Semester Concurrent Option	C. Concurrent Semester Block Option
9. Impact on seminar	Strong influence but limited by time lapses	Weakest	Strong
10. Geographical factors	Weak coordination between school and agency in structuring the quality of the field experience	Strong coordination between school and agency in structuring the quality of the field experience	Strong coordination between school and agency in structuring the quality of the field experience

Table 1

Number of Respondents in the Study

by Field Placement Option

Field Placement Option	Number	Percent
SB	41	39.4
TSC	18	17.3
CSB	45	43.3
Total	104	100.0

Note: F.P. Opt. = Type of Field Placement Option

SB = Summer Block

TSC = Two Semester Concurrent

CSB = Concurrent Semester Block

regression analysis, and factor analysis. These methods of analysis helped to explore the relationship between the independent and the dependent variables while simultaneously testing for potential intervening variables.

The Practice Orientation Scale is a thirty item, seven point Likert scale consisting of conceptual, operational, and affective domains. The respondents were asked to select their responses from a rating scale based on whether they agreed or disagreed with the statement. They also were asked to rate each item in the three domains based on how well it represented the learning and orientation experiences resulting from the field practicum and the particular model of field instruction. The possible responses ranged from very strongly agree to very strongly disagree with a mid-point category of *not sure*. Each domain contains ten factor items.

First, the researcher examined the three domains and the factor items that were statistically significant. Second, the areas of agreement among subjects by type of field placement option and factor items in each domain were identified. Third, the way in which the practice orientations of the subjects were ordered in each model of field instruction was assessed. Fourth, a summary was made of the multiple classification analysis of the dependent variables (conceptual scale, operational scale, and affective scale) with several independent variables: type of field placement option, number of years employment supervised by an MSW-level social worker, Scholastic Achievement Test scores, and college grade point average. Finally, the mean scores of factor items on the conceptual scale and the affective scale were analyzed. (See Tables 2, 3, and 4 for scale mean scores of the three domains.)

Only two conceptual factor items in the POS were found to be statistically significant. Statistical analysis using Chi Square showed that the conceptual factor (1) was statistically significant at the $p < .01$ level, and the conceptual factor (2) was statistically significant at the $p < .002$ level. Four factor items from the operational domain were statistically significant. Operational factor (4) was significant at the $p < .00$ level, factor (1) significant at the $p < .01$ level, factor (5) at the $p < .03$ level, and factor (9) at the $p < .00$ level. One factor item in the affective domain was statistically significant, affective factor (4) at the $p < .02$ level.

FINDINGS

The major null hypothesis of this study was not supported. There appears to be a difference in the postgraduate practice orientation of students according to their model of field instruction. Distinct patterns of practice orientation emerged for the students in the study. A second hypothesis, that students who participated in the summer block model of field instruction will be more agency/practice in orientation than the students in the other two models, was supported. The students in the summer block placement scored higher on the operational subscale, suggesting that they have more opera-

Table 2

Scale Mean Scores of Conceptual Domain Factor Items for

Each Field Placement Option

		Conceptual Domain		
Scale Factor Items		SB	TSC	CSB
Con	1	58.5	72.2	66.6
	2	78.0	77.8	82.2
	3	75.6	83.3	80.0
	4	90.2	88.9	80.0
	5	26.0	61.2	33.4
	6	12.2	38.9	13.3
	7	29.3	55.5	35.5
	8	73.1	66.7	72.7
	9	41.4	66.6	51.1
	10	22.0	33.4	35.5
Total Mean Score		50.63	64.45	50.03

Note: The category for a high score on the factor items is 65.0 and above; a medium score is 50.0 - 64.0; and a low score is 49.0 and below when subjected to rounding. A higher score indicates a higher percentage of agreement with the expressed factor item.

Table 3

Scale Mean Scores of Operational Domain Factor Items for

Each Field Placement Option

	Operational Domain		
Scale Items	SB	TSC	CSB
Opr 1	84.9	50.0	45.5
2	87.7	61.1	86.6
3	73.2	55.6	71.1
4	97.6	88.9	88.9
5	85.3	77.8	48.9
6	97.5	88.9	86.7
7	87.9	94.5	91.1
8	90.2	88.9	88.9
9	65.9	55.5	62.2
10	75.6	77.8	73.3
Total Mean Score	83.58	73.90	71.32

tional or agency/practice orientation than the students in the two other types of field instruction.

Students in the two-semester concurrent model had higher scores on the conceptual subscale and lower scores on the operational subscale than those in the summer block (see Table 5). These students seem to be more conceptual or classroom/theoretical in orientation. The students who participated in the concurrent semester block model of field instruction were shown to acquire a blending of the classroom/theoretical and the agency/practice orientations. The findings suggest that these students integrated the two orientations,

Table 4

Scale Mean Scores of Affective Domain Factor Items for

Each Field Placement Option

Scale Items	Affective Domain		
	SB	TSC	CSB
Off 1	75.6	44.4	68.9
2	51.2	11.2	35.5
3	75.6	61.2	68.9
4	70.8	44.5	75.6
5	31.7	44.4	24.4
6	51.2	27.9	31.1
7	39.0	33.4	42.3
8	75.7	61.1	78.8
9	65.9	55.6	51.1
10	51.1	51.3	55.6
Total mean score	58.78	43.51	53.12

earning scores falling within the intermediate range on both the conceptual and operational subscales.

Several intervening variables pertaining to (1) socioeconomic background; (2) aptitude for social work education; (3) demographic characteristics of sex and race; (4) position in college; (5) type of work setting; (6) continuing education experience; (7) self-selection features; (8) ability; and (9) employment status influence practice orientation. Demographic characteristics — age, number of years of work experience, and the number of years employment supervised by an MSW-level social worker — were shown to be statistically significant (based on the Chi Square). However, multiple classifica-

Table 5

Mean Scores for Each Practice Orientation

Domain by the Type of Field Placement Option

Field Placement Option

Cognitive Domain	SB	TSC	CSB
Conceptual	51	64	55
Operational	84	74	71
Affective	59	44	53

tion analysis of the affect of intervening variables (covariants) showed that only the number of years of supervision by an MSW had a statistically significant influence on the operational scale. The number of years of MSW supervision tended to make the students operational in their orientation. There was no significant relationship between the number of years of employment, age, and ability (student SAT scores and college GPA) and the three domains on the practice orientation scale. (See Table 6 for further details.)

Analysis also indicated that the operational scale and the affective scale were influenced by field placement options. Consequently, it appears that the model of field instruction and the number of years the subject's work is supervised by an MSW field instructor influence practice orientation and other behavioral attributes. The effects of the model of field instruction on practice orientation is independent of the covariates. All three models of field instruction are strongly related to the operational and affective attributes of the student's practice orientation.

Behavioral attributes relating to number of books and journals read, attendance at professional conferences, and the number of memberships in professional organizations were associated with the number of years the subject's work was supervised by an MSW field instructor and the type of field placement option.

Table 6

"F" Values -- Summary of Multiple Classification Analysis

of Dependent Variables (conscale, oprscale, affscale) with

F.P.Opt., YEWORK, MASUP, SAT, and COG. P.A.

Degree of Freedom			Frequencies
	Conscale	Oprscale	Affscale
F.P.Opt. 2	1.75	14.77***	4.68*
YEWORK 1	.18	.02	.15
MASUP 1	1.73	4.10*	.60
SAT 1	.43	.03	.50
COGPA 1	.00	1.06	.32

Note: YEWORK = number of years worked

MASUP   = number of years work supervised by master's level
social worker

SAT   = Scholastic Aptitude Test Scores

COGPA   = College Grade Point Average

*   = p < .05

**   = p < .01

***   = p < .00

IMPLICATIONS OF THE STUDY
FOR SOCIAL WORK EDUCATION
AND THE FIELD OF SOCIAL WELFARE

Analysis of the data revealed that the three models of field instruction investigated in this study conform to three classical modes of field instruction discussed in the social work literature — the concurrent, the block, and an amalgamation of the two. According to the social work literature, the nature of the learning experiences in the three models are work oriented (employee), educational/learning oriented (student), or an amalgam of both emphases (interns) (Dolgoff, 1974).

There are differences in the nature of the learning opportunities within each model of field instruction which produce distinct types of practice orientation. This realization is important since practice orientation is a manifestation of the social work practitioner's inner-directed conceptual frame of reference. The conceptual frame of reference guides the practitioner's assessment, intervention, and evaluation of practice situations.

As an inherent part of practice orientation, the conceptual frame of reference is significant because theoretical concepts are necessary for designing and implementing social work activities. Because of the nature of human behavior and social systems, concepts are very complex and usually cannot be expressed adequately in operational terms alone. Therefore, an orientation that is sufficiently conceptual in nature is indispensable for designing, measuring, and explaining phenomena. Comparisons and generalizations are made possible through the use of such concepts.

In order to manage practice experiences, the intern must learn to identify, integrate, and utilize many conceptual frames of reference. As one becomes a professional practitioner, the conceptual aspect of the practice orientation provides a point of view, standards, or a system of concepts to help foster the organization of experiences, perceptions, and interpretations.

The operational and affective components of practice orientation also are important. As agents for change, social workers are required to possess knowledge about a variety of theories and skills for relating to people and helping them impact on their social environment. The value base of the social worker serves as a guide to action. The operational aspect of the social worker's practice orientation requires the capacity to set into motion and to control a process of change that is highly sensitive to issues of human dignity, and the level and quality of resources and services involved.

This study provides some information about the learning opportunities in three models of field instruction that may be helpful in evaluating the structure of similar field instruction programs. The outcome of the learning experiences in these three models, and the related practice orientations, may provoke some critical thinking in social work education about the kinds of beginning level social work practitioners the schools desire to produce for the profession.

Some of the findings may be helpful in recruiting students for professional positions in the field of social welfare. Graduates with certain types of orientations may be most productive in specific kinds of practice settings. For example, where social work is not the dominant discipline (e.g., corrections), a practitioner with a conceptual (classroom/theoretical) orientation may be more effective. This orientation could help to reduce some of the tension and social distance between the profession of social work and the field of corrections by theoretically integrating their respective philosophies, principles, and practices, and reducing professional controversy. A social worker with a particular type of practice orientation may be more effective in a specific type of practice setting based on whether social work is the dominant discipline, is on an equal footing with the other disciplines, or is a subordinate discipline (Morales & Sheafer, 1983).

Practitioners who become aware of differences in practice orientation and engage in constructive self-evaluation may find the results of this study helpful in preventing "burnout," a phenomenon which occurs when service personnel are unable to cope with prolonged emotional stress. This phenomenon was identified by Maslach (1976) in a study of professionals at work. The study included poverty lawyers, physicians, prison personnel, clinical psychologists, psychiatrists, child care workers, and psychiatric nurses. Its findings suggested that a high percentage of members in all of these professional groups tend to cope with stress by a form of distancing that not only hurts themselves but was damaging to their clients. They think of clients in more derogatory terms than do non-burnout professionals, and, in its extreme form, they believe the clients deserve any problems they have.

There is little doubt that burnout plays a major role in the poor delivery of health and welfare services to the people most in need of them. Their clients wait longer to receive less attention and less care. Burnout is also a key factor in low worker morale, absenteeism, and high job turnover. Maslach (1976) found that one of the major signs of burnout was the transformation of a person with original thought and creativity on the job into a mechanical, petty bureaucrat.

Results from this study support the findings in the social work literature that practice orientations exist among social work professionals. What is missing from the social work literature are the origins of causes of the practice orientations. This study contributes to the literature in that respect. However, more studies are needed before conclusive evidence is provided. More investigation of the Practice Orientation Scale is indicated. The POS successfully measures three types of practice orientation. However, the scale needs to be rebuilt to better sort out the operational and affective components. Some of the factor items in these two domains appear to be scrambled. Items that do not load on the cognitive domain for which they were constructed need to be reassessed and the subscales subjected to more testing.

There should be further evaluation of the performance of students carrying out social work activities in field placement (e.g., evaluation of their field performance by agency field instructors). Since the number of years of employment supervised by an MSW-level social worker significantly affected practice orientation, the characteristics of the supervisor need to be pursued as possible intervening variables. Three models of supervision identified in the social work literature tend to conform or closely parallel the three classical models of field instruction (Van der Waals, 1974; Lowy, 1983). The models of social work supervision are (1) the work-oriented model, (2) the theory and method-oriented model, and (3) the learning model. Characteristics of the supervisor (i.e., type of model of supervision utilized) may have an indirect effect on practice orientation by influencing behavioral attributes of the student.

A test to determine practice orientation before the field placement option was experienced was not conducted in this study. Further studies of social work students need to include this test and a comparison of this with a test for practice orientation after experiencing any particular model of field instruction. Studies should include a more diverse and larger population of students since small groups are frequently homogeneous and receive a more intense socialization—the size of the unit has an impact on the socialization of the group (Lipset, Trow & Coleman, 1956).

It would be helpful to see if some of the professional orientation patterns identified by Billingsley (1964) and others (Corwin, 1961; Ohlin, Piven & Papenfort, 1958; Reisman, 1949) are related to particular models of field instructions experienced by practitioners when they were students. For example, would students who acquired a classroom/theoretical practice orientation when subjected to empirical testing prove to possess the "professional" type of orientation pattern? Would those with the agency/practice type of practice orientation possess the "bureaucrat" pattern. Or would those with a blending of the two types be the "conformists" and/or "innovators"? These are provocative questions about practice orientation which are worth pursuing. The results would further enhance the development of the profession of social work and contribute to models of social work education worth adopting by social work programs. These are timely research issues as the practice orientation that social work practitioners possess indeed influences how they respond to practice situations.

NOTES

1. In the Meredith College Social Work Program, Raleigh, North Carolina, the location of this study, these models of field instruction are referred to as (1) the summer block (block), (2) the two-semester concurrent (concurrent), and (3) the concurrent semester block model (an amalgamation of the two).
2. This definition of practice orientation was created by the author based on an examination of the concepts of practice and orientation as used in the professions of law, medicine, education, and social work (Black, 1979; Dorland, 1974; Good, 1973; Lowy, Blackberg & Walbert, 1971; Thomas, 1977).
3. Meredith College Self-Study and Application for Reaccreditation (1981) (Raleigh: Meredith College Social Work Program, 1981, p. 104).

REFERENCES

Billingsley, A. (1964). Bureaucratic and professional orientation patterns in social casework. *Social Service Review 38*, 400-407.

Black, H. C. (Ed.). (1979). *Black's law dictionary.* (5th ed.) St. Paul: West Publishing.

Corwin, R. G. (1961). The professional employee: A study of conflict in nursing roles. *American Journal of Sociology, 66*, 604-15.

Cronback, I. (1951). Coefficient alpha and the internal structure of tests. *Psychometrika, 16*, 297-334.

Dolgoff, R. (1974). *Report to the task force on social work practice and education*. New York: Council on Social Work Education.

Dorland's Illustrated Medical Dictionary. (1974). (25th ed.) Philadelphia: Saunders.

Gilpin, R. (1963). *Theory and practice as a single reality*. Chapel Hill: University of North Carolina Press.

Good, C. V. (Ed.). (1973). *Dictionary of education*. New York: McGraw-Hill.

Lipset, S. M., Trow, M. A., & Coleman, J. S. (1956). *Union democracy: The internal politics of the international typographical union*. New York: Free Press.

Lowy, L. (1983). Social work supervision: From models towards theory. *Journal of Education for Social Work*, *19*(2), 55-61.

Lowy, K., Blackberg, L. M., & Walbert, H. J. (1971). *Integrative learning and teaching in schools of social work: A study of organizational development in professional education*. New York: Associated Press.

Manis, F. (1972). *Field practice in social work education: Perspective from an international base*. California: Sultana.

Maslach, C. (1976). Burn-out. *Human Behavior*, *5*, 16-22.

Matson, M. B. (1967). *Field experience in undergraduate programs in social welfare*. New York: Council on Social Work Education.

Meredith College self-study and application for reaccreditation. (1981). Raleigh: Meredith College Social Work Program.

Morales, A., & Sheafor, B. W. (1983). *Social work: A profession of many faces*. (3rd ed.). Boston: Allyn & Bacon.

Ohlin, L. E., Piven, H., & Papenfort, D. M. (1958). Major dilemmas of the social worker in probation and parole (pp. 251-262). In H. D. Stein & R. A. Cloward (Eds.). *Social perspectives on behavior*. Glenco, Ill: Free Press.

Papell, C. P. (1978). A study of styles of learning for direct social work practice. (Doctoral dissertation, Yeshiva University, 1978.) *Dissertation Abstracts International*, *39*, 182A-183A.

Reisman, L. (1949). A study of role conceptions in bureaucracy. *Social Focus*, *25*, 305-310.

Schutz, M. (1969). *The potential of concurrent field instruction for learning*. In B. L. Jones (Ed.). *Current patterns of field instruction in graduate social work education* (pp. 99-107). New York: Council on Social Work Education.

Simon, B. K. (1972). Field instruction as education for practice: Purposes and Goals. In K. Wenzel (Ed.). *Undergraduate field instruction programs: Current issues and predictions* (pp. 64-79). New York: Council on Social Work Education.

Thomas, C. L. (Ed.). (1977). *Taber's cyclopedic medical dictionary* (14th ed.). Philadelphia: F. A. Davis Co.

Van der walls, J. (1974). Die frage nach dem lehrinhalt (The problem of the teaching content). In E.M.J. Siegers (Ed.). *Praxisberatung* (pp. 123-151). West Germany: Lambertus Verlag.

Impact of Sex-Role Combinations on Student Performance in Field Instruction

John C. Behling
Caroletta Curtis
Sara Ann Foster

ABSTRACT. An empirical study was performed during the spring quarters of 1974, 1976, and 1978 at a large college in the Midwest to test the impact of sex-role combinations on evaluation of students' field placement experiences. The findings imply that same sex-role combinations are more positive generally than unlike combinations.

The purpose of this study was to determine whether sex-role combinations of female student and male instructor in field instruction affect or influence student-instructor relationships and performance in field instruction. If so, what are the relative implications for social work practice? An ongoing issue in social work education is the quality of the field placement experience. One of the primary factors in the field instruction component is the teaching ability of the field instructor. A second factor of great importance is the relationship between the field instructor and the student. A basic assumption is that learning cannot occur if there are impediments to this relationship.

Students, practitioners, and most educators hold fieldwork to be the core of professional social work education (Oswald, 1966). Kolevzon (1979) wrote that distinctive characteristics of field instruction not found in the classroom are the supervisory relationship between field instructor and student, accountability through competent professional service to clients, and the range of diverse learning

Reprinted by permission by the Council on Social Work Education, from the *Journal of Education for Social Work*, Vol. 18, No. 2, Spring 1982, pages 93-97.

experiences that the supervisory relationship exposes and dissects. The most distinctive of these characteristics is the supervisory relationship between field supervisor and student. The intensity of the relationship is unparalleled in the professional education of the social work student. According to Rodgers and Williams (1977), in view of this tremendous weight carried by the field experience as it relates to the student's success or failure, one can neither overemphasize nor minimize the need for continuous striving in the effort to improve this aspect of the student's training process.

Do sex-role combinations affect or influence the nature and quality of the field experience provided by the field instructor? Since measurements of competence or evaluation of student performance vary among field instructors, one may attribute such variance to philosophical orientation of field instructors and in some degree to individual temperament or personality. Can sex-role stereotypes or sexism also contribute to this variance?

Kagan (1964) defined sex-role stereotyping as the holding of "publicly shared beliefs regarding the appropriate characteristics for males and females" (p. 144). Throughout history, two theories have emerged regarding human personality. The first theory is that the male is the prototype for humanity and the female is understood in relation to him. The second theory is that males represent the cognitive world, which is positively valued in this culture, and females represent the affective domain, which has less positive value overall (Harris & Lucas, 1976). This historically laden sexist attitude is reason for concern in the male instructor-female student sex-role combination in field instruction.

As Schwartz (1974) has noted, "the social work profession is in the process of learning the necessity of examining the effects of class, ethnicity, and race in social work thinking, but it continues to undervalue the importance of the sex factor" (p. 177). Researchers have found that the sex of both the client and the social worker is a highly significant factor affecting the helping relationship. Therefore, the sex-role combination of students and field instructors must be considered in affecting and influencing the teaching-learning relationship and subsequent student performance in field practice.

Kravetz (1976) suggested that practitioners and students should be given incentive and opportunity to reexamine their personal values and beliefs about women and become aware of sexism in relation to their practice (p. 425). Zietz and Erlich (1976) found in their study that no agency was free of sexism, and that far more women found sexism a problem than did men. In fact, 31 percent of the women in the study stated that the sex of a staff member was an important condition in work assignments, as opposed to an 11 percent response by the men. Broverman et al. (1972) indicated there is evidence to suggest that people hold stereotypes regardless of age, marital status, religion, and education.

Little published research has reported on sex-role combinations in field instruction. Is there a significant relationship between sex roles and a negative or positive evaluation of field practice? What are the factors in the field setting that offer students an optimum learning experience?

METHODOLOGY

This paper reports the results of an empirical study performed in a large Midwestern college of social work regarding sex-role combinations of graduate students and field instructors. The researchers conducted an explanatory descriptive survey. The data collection schedule included an evaluation instrument for assessing negative to positive student reaction to specifically assigned field placement.

In addition to this instrument, a student evaluation of his or her field instructor, demographic and background data for each student, and sex-role combination of student and instructors were included. The data collection schedule was administered to all first- and second-year graduate students during the spring quarters of 1974, 1976, and 1978.

The origins of the sex-role combination research to which this paper is addressed had its beginnings in a graduate course in social research methods for social work students. The original instrument was constructed around a 20-item scale designed for students to evaluate their field placements. This field placement evaluation scale was constructed and tested for reliability and validity using the Thurstone Method of Equal Appearing Intervals. Other variables were designed as independent measures in the hope of explaining negative and positive field placement evaluation (the dependent variable).

Table 1 shows the sex-role combinations as (1) female student-male instructor, (2) female student-female instructor, (3) male student-female instructor, and (4) male student-male instructor for each year the study was conducted. It can be seen that the number of students in each combination was approximately the same each year.

These sex-role combination groups were tested against a series of variables that cluster around the perception of the student in regard

Table 1

Number and Percent of Students

In Sex-Role Combinations by Year

Gender Combination	1974		1976		1978	
	N	%	N	%	N	%
Female Student- Male Instructor	27	27	21	29	28	27
Female Student- Female Instructor	42	42	34	47	46	45
Male Student- Female Instructor	13	13	6	8	16	16
Male Student- Male Instructor	18	18	12	16	13	12
TOTAL	100	100	73	100	103	100

to the instructor and field placement. The seven variables of importance in this cluster were as follows: (1) evaluation of field placement, (2) grade received by the student for field placement, (3) rating of the field instructor as a person, (4) the average amount of time spent with the field instructor each week, (5) the feeling of being forced to compete with the other students placed at the agency, (6) the student's need for better supervision at times, and (7) the student rating of the field instructor as a teacher.

FINDINGS

The data showed that for each year field placement was positively evaluated when the student had a positive perception of the instructor (p = .01). In fact, no other variable seemed to play a more important role in the student assessment of field placement. This finding was confirmed for each year (at p = .01 or less) and was not surprising. What was surprising was the pattern of statistical significance when sex-role combinations were analyzed in relation to those factors clustering around the field instructor. On examination of the four sex-role combinations in relation to perceptions regarding the seven instructor-related variables, the pattern varied from year to year. However, of the four combinations, male-male and female-female were significantly more positive in their response to the field instructor when compared to the female student and male instructor combination.

The following results have convinced these researchers that the most problematic sex-role combination is female student-male instructor. These findings may well suggest some underlying sexism that is being identified and expressed by the female graduate student. The authors looked more closely at the findings in regard to the seven instructor-related items discussed above:

1. Evaluation of Field Placement — The data from all three years showed that the female student and male instructor sex-role combination was perceived as significantly more negative (p < .05) when tested against other combinations in regard to field placement evaluation. The male-male combinations showed up significantly more positive (p < .01) for 1974 and 1978 data.

2. Grades Received by the Student for Field Placement — The 1976 data revealed students in female student-male instructor sex-role combinations received significantly lower grades (p < .05) than any other combination.

3. Rating of the Field Instructor as a Person — The 1974 and 1978 data showed a significant difference (p < .001) between the ratings of the instructor for female-male sex-role combinations and all other combinations. The ratings of the instructor were more negative.

4. The Average Amount of Time Spent with the Field Instructor Each Week — This variable produced consistently negative results for female-male sex-role combinations when "time with the instructor" was asked of the student. Data from all three years produced negative results when compared with the other sex-role combinations. Obviously, time spent with the field instructor is of great value in the learning process. There is some evidence to suggest that this conclusion is a result of the multiple roles of the instructor — that is, male instructors tend to hold positions of an administrative nature and frequently give less time to the task of student supervision.

5. The Feeling of Being Forced to Compete with the Other Students Placed at the Agency — The data from 1976 and 1978 indicated that female students with male instructors tended to feel forced to compete with other students for their grades. This corroborated the feeling of many students in this sex-role combination that such competition interferred with their effectiveness as social workers in placement.

6. The Student's Need for Better Supervision at Times — The 1974 and 1976 data showed a significant difference (p < .001) between the female student and male instructor and other sex-role combinations in regard to quality of supervision. The female student with the male instructor again perceived this aspect of her field experience as negative or more negative than other combinations. The 1978 data did not show the same pattern.

7. The Student Rating of the Field Instructor as a Teacher — The 1974 and 1978 data indicated that the female students gave significantly lower (p < .01) ratings to their male instuctors compared to other sex-role combinations. Also, the data for

1974 and 1976 showed that students rated their instructors negatively for failure to give individualized assessment in the teaching process.

RECOMMENDATIONS AND IMPLICATIONS FOR PRACTICE WITH CLIENTS

Our findings indicated that the female student-female instructor was the most positive sex-role combination for the advancement of learning in field instruction. Further, same sex-role combinations were more positive generally than unlike combinations. The female student-male instructor combination was the most stressful and problematic. The stresses in this combination primarily were attributed to traditional sexist attitudes held by the male instructor. These attitudes must be recognized, acknowledged, and modified by field instructors who influence and facilitate the learning processes of students and ultimately social work practice with clients.

It cannot be decried that sexism, like racism, is incompatible with the values of the profession, but also in practice sexism reinforces rank discrimination against women. The patterns of student reaction to sexist attitudes serve to weaken our commitment to equal justice. Students cannot confront their antidemocratic biases if they are reflected in the instructor's values and teaching style.

We suggest that the field placement of students and instructors must be matched carefully and thoughtfully. However, matching may not counter the combination in relationship to quality of services delivered to female clients in a nonsexist way. Moreover, many women students and clients may not recognize sexism in service delivery, which might interfere with their best possible functioning.

REFERENCES

Broverman, I., Vogel, S. R., Broverman, D. M., Clarkson, F. E., & Rosenkranz, P. S. (1972). Sex-role stereotypes: A current appraisal. *Journal of Social Issues*, *28*, 59-78.

Harris, L. H., & Lucas, M. (1976). Sex role stereotyping. *Social Work*, *21*, 390-395.

Kagan, J. (1964). Sex typing and sex role identity. In L. Hoffman & M. Hoffman

(Eds.). *Review of child development research* (p. 144). New York: Russell Sage.

Kolevzon, M. (1979). Evaluating the supervisory relationship in field placements. *Social Work, 24,* 241-244.

Kravetz, D. E. (1976). Sexism in a woman's profession. *Social Work, 21,* 421-426.

Oswald, I. (1966). Field instruction: Facts and outlook. In *Trends of field work instruction* (p. 7). New York: Family Service Association of America.

Rodgers, A., & Williams, E. G. (1977). Field instruction and evaluation: Some continuing and some new issues. *Arete, 4*(4), 225-234.

Schwartz, M. C. (1974). Importance of the sex of worker and client. *Social Work, 19,* 177-185.

Zietz, D., & Erlich, J. L. (1976). Sexism in social agencies: Practitioners' perspectives. *Social Work, 21,* 434-438.

The Influence of Field Instructor-Student Gender Combinations on Student Perceptions of Field Instruction Quality

Bruce A. Thyer
Karen Sowers-Hoag
J. P. Love

ABSTRACT. The currently available studies investigating the influence of field instructor-student gender combinations on the perceived quality of field work yield ambiguous findings. Given the importance of arranging a satisfactory field placement in the student's overall professional education, the authors conducted an empirical investigation to isolate the relative influence gender considerations contribute to the field experience. Results indicate that although same-gender combinations produce the most favorable rating of field instruction, the effects of both student gender and field instructor gender were of little practical meaning, accounting for only five percent of the variance in student satisfaction with field instruction.

As a profession, social work has an admirable history of attending to minority, racial, and ethnic concerns. This is reflected in the Council on Social Work Education's *Curriculum Policy Statement* which mandates that such content be included in the coursework of BSW and MSW professional education (Social Work Education Reporter, 1982). The *Code of Ethics* of the National Association of Social Workers further stipulates that professional practices be free from discriminatory actions and attitudes (National Association of

Reprinted by permission of The College of Social Work, University of South Carolina, from *Arete*, Vol. 11, No. 2, Winter 1986, pages 25-29.

Social Workers, 1980). In recent years, a number of empirical articles have appeared in the professional literature examining the possible existence of sexism within the profession itself (Scotch, 1971; Williams, Ho, & Fielder, 1974; Kadushin, 1976), apparent differential publications rates occurring between male and female social work faculty (Kirk & Rosenblatt, 1980, 1984; Faver & Fox, 1984), the role of student gender in influencing choice of professional specialization (Brager & Michael, 1969), and social worker bias in perceiving clients, based upon unwarranted gender considerations (Schwartz, 1974; Diangson, Kravetz, & Lipton, 1975).

One area which has been relatively neglected is the influence which field instructor-student gender combinations may have on the quality of the field work experience. This omission is puzzling since there is a comparatively large literature on the related topic on how gender may affect supervisor-supervisee relationships (Munson, 1979; Schein, 1973, 1975). The relationships occurring in field instruction supervision are sufficiently distinct from traditional professional supervision as to warrant empirical inquiry in its own right. The primary role of students serving in the field is that of student, and the primary goals of the field experience are educational in nature. Likewise, the field instructor, while providing supervision of the student's practice, also fulfills a strong educative role. The field instructor-student relationship is likely to possess greater age disparities between the two principals than in subsequent practice, and the evaluative component, wherein the field instructor is largely responsible for critiquing and grading the student's performance, is also distinct from the more commonly encountered collegial supervision occurring after graduation.

Recently, Behling, Curtis and Foster (1982) conducted a study of the impact of sex-role combinations on student performance in the field, employing a sample of 276 MSW students. Of the four possible gender combinations (female student-female field instructor; female student-male field instructor; male student-female field instructor; male student-male field instructor), it was apparently shown that the female student-female field instructor combination was the arrangement most favorably rated by the student, and that, in general, same sex combinations were more positively evaluated than unlike combinations. The female student-male field instructor relationship appeared to be the most stressful and problematic. The validity of these results is difficult to evaluate since statistical summarization of the data was not provided, only probability levels. Furthermore, the authors ascribed these apparent differences to the existence of traditional sexist attitudes held by the male field instructors. This was unwarranted. Even assuming that the results they obtained are valid, the design of their study did not permit a determination of the cause of such variance.

Related studies have failed to replicate the findings of Behling et al. Raskin (1982) examined student evaluations of their field experience using a sample of 170 BSW students. Neither student gender nor field instructor gender were found to be significantly related to student satisfaction in field placement. In a similar study reported by Kolevzon (1979) using a sample of forty-two MSW students, student and field instructor gender combinations were not found to significantly affect the quality of the supervisory relationships. A nonstatistically significant trend was present, however, for students to more poorly evaluate those supervisory relationships of disparate gender.

In summary, the available studies do not permit unambiguous conclusions as to the influence which field instructor-student gender combinations have on the perceived quality of field work. Given the importance of arranging a satisfactory field placement in the student's overall professional education, we undertook the following study to isolate the relative influence gender considerations contribute to the field experience.

METHODOLOGY

We employed a retrospective review of student evaluations of their field experience, using a standardized questionnaire developed in our Office of Field Instruction.[1] The questionnaire consists of two main parts: demographic information about the student, field instructor, and agency; and rating scales on which the student evaluates their field instructor and agency.

The field instructor evaluation component consists of thirteen items rated on a six point scale. The potential scores range from thirteen to seventy-eight, with higher scores indicating a more favorable rating. This questionnaire is depicted in Table I.

We employed as the dependent variable the individual student's total score on the evaluation of field instructor items. Student and field instructor gender served as the independent variables.

The sample consisted of 413 student evaluations, completed between the years 1981-1984. The sample was eighty-two percent female, ninety percent Caucasian, eight percent black, and two percent Hispanic. Evaluations from MSW students formed sixty-nine percent of the sample, while BSW students contributed the remaining thirty-one percent of the questionnaires. The students' mean age was 27.3 years (S.D. = 7.2).

The student's mean total scores and standard deviations for the evaluation of the field instructor items are depicted in Table II. These data were subjected to a two (student gender) by two (field instructor gender) analysis of variance. An overall main effect was found for the students' evaluation of their field instructor [$F(2,409) = 7.99$; p = .001], and the individual effect of field instructor gender was also significant [$F(1,409) = 11.06$; p = .001], whereas the effect of student gender was not statistically significant [$F(1,409) = 2.46$; p = .11]. The source of this variance is more clearly displayed in Table III which presents the significance levels of Scheffe post-hoc comparisons and indicates that the results obtained with the 2 × 2 analysis of variance are solely due to the more favorable ratings obtained with the female student-female field instructor gender combination.

DISCUSSION

At first glance, our results appear to partially replicate those of Behling et al. in that we found the female student-female field instructor gender combination to produce the most favorable ratings of the field instructor. The next most favorable gender combination we found was the male student-male field instructor relationship, a result also congruent with that obtained by Behling et al. However it should be noted that the combined effects of both student gender and field instructor gender accounted for only five percent of the variance in the students' evaluation of their field instructor (Fletcher, 1981).

This suggests that the finding of "statistically" significant differences in student field evaluations, based upon student-field instructor gender may be "much ado about nothing" in that the results have little apparent practical utility.

Given the small proportion of the variance in student evaluations accounted for by gender combinations, it would not be warranted to differentially assign male and female students in order to obtain same-gender field instruction placements in the hopes of enhancing the field work experience. This research provided further evidence that schools of social work should maintain a gender-neutral policy with respect to the field work placement process.

Table I

Items Used by the Student to Evaluate the Field Instructor

In your opinion, how well did your Field Instructor:	Extremely Well				Not Very Well
1. Help you feel comfortable with your work?	6	5	4	3	2	1
2. Establish a comfortable working relationship with you?	6	5	4	3	2	1
3. Give you the amount of time you felt you needed?	6	5	4	3	2	1
4. Assist you in learning and developing work skills and techniques?	6	5	4	3	2	1

5. Help you integrate classroom learn-
   ing with field practice?   6   5   4   3   2   1

6. Plan your orientation to the agency?   6   5   4   3   2   1

7. Offer constructive criticism?   6   5   4   3   2   1

8. Listen to your points of view?   6   5   4   3   2   1

9. Provide support when needed?   6   5   4   3   2   1

10. Provide regularly scheduled
    conference times?   6   5   4   3   2   1

11. Organize your learning experience?   6   5   4   3   2   1

12. Provide help in times of crisis?   6   5   4   3   2   1

13. Assist you in learning about and
    working with minority groups served
    by the agency?   6   5   4   3   2   1

175

Table II

Mean Scores and Standard Deviation of Students Total Scores

In Evaluating Their Field Instructor

Gender Combination	N	M	S.D.
Female Student/Female Field Instructor	217	68.4	8.6
Female Student/Male Field Instructor	122	63.9	11.6
Male Student/Female Field Instructor	30	63.0	10.0
Male Student/Male Field Instructor	44	64.6	9.4

Table III

Scheffe Post-hoc Comparisons of Student Total Scores in

Evaluating Their Field Instructors

Gender Combination

	1	2	3	4
1. Female Student/Female Field Instructor	--			
2. Female Student/Male Field Instructor	.05	--		
3. Male Student/Female Field Instructor	.05	n.s.	--	
4. Male Student/Male Field Instructor	.05	n.s.	n.s.	--
	FS/FFI	FS/MFI	MS/FFI	MS/MFI

FS - Female Student

FFI - Female Field Instructor

MFI - Male Field Instructor

MS - Male Student

NOTE

1. A copy of the complete Field Instruction Evaluation Questionnaire is available from the senior author. Gratitude is extended to Reggie Black-Stock who was instrumental in designing the questionnaire and to Lisa Geilenkeirchen who aided with the analysis of the data.

REFERENCES

Behling, J., Curtis, C., & Foster, S. A. (1982). Impact of sex-role combinations on student performance in field instruction. *Journal of Education for Social Work, 18*(2), 93-97.

Brager, G., & Michael, J. A. (1969). The sex distribution in social work: Causes and consequences. *Social Casework, 50*, 595-601.

Council on Social Work Education (1982). Curriculum policy for master's degree and baccalaureate degree programs in social work education. *Social Work Education Reporter*, September, 5-12.

Diangson, P., Kravetz, D. E., & Lipton, J. (1975). Sex role stereotyping and social work education. *Journal of Education for Social Work, 11*(3), 44-49.

Faver, C., & Fox, M. F. (1984). Publication of articles by male and female social work educators. *Social Work, 29*, 488.

Fletcher, H. J. (1981). Reporting explained variance. *Journal of Research in Science Teaching, 18*, 1-7.

Kadushin, A. (1976). Men in a woman's profession. *Social Work, 21*, 440-447.

Kirk, S. A., & Rosenblatt, A. (1980). Women's contribution to social work journals. *Social Work, 25*, 204-209.

Kirk, S. A., & Rosenblatt, A. (1984). The contribution of women faculty to social work journals. *Social Work*, 67-69.

Kolevzon, M. S. (1979). Evaluating the supervisory relationship in field placements. *Social Work, 24*, 241-244.

Munson, C. E. (1979). Evaluation of male and female supervisors. *Social Work, 24*, 104-110.

National Association of Social Workers. (1980). *Code of ethics*. Washington, D.C.: Author.

Raskin, M. S. (1982). Factors associated with student satisfaction in undergraduate social work field placements. *Arete, 7*(1), 44-54.

Schein, V. E. (1973). The relationship between sex role characteristics and requisite management characteristics. *Journal of Applied Psychology, 57*, 95-100.

Schein, V. E. (1975). Relationships between sex role stereotypes and requisite management characteristics among female managers. *Journal of Applied Psychology, 60*, 340-344.

Schwartz, M. C. (1974). Importance of the sex of worker and client. *Social Work, 19*, 177-185.

Scotch, C. B. (1971). Sex status in social work: Grist for woman's liberation. *Social Work, 16*, 5-11.

Williams, M., Ho, L., & Fielder, L. (1974). Career patterns: More grist for women's liberation. *Social Work, 19*, 463-466.

PART III:
FIELD INSTRUCTORS:
MYTHS AND CHALLENGES

Introduction

Part III and Part IV of the volume will examine two of the major participants in field placement: field instructors and students. Dina Rosenfeld's timely study, "Field Instructor Turnover," examines the intrinsic and extrinsic rewards of field instructors and the relationship of these rewards with plans to continue supervising students. One-third to one-half of the field instructors are new to schools each year. It is time consuming (and costly) to recruit, screen, and train field instructors. Rosenfeld observes that schools, agencies, and field instructors need to discuss the following factors that enhance retention of field instructors: (1) field instructors are more likely to plan to continue supervising students if their agencies are supportive of their efforts; (2) the faculty liaison is perceived to be more helpful to field instructors as communication increases (in-person, telephone, and least by mail); (3) satisfaction with their jobs and working conditions influences field instructors' plans to continue supervising; and (4) the quality of the student.

Providing library privileges, certificates, or tickets to football games did not directly contribute to a reduction in field instructor turnover. These approaches have been adopted by many schools to show appreciation to field instructors, to make them feel that they

© 1989 by The Haworth Press, Inc. All rights reserved.   *181*

are part of the school, and to encourage them to continue their affiliation. Turnover, however, seems to be related to variables other than fringe benefits provided by the school, although they help in providing a positive feeling towards the school.

Beverly Hartung Hagen's article, "The Practicum Instructor: A Study of Role Expectations," identifies the importance of various expected role behaviors for practicum instructors as expressed by agency executives, graduate students, practicum instructors, and practicum coordinators (directors).

The study shows areas of agreement and (sometimes considerable) disagreement between the groups. Role behavior items dealing with student progress and evaluation received the most "very important" role behavior responses from all four groups. All field directors rated "communication with the school" as a very important role of the supervisor, while only sixty-nine percent of the field instructors rated this item as very important. (The difference between the groups was significant at the .05 level.)

Hagen found that each group gave priority to role behaviors of field instructors that related to their own orientation. Practicum directors stressed professional items or school-related areas; students gave priority to skill development, evaluation, and socialization to the profession; field instructors emphasized skills, professionalization, student orientation, and teaching methods; and agency executives stressed skill areas, supervision, and development of students as professional social workers.

Field instructors can find themselves in highly stressful situations. Areas of conflict about expected role behaviors may lead to feelings of alienation toward the school (perhaps contributing to turnover) and role overload contributing to burnout. Shapiro's article, "Burn-Out in Social Work Field Instructors," adds a new dimension to the understanding of field instructors' job burn-out from a systems perspective. Burn-out is focused on organizational demands that produce role overload rather than burn-out being attributed to individual problems. Preventing job burn-out of field instructors includes clarifying role expectations and negotiating realistic responsibilities.

Hagen's study points to the areas in which role expectations of field instructors are in conflict. Shapiro sees this conflict as a systems problem that leads to burn-out. In addition, if the field instructor is faced with a lack of agency support or is dissatisfied with his/her job, a decision not to continue supervising students is likely to occur.

Can creative solutions be found to a situation which seems to be difficult at best? Do individuals understand what they are getting into when they "volunteer" to become a field instructor? Do schools and agencies expect more than one person can handle?

The next two articles have significant implications for the accreditation standards of the Council on Social Work Education. Researchers such as Thyer, Williams, Love, and Sowers-Hoag have begun to look for answers to the question they pose in the title of their paper, "The MSW Supervisory Requirement in Field Instruction: Does it Make a Difference?" The researchers surveyed 410 students (MSW and BSW) and asked them to evaluate their satisfaction with their field instructor and with the agency as a training site. Approximately three hundred (300) students had a field instructor with an MSW, and the rest were supervised by individuals with a masters degree or a doctorate in a related field. The authors conclude that, although the profession may continue to mandate such a requirement, no empirical evidence exists to justify the requirement for supervisors to have the MSW.

Thyer et al., found no statistically significant differences in satisfaction between those students who had an MSW supervisor and those who did not. Perhaps, satisfaction of the student is not a sufficient criteria upon which to base the need for an MSW supervisor. The article by Smith and Baker, "The Relationship Between Educational Background of Field Instructors and the Quality of Supervision," is supportive of this finding, at least from the students' perspective. The results of the multivariate analysis showed that there is no statistically significant difference in student perception of the *quality of supervision* between those who had an MSW supervisor and those who did not.

Smith and Baker found that ratings of field faculty were statistically significant when MSW and those with other degrees were compared. Upon closer examination of the results, the researchers conclude that there is no statistically significant difference in ratings between MSW and MA level supervisors and between BSW and

MA level supervisors. Most of the differences occurred between the comparison of BA level and MSW/MA level supervisors. The authors suggest that there may be substitutability of the MA and BSW level supervisor for the MSW. However, at least from the faculty perspective, individuals with a BA from a non-social work area might not be adequate as supervisors.

An additional study that looks at student satisfaction in field placement ("Factors Associated with Student Satisfaction in Undergraduate Social Work Field Placements") appears in the next section of the book. The focus of this paper is broader than the relationship of the educational background of the supervisor and student satisfaction. However, in this study, students were more satisfied in field placement when their supervisor did not possess the MSW degree.

In the article by Julianne Wayne, "A Comparison of Beliefs About Student Supervision Between Micro and Macro Practitioners," eighty (80) field instructors were interviewed in order to compare beliefs about student supervision between micro and macro practitioners. Supervisors of micro and macro practice were shown to have different attitudes toward, and beliefs about, the education and supervision of social work students. Micro supervisors engage in a retrospective analysis of student behaviors while macro supervisors focus more heavily on helping students plan future strategies. Micro supervisors perceive greater agency support for their student supervision responsibilities than do macro supervisors. Macro supervisors emphasize the cognitive over the affective aspect of the educational process while micro supervisors do the reverse. Macro supervisors value the development of a student evaluation instrument that focuses on problem-solving and strategy building, rather than on interactional processes.

The differences in the style of supervision between micro and macro practitioners need to be recognized. The schools have to pay more attention to variations in the motivation to supervise students and in level of agency support for supervision. Is the emphasis of field instructor training, class assignments related to field, and evaluation forms too heavily weighted toward either micro or macro skills?

The increasing pressure on field instructors to serve client, organizational, student, and university needs, and a growing field curriculum required by the Council on Social Work Education accreditation standards, may contribute to higher turnover rates and burn-out of field instructors. Many schools outline the responsibilities of the agency, field instructor, and school in their field instruction manuals. Yet, how many agency executives, field instructors, students, and school faculty engage in creative discussions with regard to the feasibility and reality of carrying out such expectations? If students cannot perceive a difference in the quality of supervision between an MSW and a non-MSW supervisor, how do we proceed? Even field instruction experts are not fully convinced about the MSW requirement for supervision. They could not reach consensus on the following statement: "we can justify having individuals with other than social work degrees supervise students in the field" (Part I of the book, "A Delphi Study in Field Instruction: Identification of Issues and Research Priorities by Experts").

The time is ripe to fine tune research questions, to strengthen methodology and measurement. A willingness to test traditions and to defend those that remain valid after scientific review is a test of the profession itself. Agency personnel need to be supported and satisfied with their jobs before taking on field instruction responsibilities. Expectations of the field instructor should be clear and realistic, and, perhaps, even individualized.

The need for the MSW degree by a field instructor has been debated for a long time. The studies presented in this volume will not end the debate. The results may encourage those on both sides of the issue to explore the values, knowledge, and skills needed to provide effective field instruction for the social workers of the next decades. This exploration *may* show that the possession of the MSW degree in combination with other variables is necessary and/or sufficient to warrant its continuation as a requirement by the schools.

Field Instructor Turnover

Dina Jordana Rosenfeld

ABSTRACT. This study examined the turnover of field instructors in relation to agency and university support, and to the intrinsic satisfaction from field instruction. As expected, both agency and university supports positively influenced the decision of field instructors to continue taking students. The intrinsic rewards that evolved from the content of the work were: teaching and sharpening practice skills; learning new ideas; contributing to the profession; and relieving the boredom of the job. As hypothesized, all the above variables correlated positively with the plans of field instructors to take students the next year. The quality of the student correlated with all the major variables of the study.

INTRODUCTION

Given the centrality of field instruction, the high rate of turnover among field instructors is a source of concern to agencies and universities. Field work directors in the New York area estimate that they train approximately 400 new field instructors a year, and several authorities estimate the general turnover to average 50 percent (Berengarten, 1962). The quality of field instruction is threatened by the high turnover rate of field instructors.

Social work had its beginning exclusively in field experience, and even today field instruction occupies close to half the learning time of social work students. Most social work students and alumni see field work as the most valuable aspect of their personal and professional training (Gizyniki, 1978). Within field instruction, the quality of the field instructor is one of the important variables in contributing to a positive field experience (Kahn, 1981).

The dropout rate requires constant recruitment and training of new field instructors. Agencies carry the cost by offering release time for staff so that they can attend seminars for new field instruc-

© 1989 by The Haworth Press, Inc. All rights reserved.

tors. The schools contribute by providing seminars for new field instructors and by increasing faculty follow-up in the first year of field instruction. Students are most adversely affected since they must continually deal with inexperienced field instructors.

Analysis of factors entering into the high drop-out rate of field instructors is the subject of this study. Three major factors and their relationship to field instructors' plans to continue supervising students were investigated: agency supports, university supports, and intrinsic rewards of field instruction.

METHODOLOGY

A questionnaire was sent in 1982 to all field instructors associated with the New York University (N.Y.U.) School of Social Work. The total population consisted of 358 field instructors who were located in 197 agencies and were involved in the training of 418 students. Of the total population, 327 field instructors (91 percent) participated in the survey.

The instrument used was a mail questionnaire, encompassing 55 multiple-choice questions and 3 open-ended questions. The major hypothesis of the study was that when the intrinsic and extrinsic rewards from field instruction outweigh the costs of this instruction, field instructors will be more likely to want to continue to serve as supervisors.

The following were the subhypotheses to be tested:

H 1. Field Instructors will be more likely to want to continue supervising if their agency is supportive of field instruction. The intention to continue supervising is the dependent variable, and agency support is the independent variable.

The following components of agency support were studied:

a. Recognition of field instruction experience as part of career enhancement and job mobility
b. Alleviation of field instructor's heavy caseload
c. Facilitation in finding appropriate cases
d. Relationships of field instructor with other staff, including professional status

e. Availability of release time necessary for university-associated activities
f. Provision of office space and secretarial help

H 2. Field instructors will be more likely to want to continue supervising if they perceive the university as being supportive of their efforts.

The intention to continue supervising was the dependent variable, and university support was the independent variable. The following components of university support were studied:

a. Quality of the training program for field instructors
b. University bonuses (e.g., library card, half price courses, and adjunct status)
c. Amount, quality, and content of contact with faculty advisor

H 3. Field instructors will be more likely to want to continue supervising if they are satisfied with the intrinsic aspects of field instruction.

The intention to continue supervising was the dependent variable, and satisfaction with the intrinsic aspects of field instruction was the independent variable. The following components of intrinsic satisfaction were studied:

a. Satisfaction with teaching
b. Relief of job-related boredom
c. Contribution to the profession
d. Sharpening of practice skills
e. Learning new ideas in the field
f. Quality of the student assigned to the field instructor

The following are examples of items from the questionnaire representing each category of hypothesis:

1. How many contacts have you had this academic year with your student's university faculty advisor? (circle number in each category)

In-Person	0	1	2	3	4	5+
By phone	0	1	2	3	4	5+

In group	0	1	2	3	4	5+
By mail	0	1	2	3	4	5+

2. Does supervising social work students in your agency have:

a. High status
b. Medium status
c. Low status
d. No status

3. How would you rate your student's performance in the field?

a. Excellent
b. Good
c. Fair
d. Poor

The following were the open-ended items on the questionnaire. These questions examined the dependent variables of the study:

1. Assuming no significant personal and agency changes from the past year, would you take a student next year?

1 DEFINITELY YES (ANSWER QUESTION 3)
2 PROBABLY YES (ANSWER QUESTION 3)
3 NOT SURE (ANSWER QUESTION 2)
4 PROBABLY NOT (ANSWER QUESTION 2)
5 DEFINITELY NOT (ANSWER QUESTION 2)

2. If your answer to the above is NOT SURE, PROBABLY NOT, or DEFINITELY NOT, please describe the reasons you are considering not taking a student next year.

3. If you are planning on taking a student, but prefer that he/she come from a school other than N.Y.U., please briefly state your reasons for wanting a student from another school.

4. What was the greatest source of satisfaction in your experience as a field instructor?[1]

The scale used to rate answers was a Likert-type scale; respondents were asked to reply in various degrees of agreement or disagreement. Analysis of the material relied on crosstab statistics and chi-square as a test of statistical significance. Computerized statistical analyses used SPSS (Statistical Program for Social Sciences).

AGENCY RELATIONSHIP TO FIELD INSTRUCTION

The field instructor is the central figure and often the only agency representative involved in student training. The agency-university relationship, however, has been criticized for relying too heavily on one staff member, the field instructor, in carrying out the mandate of training students. It is felt by many that the whole agency, which benefits from having students, should be involved in the educational endeavor (Pins and Ginsberg, 1971).

The agency director and other staff often are enthusiastic at the thought of students coming, but when the students arrive the field instructor stands alone. In those situations where the agencies accepted students solely to comply with the instructors' wish to be involved in teaching, field instructors may have even less cause to expect agency support in handling the varied needs of students (Kahn, 1981).

Since an organization's support of its workers has a major impact on job satisfaction, and job satisfaction results in decreased turnover of staff, the area of organizational support is important to examine. This study investigates the self-reported satisfaction of field instructors with agency support and the various aspects of that support.

FINDINGS

The following is a summary of the findings on the impact of agency support on the plans of field instructors to continue supervising students. Field instructors were more likely to want to continue taking students if they were satisfied with the general support provided. The more they liked working for their agency, the better the relationship with their social work director and the more positively they felt about their agency's support. The effects of serving as a field instructor on the relationship with colleagues, job mobility, and professional status also were positively related to the degree of satisfaction with agency support. The agency's willingness to provide release time for university meetings, office space, and secretarial assistance were seen as important characteristics of a supportive agency. The supervisors who had autonomy over their units perceived their agencies as being more supportive.

Respect, status, and recognition are seen to be important variables in agency satisfaction (Glicken, 1980). Of all the variables studied in this section, status had the strongest correlation with satisfaction of the field instructor with respect to the agency's support. The correlation is at Pearson R of .346 and .0000 level of significance (Table 1).

Over 60 percent of the field instructors reported an increase in their workloads as a result of having students. They reported working an extra six hours. Analysis showed no correlation between increased workload and satisfaction with agency supports.

Field instructors may view the additional workload as an appropriate and expected aspect of field instruction. In response to the open-ended question, ". . . please describe the reason you are considering not taking a student next year," of the 45 respondents for whom their agencies assumed a central role in the dissatisfaction, the majority reported their workloads to be overwhelming and with little support or understanding received from their agencies. The following are some examples: "Increases my workload, and it means I have to take time from my off hours to provide adequate student supervision and keep up with my job responsibilities"; "Involves extra emotional investment and usually presents additional problems at work"; and, "Not enough time given by agency freely to provide good supervision, since the agency doesn't really want students."

Approximately 60 percent of the field instructors who complained that student instruction required additional workload stated that poor students are not worth the extra time involved: "Since it adds work, I don't want to risk having another mediocre student"; and, "Students increased my workload, and I also had a very poor student who was not satisfying."

Thus, in re-examining the question of workload, it seems that working extra hours and carrying additional cases were not necessarily perceived as a burden by the field instructors. The work became troublesome when the actual experience with the student was not gratifying enough to make the exchange worthwhile.

THE UNIVERSITY'S RELATIONSHIP TO FIELD INSTRUCTORS

With the historical movement of social work education away from agency auspices and toward academic settings, the relationship between university and agency had to be continually redefined. Many educators have lamented the lack of "coordination" and "cooperation" between the schools of social work and agencies (Kahn, 1981).

When the literature speaks of the "agency" and of the "school" interacting, it refers primarily to what actually takes place between the field instructor and the student's faculty advisor: the faculty advisor is the pivotal figure in the field instructor's relationship to the school (Rosenblum and Raphael, 1985). As illustrated in Table 2, a Pearson's R of .3387 at a .000 significance level was obtained in correlating how the field instructors felt about the association with N.Y.U., and how helpful the student's University faculty advisor was perceived to be. As a consequence of the school's recognition of the importance of the faculty advisor in agency relations, an attempt is made to maintain the same faculty advisor with a given set of agencies year after year. This ensures continuity and a further building of the relationship between the faculty advisor and the field instructor.

When correlating how helpful faculty advisors were to field instructors with the number of actual contacts (in-person, phone, group meetings, and mail), there is a clear indication that increased frequency of contact is experienced as being helpful to the field instructor. As illustrated in Tables 3 and 4, there was a strong correlation of helpfulness of faculty advisor as demonstrated by the number of phone contacts and in-person contacts. Group contacts and mail (an impersonal form of contact) were seen as least helpful to

Table 1

SATISFACTION WITH AGENCY SUPPORT OF FIELD INSTRUCTION

CORRELATED WITH THE STATUS OF SUPERVISING STUDENTS

Satisfaction With Agency Support	Status Associated with the Supervision of Students			
	None	Low	Medium	High
Very dissatisfied	5	1	0	0
	6.8%	8.3%	.0%	.0%
Moderately dissatisfied	11	3	9	2
	14.9%	25.0%	5.6%	2.4%

	74	12	160	84
Not sure	10	0	5	0
	13.5%	.0	3.1%	.0%
Moderately satisfied	20	7	61	2
	27.0%	58.3%	38.1%	29.8%
Very satisfied	28	1	35	57
	37.8%	8.3%	53.1%	67.9%
Total	74	12	160	84
	100.0%	100.0%	100.0%	100.0%
	100.0%	100.0%	100.0%	100.0%

R= .34641   Significance= .0000

195

Table 2

FEELINGS ABOUT PRESENT ASSOCIATION WITH N.Y.U.

BY THE PERCEIVED HELPFULNESS OF

THE STUDENT'S FACULTY ADVISOR

	Perceived Helpfulness				
	Not at All	A Little	Somewhat	Very	Total
Feelings					
Negative	5	1	1	1	8
	11.4%	4.5%	2.0%	1.2%	4.0%

Neutral	15	7	6	8	36
	34.1%	31.8%	11.8%	9.9%	18.2%
Positive	24	14	44	72	154
	54.5%	63.6%	86.3%	88.9%	77.8%
Total	44	22	51	81	198
	22.2%	11.1%	25.8%	40.9%	100.0%

R = .33868   Significance = .0000

Table 3

HELPFULNESS OF STUDENT'S FACULTY ADVISOR

BY NUMBER OF PHONE CONTACTS

Helpfulness of Students' Faculty Advisor	Number of Phone Contacts						
	0	1	2	3	4	5+	Total
Not at all	16	14	6	1	2	1	40
	72.7	50.0	20.7	2.9	6.9	2.2	21.3%
A little	1	2	7	5	3	3	21
	4.5	7.1	24.1	14.7	10.3	6.5	11.2%

							Total
Somewhat	3	6	7	11	9	12	48
	13.6	21.4	24.1	32.4	31.0	26.1	25.5%
Very	2	6	9	17	15	30	79
	9.1	21.4	31.0	50.0	51.7	65.2	42.0%
Total	22	28	29	34	29	46	188
	11.7%	14.9%	15.4%	18.1%	15.4%	25.4%	100.0%

$R = .54750$ Significance = .0000

199

Table 4

HELPFULNESS OF STUDENT'S UNIVERSITY FACULTY ADVISOR

BY NUMBER OF IN-PERSON CONTACTS

Helpfulness of Student's University Faculty Advisor	In-Person Contacts						
	0	1	2	3	4	5+	Total
Not at all	27	10	1	1	1	0	40
	47.4	15.9	3.4	6.7	50.0	0	22.1%
A Little	7	12	1	0	0	0	20
	12.3	19.0	3.4	0	0	0	11.0%

Somewhat	6	20	8	3	1	8	46
	10.5	31.7	27.6	20.0	50.0	53.3	25.4%
Very	17	21	19	11	0	7	75
	29.8	33.3	65.5	73.3	0	46.7	41.4%
Total	57	63	29	15	2	15	181
	31.5%	34.8%	16.0%	8.3%	1.1%	8.3%	100.0%

R = .35455   Significance = .0000

field instructors. The correlation of group contacts and mail contact with helpfulness of faculty advisor was, respectively, Pearson's R = .22388 with a .0023 significance, and R = .19618 with a significance of .0072.

Seminars for the new field instructors are the major vehicle by which social work professionals are taught about becoming field instructors. In these seminars, field instructors learn the skills of supervising, discuss possible problems that may arise with students, review reading material, and receive support from the school and other beginning field instructors in their new task of teaching.

Berengarten (1961) suggested that group meetings represented the most helpful format for new field instructors. With the increased coordination of metropolitan area schools of social work, there is a more defined and uniform body of knowledge that is being transmitted in these seminars.

Based upon the researcher's experience and observations of field instructors, it appears that the seminars have a significant influence on the satisfaction of field instructors with the school and on the quality of their teaching. As illustrated in Table 5, satisfaction with contacts with the N.Y.U. School of Social Work is positively correlated with the rating of the seminar for new field instructors.

In addition to the contact field instructors have with the school through students, other contact includes adjunct faculty status, use of the library, bookstore discounts, and educational conferences.

Even though the majority of the field instructors (74 percent) do not utilize the library or the bookstore, there is a correlation between how field instructors feel about their association with N.Y.U. and their use of these services. Feelings about association with N.Y.U. correlated with the use of library and bookstore at a R = .25568 with a significance = .0000, and with the use of all-day institutes at R = .16187 and a significance of .0019. The positive feelings about N.Y.U. and the use of concrete supports probably affect each other reciprocally. A field instructor who utilizes the school's various services may experience contacts with N.Y.U. more positively; someone who generally has positive feelings about N.Y.U. may be more motivated to seek out these services.

INTRINSIC REWARDS OF FIELD INSTRUCTION

In Kahn's (1981) survey and analysis of the motivations of social workers who choose to become field instructors, the three strongest factors reported were the field instructor's enjoyment of teaching, their perception of field instruction as an additional learning experience, and furthering of the profession. She reported that these motivators were ranked as "major factors" by 72.8 percent, 57.2 percent, and 40 percent of field instructors, respectively. In contrast, motivators such as status and prestige ranked as "major factors" for only 19.4 percent of field instructors.

"Relieving the boredom of the job" was included as one of the areas to be examined. Field instructors frequently talked about student supervision as being the most interesting aspect of their jobs, serving as an antidote to jobs they found no longer stimulating. Job satisfaction researchers have demonstrated a strong correlation between the variety available in a job and job satisfaction (Hackman and Lawer, 1971). In addition, task variety has been shown to be positively correlated with feelings of self-esteem and personal growth associated with a job (Tuggle, 1978).

The findings in this study support the research results of Kahn. The respondents indicated the following order as most important in their choosing to continue as field instructors: enjoyment of teaching, sharpening practice skills, learning new ideas, contributing to the profession, and relieving the boredom of the job.

In an examination of the cross tabulation of five factors with plans to continue field instruction, the correlation with relieving boredom was the most significant (Table 6 and Table 7). This is interesting because when asked to rank the areas of importance, 85.6 percent of the field instructors regarded teaching to be a very important consideration, while only 28.7 percent cited relieving the boredom of the job as very important.

One possible theory explaining this discrepancy is that the two questions, although similar, tapped different needs of the field instructors. The direct questioning of the field instructors about the relative importance of various factors in continuing field instruction may have evoked consideration of professional values as to what is or ought to be important. In contrast, the importance of relieving

Table 5

SATISFACTION WITH N.Y.U. SCHOOL OF SOCIAL WORK

BY RATING OF THE NEW FIELD INSTRUCTOR'S SEMINAR

Satisfaction With N.Y.U.	Rating of New Field Instructor's Seminar				
	Poor 1	Fair 2	Good 3	Excellent 4	Total
Very dissatisfied	3 20.0	1 2.3	4 2.0	0 0	8 2.9%
Moderately dis-satisfied	2 13.3	5 11.4	10 7.5	7 8.0	24 8.6%

Not Sure	.1 6.7	6 13.6	8 6.0	3 3.4	18 6.5%
Moderately satisfied	4 33.3	20 45.5	68 51.1	27 31.0	119 42.7%
Very satisfied	5 33.3	12 27.3	43 32.3	50 57.5	110 39.4%
Total	15 5.4%	44 15.8%	33 47.7%	87 31.2%	279 100.0%

$R = .24098$ Significance $= .0000$

Table 6

PLANS TO TAKE A STUDENT NEXT YEAR
BY RATING OF SATISFACTION WITH RELIEVING
BOREDOM OF JOB

Satisfaction with Relieving Boredom of Job

Plans to Take Student	Very Dissatisfied	Moderately Dissatisfied	Not Sure	Moderately Satisfied	Very Satisfied	Total
Definitly No	0 .0	2 33.3	5 7.1	2 2.0	2 1.7	11 3.7%
Probably No	0 .0	0 .0	5 7.1	2 2.0	4 3.4	11 3.7%

	1	2	6	9	3	21 7.1%
Not Sure	25.0	33.3	8.6	9.2	2.6	
	0	1	23	20	11	55
Probably Yes	.0	16.7	32.9	20.4	9.4	18.6%
	3	1	31	65	97	197
Definitely Yes	75.0	16.7	44.3	66.3	82.9	66.8%
	4	6	70	98	117	295
Total	1.4%	2.0%	23.7%	33.2%	39.7%	100.0%

R = .28434   Significance = .0000

207

Table 7

PLANS TO TAKE A STUDENT NEXT YEAR

BY RATING OF SATISFACTION WITH TEACHING

Plans to Take a Student	Satisfaction with Teaching					
	Very Dissatisfied	Moderately Dissatisfied	Not Sure	Moderately Satisfied	Very Satisfied	Total
Definitely No	0	0	1	1	10	12
	.0	.0	20.0	1.2	4.3	3.7%
Probably No	0	0	0	4	8	12
	.0	.0	.0	4.8	3.4	2.7%

						Total
Not Sure	0	1	2	8	13	24
	.0	33.3	40.0	9.6	5.5	7.3%
Probably Yes	0	1	1	25	30	57
	.0	33.3	20.1	30.1	12.8	17.4%
Definitely Yes	1	1	1	45	174	222
	100.0	33.3	20.0	54.2	74.0	67.9%
Total	1	3	5	83	235	327
	.3%	.9%	1.5%	25.4%	71.9%	100.0%

$R = .11605$ Significance $= .0180$

boredom, a finding resulting from a crosstabulation of the satisfaction with various aspects of field instruction with plans to take students, may reflect the actual needs of field instructors in their everyday work. Put another way, the first question asked the field instructors to do the correlation in their own minds and represents their image of what is important. The correlations shown in Tables 6 and 7, however, illustrate what is actually important to them — the image does not coincide with the reality.

It is instructive to examine the write-in answers to the question, "What is the greatest source of satisfaction in your experience as a field instructor?" The majority of the answers referred to the successful end product: "Feeling that I made a contribution to creating competent, ethical, and creative social workers"; "Seeing students reach their learning goals"; and, "The student with whom I worked was delightful, bright, motivated, perceptive, and empathic." The following comment makes beautifully clear the implicit connection between student progress and the instructor's satisfaction: "Student's growth generated feelings of my own competence." In the 200 write-ins to the above questions, only 6 answers reflected satisfaction in the struggle over a poor student.

Field instructors were asked to rate their students' performance in the field. Only 3.4 percent rated their students as being "poor," 13.9 percent "fair," 43.7 percent "good," and 39 percent "excellent." When crosstabulating student performance in the field with whether the field instructor planned to take a student the following year, a positive correlation of .116 was found at a .02 level of significance (Table 8). In considering the weakness of the correlation, it is important to note that there is no difference (72 percent and 71.8 percent) between those who rated their students excellent and good, while there was a 35.6 percent absolute difference between those who rated their students excellent and those who rated them poor. In other words, in their decisions to continue supervising, field instructors divide their students into "good" and "bad," with less marked differences in the categories in-between.

The quality of the student also seemed to correlate positively with the other variables in the study: satisfaction with agency supports; satisfaction with N.Y.U.; and satisfaction with teaching.

Number of Years Supervised

Research has indicated that the largest percentage of turnover in field instructors occurs after the first year of field instruction (Gitterman, 1972). Thus, it is appropriate to examine how satisfaction with teaching correlates with the number of years that field instructors have supervised students. As illustrated in Table 9, a positive correlation exists with particularly marked differences occurring at the first year and 5 + years, with the second, third, and fourth years being fairly similar. It might be that those social workers who continued for 5 + years are enjoying teaching and, through experience, are fairly comfortable with it. The lowest satisfaction with teaching seems to occur in the first year, when the new field instructor's lack of experience and insecurity in his/her ability to supervise may make it difficult to enjoy teaching.

Wilson (1981) suggests that the new supervisory role leads to a great deal of self-examination and a questioning of previously assumed competence and effectiveness. Field instructors become aware of the responsibility of introducing a new person into the profession, and they question whether they can translate their knowledge of practice into educational principles for their students. The first year of field instruction is described as being a difficult one, fraught with anxiety and self-doubt.

DISCUSSION AND IMPLICATIONS

When negotiating an agency-university working relationship, universities should make clear to the field work liaison or the agency director the importance of giving field instructors the release time for meetings at school, secretarial assistance, adequate work space for the student, and the ability to choose appropriate student cases.

The most important and the most difficult recommendation is for the agency to accord higher status to field instruction. It is possible that the more concrete the supports that are offered, the higher the status experienced by the field instructors. In addition, *with fewer field placements needed by schools*, selection to be a field instructor may be seen as special and selective, conferring higher status. Since

Table 8

PLANS TO TAKE STUDENTS NEXT YEAR

BY RATE OF STUDENT'S PERFORMANCE

IN THE FIELD

Plan to Take Students	Student's Performance in the Field				
	Poor	Fair	Good	Excellent	Total
Definitely No	1	1	5	5	12
	9.1	2.1	3.5	4.0	3.7%
Probably No	0	3	5	4	12
	.0	6.4	3.5	3.2	3.7%

					Total
Not Sure	2	6	9	7	24
	18.2	12.8	6.3	5.6	7.4%
Probably Yes	4	14	21	19	58
	36.4	29.8	14.8	15.2	17.8%
Definitely Yes	4	23	102	90	219
	36.4	48.9	71.8	72.0	67.4%
Total	11	47	142	125	325
	3.4%	14.5%	43.7%	38.5%	100.0%

$R = .11556$ Significance $= .0187$

213

Table 9

SATISFACTION WITH TEACHING

BY NUMBER OF YEARS SUPERVISING

	Number of Years Supervising				
Satisfaction with Teaching	1	2	3	4	5+
Very Dissatisfied	0 .0%	1 1.5%	0 .0%	0 .0%	0 .0%
Moderately Dissatisfied	2 2.6	0 .0	1 2.2	0 .0	0 .0

Not Sure	4	1	0	0	0
	5.3	1.5	.0	.0	.0
Moderately Satisfied	26	16	10	18	5
	34.2	24.2	21.7	25.0	9.3
Very Satisfied	44	48	35	54	49
	57.9	72.7	76.1	75.0	90.7
Total	76	66	46	54	54
	100.0%	100.0%	100.0%	100.0%	100.0%

R = .23059   Significance = .0000

travelling to the university is very time consuming, it may be possible in larger agencies to offer advanced seminars for field instructors at the agency, taught by either a senior agency supervisor or university faculty. The more welcoming and supportive the total agency is to the student, the higher the actual or perceived status of the field instructor.

Phone contacts had the strongest correlation with how helpful the faculty advisor was perceived—phone contact is the least expensive and the most readily available form of contact between faculty advisor and field instructor. This particular researcher values both visits to the agency by the faculty advisors and group meetings of full instruction at the school. However, the findings of this study, as well as the lean economic times, suggest that the telephone should be utilized more frequently as a way of communicating the university's continued need for, and investment in, field work.

According to the ranking by the field instructors of the content of the field instructor-faculty advisor meeting, more direct references to, and working from, process recordings may serve to improve communication between faculty advisor and field instructor. In addition, the field instructor's initial impression of the university can be enhanced by offering a positive experience in the seminars for new field instructors. Since all universities seem to offer some concrete "gifts" to field instructors for their services, it seems important to emphasize their availability and encourage their use.

The apparent impact of the quality of the student on field instructors' perceptions of their supervisory experience becomes even more important in light of the present trend of decreasing applications to schools of social work. Some schools of social work may increasingly accept students of lower quality in order to maintain a viable level of enrollment. The findings of this study suggest that the standards for social work applicants need to be upheld in order to retain the interest of field instructors in the supervision of students. Obviously, these standards must be maintained as well for the sake of the profession and the clients that are served.

While student supervision does generate its own rewards for field instructors, those same field instructors also feel the burdens of that supervision. Field instructors will undertake supervision when they expect the positive rewards to outweigh the burdens, and they will discontinue supervising when the exchange is no longer expected to be positive overall.

The request by social workers to take on the responsibility of students demonstrates the normative power that universities exert upon the profession. However, commitment may waver once the exact nature of the work is discovered. Because many of the positive rewards of the relationship between field instructors and the universities may be enjoyed, and any sense of obligation to the profession may be satisfied, after the first year of supervising a continuing commitment to field instruction is less likely.

Based upon the research findings of this study, recommendations were made whereby agencies and universities can modify their policies to improve the context in which field instructors operate. Such modifications should, in turn, increase field instructors' perceptions of the positive rewards of supervision. In addition, emphasis on the (net) positive aspects of student supervision should help to decrease the turnover rate of field instructors.

NOTE

1. Uncopyrighted questionnaire developed by author.

REFERENCES

Berengarten, S. (1961). Educational issues in field instruction in social work. *Social Service Review*, *XXXV*(3).

Berengarten, S. (1962). Educational issues in field instruction in social work. In *Field Instruction and Casework*. New York: The Jewish Guild for the Blind.

Gitterman, A. (1972). The field instructor in social work education: A study of role strain. Doctoral Dissertation, Columbia University, Teachers College.

Gizyniki, M. (1978). Self awareness of the supervisor in supervision. *Clinical Social Work Journal*, 6(3).

Glicken, V. (1980). Enhancing work for professional social workers. *Administration in Social Work*, 4(3), 61-74.

Hackman, J. R., & Lawler, E. E. (1971). Employee reactions to job satisfaction characteristics. *Journal of Applied Psychology*, 55, 259-286.

Kahn, S. L. (1981). An analysis of the relationship between social work schools and field placement agencies in their joint task of educating social workers. Doctoral Dissertation, Columbia University School of Social Work.

Pins, A., & Ginsberg, L. (1971). New developments in social work education and their impact on Jewish communal service and community center work. *Journal of Jewish Communal Services, XLVIII*(1).

Rosenblum, A. F., & Raphael, F. (1983). The role and function of the faculty field liaison. *Journal of Education for Social Work, 19*(1), 67-73.

Tuggle, F. D. (1978). An analysis of employee turnover. *Behavioral Sciences, 23*(1), 32-37.

Wilson, S. J.(1981). *Field instruction techniques for supervisors.* New York: Free Press.

The Practicum Instructor:
A Study of Role Expectations

Beverly J. Hartung Hagen

ABSTRACT. This paper focuses on the differences among four respondent groups (students, practicum coordinators, practicum instructors, and agency executives) in their perception of the importance of various role behaviors of practicum instructors in social work. A random sample of the 84 accredited graduate schools of social work in the United States and Puerto Rico was studied. Both significant differences and areas of agreement concerning perception of role behavior were found among the four groups.

The social work practicum is a vital part of the master's degree in social work programs in colleges and universities throughout the United States. It provides the student the opportunity to apply knowledge gained in the classroom and to learn the practice skills necessary for effective social work service. The relationship between the practicum or field instructor and the social work student is an important element in this educational process. In this study, role theory, which involves the definition of certain interactions between people, provides a framework to study the supervisory role in the field practicum.

The importance of the supervisory role in the formal education process and in the continued growth toward autonomy of the agency professional is summarized by Kadushin (1976):

> The objective of professional training is not only to teach the knowledge, skills, and attitudes that would enable the recruit to do a competent job but also to socialize the student to the ways of the profession, to develop a professional conscience.

This paper originally appeared in the *Journal of Sociology and Social Welfare*, Vol IX, No. 4, 1982, pages 662-670.

It is the elaborate process of professional socialization, during a prolonged program of intensive training, which permits workers in all professions to operate autonomously, free of external direction and control on the basis of competence and values incorporated during training. The supervisor is, in effect, internalized during the transformation of the lay person into a professional, and supervision does not then need to be externally imposed. (pp. 30-31)

The goal of the social work practicum program broadly stated is to provide the student an opportunity to obtain experience working in various social work settings. Agencies and social work educational institutions, therefore, experience a mutual dependency which has the potential to be both harmonious and mutually satisfying. As Tropman (1977) observes:

Perhaps the most obvious link is the agency's dependency on the educational institution for the preparation of its professional staff, and the educational institution's dependency upon the agency for fieldwork experience. (p. 8)

Tropman points out that a mutually satisfying relationship between an agency and an educational institution is sometimes confronted by obstacles such as: (1) agency history and tradition which are in conflict with educational goals; (2) agency responsibility which may focus on present rather than future concerns; and (3) agency organization and support which may include boards or directors whose philosophy, values, and ideas may not be supportive of education. One of the most obvious obstacles to which Tropman (1977) alludes is that of the differences in responsibility experienced by agencies and educational institutions (i.e., the possible conflict between service roles and educational roles).

The role of the practicum instructor varies among schools and agencies according to the demands placed on the instructor by students, faculty, agency administrators, and other people throughout the community. Ramsay (1974) uses an allegory to describe the practicum student as "standing on the bridge between academic studies and reality" (p. 45). This author suggests that the role of the agency supervisor has to do with "assisting him in crossing this bridge and seeing the view from its span'' (p. 45). He also views the supervisor as a special kind of educator who must respond to the varied objectives of students' individual differences with special approaches in guiding them through field work experiences. Ramsay (1974) clarifies the practicum supervisor's role by stating:

> The agency supervisor has a double role in relation to students engaged in field experience. He must see the student as both worker and learner. His special contribution to the student's development is helping the student relate through his work to the real world. (p. 50)

Ramsay believes that the practicum supervisor has an interpretive role which is part of the teaching function. He concludes:

> In general, supervisors are responsible for some output in terms of product or service, they must see that the objectives of the organization are met and that the labor under their supervision is directed toward that end. However, the student laborer is an end in himself and success is measured in part by his development. (p. 50)

It is clear that the supervisor's position requires satisfying both agency and student needs, and this may result in conflicting role demands. The practicum supervisor also may be faced with conflicting expectations from other groups such as the faculty of the school of social work, the practicum coordinator for the school, or the community in which the supervisor practices. Merton (1964) observes that "the professional social worker has become more aware of conflicting demands and that the resulting problems have become acute in supervision" (p. 388). Merton (1964) suggests, however, that conflict has the potential to be beneficial and that:

> When it becomes plain that the demands of some are in full contradiction with the demands of others, it becomes, in part, the task of members of the role-set . . . to resolve these contradictions either by a struggle for over-riding power or by some degree of compromise. (p. 383)

Before being able to "resolve contradictions," however, the practicum supervisor must be aware of the role expectations coming from the various groups with which professional contact is experienced.

RESEARCH OBJECTIVES AND QUESTIONS

The purpose of this study is to determine the importance of expected role behaviors for practicum instructors in social work. Specifically, the objectives of this study are to: (1) identify and indicate the importance of various expected role behaviors for practicum instructors in social work as determined by agency executives, graduate students in social work, practicum instructors in social work, and practicum coordinators in schools of social work; and (2) determine whether these groups believe that an appropriate amount of practicum time is spent in various role activities.

The following questions are addressed: (1) What expected role behaviors for practicum instructors in social work are identified as important by students, practicum instructors, practicum coordinators, and agency executives? (2) Does conflict exist between the various groups responding in terms of their determination of the importance of the practicum instructor's role behaviors? (3) Are the four respondent groups in agreement as to how practicum instructors should spend practicum time? (4) Are there differences in the way in which the groups give priority to the role expectations?

METHODOLOGY

The multistage, stratified, systematic random sample of respondents (on the basis of school size) was taken from the 84 accredited graduate schools of social work in the United States and Puerto Rico listed in the *Statistics on Social Work Education in the United States (1977)*. Sixteen schools were chosen by this system from which 564 students, 16 practicum coordinators, 200 practicum instructors, and 200 agency executives were randomly selected. Of these respondents, 71 percent (398) of the students, 81.5 percent (163) of the practicum instructors, 67 percent (134) of the agency executives, and 87.5 percent (14) of the practicum coordinators returned usable questionnaires in time for participation in the study.

Data Gathering Instrument

A basic questionnaire comprised of dependent variables was developed and divided in two parts. The first section consisted of forty-two possible practicum instructor roles such as "helps the student incorporate professional values" or "communicates actively with the School of Social Work." For each role, the respondent was given a choice of responses ranging from "No, not a role," to "Yes, a very important role."

The second part of the questionnaire consisted of eleven statements which were summaries of the forty-two previous role expectation statements (e.g., "Formal Teaching" or "Student Skill Development"). In this section, the respondent was asked to indicate if practicum instructors should spend less time, the same time, or more time in the described activities. A "Don't know" response also was provided.

From this basic questionnaire, four versions were made with independent variables which would be appropriate to the respondent group. For example, the student questionnaire asks for years in school, whereas the practicum instructor version asks for position in agency.

Analysis of Data

A test for proportional differences between percentages was used in the statistical analysis reported in this research. Because the sample of practicum coordinators is much smaller proportionately than the other three groups, a conservative bias will tend to occur since differences between the practicum coordinators and other groups are less likely to be found.

FINDINGS

The first question was: "What role behaviors for practicum instructors in social work are identified as important by students, faculty members, practicum coordinators, agency administrators, and practicum instructors?" In order to answer this question, all role behaviors which were perceived by 80 percent or more of all four respondents as "Very Important" were considered "Important" in this study and are presented in Table 1. Role behavior items having to do with student progress and evaluation received the most "Very Important" responses. The Summary area of student skill development and orientation both had two items which were rated "Very Important" by 80 percent of all four groups. Teaching modalities

Table 1

Role Behavior Items Which Were Considered

"Very Important" by 80% or More of Respondent Groups

Summary Statement

    Role Behavior Item

The Practicum Instructor's Role is to:

Orient Student to Agency

    Define Student's Role in Agency

    Orient Student to Agency Procedures

Formal Teaching

    Teach Specific Treatment Modalities

Student Skill Development

    Points Out Student's Weaknesses

    Points Out Student's Strengths

Supervision and Case Selection

    Help Student with Awareness of Self

    Help Student Clarify Feelings

Evaluation of Student

    Evaluate the Student

    Confer with Student Regarding Progress

    Provide Supervisory Time for Student

also might be included in the area of skill development. Finally, all four groups indicated that the practicum instructor is responsible for helping students develop awareness and use of self, as well as definition about feelings experienced toward clients.

The second research question asked was whether conflict existed between the various respondent groups as to their determination of the importance of the practicum instructor's various role behaviors. The findings suggest that conflict does exist among the four respondent groups on the importance of some of the role behaviors. Of the 42 role behavior items on section one of the questionnaire, 12 items were found to have significant differences in the total percentage of "Very Important" responses between two groups or more. The role behaviors for which two or more respondent groups had conflicting views about their importance are grouped together in Table 2.

The third research question asked: "Are the groups in agreement with how the practicum instructor should spend practicum time?" The findings show that there was disagreement on more than half of the summary statements as to how much time should be spent in the various broad areas of activity. Of the summary statements in section two of the questionnaire, there was general agreement between the four groups on four of the statements as to whether or not the practicum instructors should spend less time, the same amount of time, or more time on the listed behaviors. The four summary statements in which relative agreement was found were: (1) Formal teaching; (2) Student skill development; (3) Supervision of client care and case selection; and (4) Socializing the student to the profession.

In six summary statements there was significant disagreement between two or more groups as to whether or not more or less time should be spent in a particular activity. Table 3 summarizes the responses in which significant disagreement was found.

For more than half of the summary items, significant disagreement occurred between one or more of the groups as to whether more or less time should be spent in a particular role behavior. On all but one summary statement, disagreement was focused on whether or not the practicum instructor should spend more time in a role behavior. All but one of the differences occurred between practicum instructors and students—in the area of professional development of the practi-

Table 2

Role Behavior Items on Which One or More Respondent Groups
Had Significant Disagreement on "Very Important" Responses

Role Behavior Items	Percentage of "Very Important" Responses By Respondent Group			
	Practicum Coordinator	Students	Practicum Instructor	Agency Executive
The Practicum Instructor's Role is to:				
1. Communicate with School	100%[a]	66%[b]	69%[b]	85%
2. Serve on Committees	67%[a]	31%[b]	36%[b]	42%[b]
3. Be Aware of Other Employee Feelings Toward the Student	69%[b]	48%[a]	71%[b]	75%[b]
4. Teach About Minority	100%	72%[a]	84%[b]	81%

5. Demonstrate Treatment Methods	85%	70%[a]	80%[b]	73%
6. Improve Listening Skills of Students	85%	73%[a]	87%[b]	91%
7. Help Student Develop a Work Schedule	93%[b]	41%[a]	71%[b]	76%[b]
8. Review Assignments of Students	93%	67%[a]	81%[b]	81%
9. Challenge Student Attitudes	100%	77%[a]	86%	90%[b]
10. Write Letters of Recommendation for Student	31%[b]	73%[a]	55%[b]	49%[b]
11. Set Up Opportunities for Students to Observe Other Professionals	58%	59%[b]	59%[b]	73%[a]
12. Interview the Student for Suitability for Agency	46%[a]	67%	80%[b]	79%

a, b The difference between two groups "a" and "b" significant; $p < .05$.

Table 3

Significant Differences in Percentage Responses

on Summary Statements by Respondent Groups

Summary Statements		Response Percentage			
		Practicum Coordinator	Students	Practicum Instructor	Agency Executive
1. Assessment of Suitability of Student for Placement	"More Time"	23%	19%	*38%	24%
2. Orienting the Student to Agency	"More Time"	31%	32%	*17%	28%
3. Advocating for the Student in Agency	"More Time"	8%	18%	* 6%	6%

4. Involvement in Personal Concerns of Student	"More Time"	54%	16%	*32%	39%
5. Professional Development of P. I.	"More Time"	54%	22%	*68%	36%
6. Evaluation of Student	"More Time"	36%**	26%	11%	19%

* The Difference between Student and Practicum Instructor was significant at $p < .001$

** The Difference between Practicum Coordinator and Practicum Instructor was significant at $p < .05$.

cum instructor, the agency executives responded "More Time" at a much lower rate than did the practicum instructors.

The final research question was: "Are there differences in the order in which the groups gave priority to the expected role behaviors?" The findings suggest that there are differences. But six role behaviors were chosen by all four respondent groups as first through ninth in priority in terms of the percentage of "Very Important" responses received. These findings are summarized in Table 4.

As is shown by Table 4, each group gave priority to items which had to do with their own orientation in the situation. For example, practicum coordinators tended to stress educational-professional items or areas which were related to the school (e.g., teaching minority issues, communication with the school, and incorporation of professional values). Students seemed to emphasize skills, evaluation, and socialization to the profession. Practicum instructors also emphasized skills and professionalization with the addition of student orientation and teaching methods or modalities. Finally, agency executives also stressed skill areas as well as supervision of the student and development of the student as a professional social worker.

Although there is disagreement over the importance of some of the role behaviors, Table 4 shows there is a good deal of agreement among students, practicum instructors, and agency executives as to the ten most important behaviors, with only one or two questions not appearing in the top ten ratings for all three of the groups. Practicum coordinators also agreed with many of the rankings of the other three groups — only three of the questions rated as the top nine by coordinators did not appear in the other three lists.

CONCLUSIONS

There are many ways to deal with conflicts in role behavior expectation, ranging from ignoring the conflicting views to using the conflicts to further the understanding and improvement of relationships among people. There are areas of both consistent agreement and considerable disagreement, illustrated by the responses of the four groups which participated in the study. Recognition of such disagreements must occur on the local level as well since such conflicts may be the basis for misunderstandings and feelings of alienation by practicum instructors toward Schools of Social Work. The potential of schools to build upon similarities and to learn from differences through discussions, meetings, liaison activities, and other forms of communication between the school faculty, agencies, and students is one obvious remedy, especially if conflicts are acknowledged, specified, and discussed. It is possible for compromise and resolution to be developed.

The general area of practicum, field work, internship, practice teaching, or whatever term a specific profession uses to describe the practical training of its students, has potential for further study. A review of the literature indicates that there is very little transfer of information from one profession to another in this area. Although there are, of course, differences in subject matter and approaches among professions, much could still be learned from the research and experience of other professions.

The practical application of a student's learning experience has been an area of concern for educators in all professions. Although many of the problems involved in providing field work experiences have been either lessened or alleviated, a considerable number still exist, not the least of which is that of conflicting role expectations. Further investigation of specific role behaviors in training is needed to provide students with consistent excellence in their educational experience and to produce professionals who will make viable contributions to our society.

Table 4

Items Ranked as the Ten Highest by Each Group According
to the Percentage of "Very Important" Responses

Ranking by				Item
Practicum Coordinator	Student	Practicum Instructor	Agency Executive	
1	3	4	4	Serves as a role-model of a social work professional
2	7	6	2	Helps the student incorporate professional values
3	1	1	3	Regularly confers with the student regarding the process
4				Challenges students' attitude not in harmony with social work values

232

5	4	8	7	Points out the students' weaknesses in skills and techniques
6	5			Teaches the student about minority issues
7	5	7	5	Provides weekly supervisory time for the student
8				Communicates with the school of social work
9	2	2	1	Points out the strengths of the student in the area of skills
	6	3	9	Helps student develop an awareness of self
	8			Evaluates the student's progress formally twice per semester
	9	5	6	Helps identify and clarify feelings about the client

Table 4 Continued

Ranking by			
Practicum Coordinator	Student Practicum Instructor	Agency Executive	Item
10			Introduces the student to agency employees
	9		Orients the student to policies and procedures of the agency
	10	10	Helps the student learn one or more methods of working with people
		8	Defines the student's role within the agency

*Only the top nine items were ranked for the practicum instructor since they all received 100% rating.

REFERENCES

Kadushin, A. (1976). *Supervision in social work*. New York: Columbia.

Merton, R. K. (1964). The role set: Problems in sociological theory. In L. A. Coser & B. Rosenberg (Eds.). *Sociological theory: A book of readings* (pp. 379-384). New York: MacMillan.

Ramsay, W. R. (1974). Role of the agency supervisor. *New directions for higher education, 2*, 45-54.

Statistics on social work education in the United States. (1977). New York: Council on Social Work Education.

Tropman, E. O. (1977). Agency constraints affecting links between practice and education. *Journal of Education for Social Work, 13*, 8-14.

Burnout in Social Work Field Instructors

Constance Hoenk Shapiro

ABSTRACT. Striving to respond to clients' pressing social needs while simultaneously providing solid educational experiences for students leaves many field instructors vulnerable to burnout. Rather than viewing burnout as an individual ailment, this article focuses on the organizational demands that produce role overload in the field instructor. Preventive responses emphasize the importance of replenishing energy, clarifying role expectations, and negotiating realistic responsibilities. Efforts which the university-based fieldwork liaison can take to reduce burnout in fieldwork instructors include careful assessment when recruiting field instructors, problem exploration, clarification, and advocacy with ongoing field instructors, and providing ample opportunities for field instructors to acquire new learning.

Burnout or "occupational battle fatigue" is a phenomenon experienced by persons in many professions, including social work. Burnout has been defined as a wearing out, exhaustion, or failure resulting from excessive demands made on energy, strength, or resources. For social workers who are in daily and often intense contact with troubled people, the risk of burnout is ever prevalent. Symptoms of burnout demonstrated by individuals include high resistance to going to work, postponing professional responsibilities, stereotyping clients, becoming emotionally detached from clients, and treating clients in a dehumanizing way. The impact of burnout in the work setting can result in poor staff morale, high absenteeism, reduced organizational effectiveness, delays in service delivery, and high staff turnover.

One population of social workers that has not been studied with respect to burnout is that of field instructors. This group, trying to

© 1989 by The Haworth Press, Inc. All rights reserved.

meet agency and university expectations, juggling needs of students and clients, and striving to integrate roles as educators and social workers, is potentially vulnerable to experiencing burnout. Especially in the 1980s when social programs are being cut and remaining programs must pick up the slack, field instructors may feel torn between bolstering clients above the survival level and providing a solid educational experience for social work students.

This article utilizes the theoretical perspectives of systems theory and role analysis to identify the social and organizational factors associated with burnout in field instructors of undergraduate social work students. Preliminary findings from a survey of 20 undergraduate fieldwork liaison representatives[1] will provide further data regarding the impact of burnout on field instructors.

Research on burnout that has focused on social workers includes studies of workers in child welfare services (Daley, 1979; Jayaratne et al., 1983, 1986; Davis-Sacks et al., 1985; Jayaratne and Chess, 1983; Harrison, 1980); child care (Freudenberger, 1977; Barrett and McKelvey, 1980); middle management (Haynes, 1979); mental health (Pines and Maslach, 1979); and social services (Pines and Kafry, 1978).

Much of the current literature on burnout among social workers emphasizes the psychological and emotional precipitating factors. In addition to identifying stressors that social workers encounter, most of these studies also propose self-help techniques that individual workers can use to reduce the extent of burnout they are experiencing on the job. While individual approaches to burnout can be helpful, they tend to overlook the organizational factors which contribute to the emotional depletion experienced by many social workers. Given the emphasis in social work on the person-in-situation, it seems logical to extend this perspective to the organizational context in which burnout occurs.

For the field instructor, the occupational environment encompasses both agency setting and educational institution. These environments have the potential to exhaust or to replenish the reserves of energy on which the social work field instructor needs to draw in order to meet expectations of persons in both settings. Systems theory provides a particularly useful framework for examining the organizational deficits that contribute to burnout among field instructors. Such a perspective highlights the interlocking and interactive components of the field instructor's experience in the work setting, assumes that change in one part of the system will generate change in other parts, and emphasizes the potential impact of new energy as a means of preventing or reducing burnout.

SYSTEMS THEORY

A systems approach assumes that the essential problems are the organizing relations that result from dynamic interaction and make the behavior of parts different when studied in isolation or within the whole (Janchill, Spring 1969). Realizing that the field instructor is a participant in two systems—agency and undergraduate social work program—is crucial to an appreciation of the field instructor's vulnerability to burnout. In order to avoid burnout, the field instructor needs a ready input of new energy to keep pace with the demands for energy output. Examples of sources of energy input for the field instructor are depicted in Figure 1. This figure also depicts the demands for energy output to which a field instructor must respond. Energy replenishment is crucial to preserving the negative entropy of the systems in which the field instructor is engaged. Negative entropy occurs when a system imports more energy from its environment that it spends. The system is less vulnerable to decomposition and stagnation as it draws on excess reserves of energy. Homeostasis, or the capacity of the system to remain in a state of dynamic balance, is facilitated by a ready supply of new energy available to be transformed into the outputs expected of the system.

The systems in which field instructors find themselves vary greatly. On the whole, most field instructors consider that their primary affiliation is with their agency of employment, and that affiliation with an undergraduate social work program is secondary to their agency responsibilities. Many social workers do not receive a reduced agency workload when they are field instructors but, instead, believe that the educational stimulation and professional challenge of supervising students offers rewards that are distinctly different from client feedback.

Current economic hardships and the social problems stemming from them have resulted in additional demands for agency output,

Figure 1

Energy Input and Output Experienced by the Field Instructor

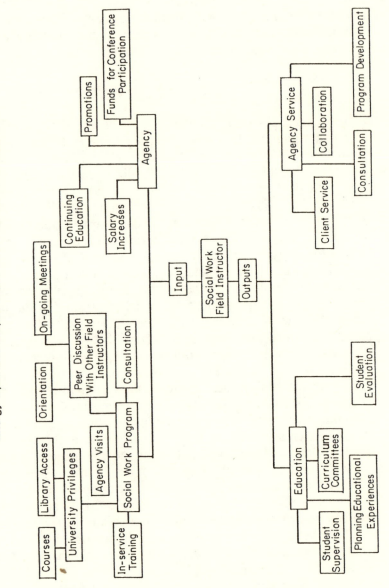

while agency inputs in the form of salary increases, continuing education, and promotions often are less available than before. Many social workers who also are field instructors find that their work with students is affected by the increased workloads and the serious client hardships accompanying this country's recent economic recession.

Inputs of energy to field instructors from university social work programs often are curtailed as well. This may take the form of reduced agency visits, less elaborate orientation or in-service activities, restricted university privileges, or limited collaborative endeavors between field instructors and social work faculty. Thus, with less energy input available and additional demands for energy output, field instructors may find themselves increasingly encountering entropy. The feeling of professional stagnation can leave the field instructor vulnerable to burnout unless some aspect of the system can be stimulated to generate new energy.

ROLE ANALYSIS

Having utilized systems theory for identifying situational components of the person-in-situation, it is now possible to look more closely at the *person* via role analysis.

According to Nathan Ackerman (1954), roles can be conceived of as "a bridge between psychological and social processes." Perlman (1962), in her definition of *role* for social caseworkers, viewed the construct as a person's organized pattern of modes of behaving, fashioned by the status of functions the person carries in relation to one or more other individuals. Such a behavior pattern is selected, shaped, and colored by several dynamic factors: (1) The person's needs and drives (i.e., what the person wants, consciously and unconsciously); (2) the person's ideas of the mutual obligations and expectations that have been invested (by custom, tradition, or convention) in the particular status and functions undertaken; and (3) the compatibility or conflict between the person's conceptions of obligations and expectations and those held by other person(s) with whom the person is in reciprocation. Merton (1957), in defining role set as the complement of a person's role relationships, offers a perspective from which one can examine the role strain experienced by a person carrying multiple professional roles.

Role overload is one way of conceptualizing the experience of some field instructors. Because of agency cutbacks, it is not unusual for a social worker to be asked to assume new and unfamiliar professional responsibilities. Preparation for assuming such new roles, and the anxiety accompanying their early performance, can be both time consuming and energy depleting.

In those situations where new responsibilities are not expected of the worker, other agency pressures can contribute to a sense of role overload: an increased caseload; clients with complex problems or especially pressing needs; the expectation that clients be terminated as soon as feasible in order to shorten the agency waiting list; and the inability of other agencies to provide the strength of collaborative service that has been experienced in better economic times. Any of these experiences can make social workers feel less energetic toward their responsibilities as field instructors.

THE SOCIAL WORK PROGRAM'S RESPONSE

With an awareness of expectations and energy demands faced by field instructors in the tight economy of the 1980s, what can social work programs do to prevent or reduce the impact of burnout? Interventions can be made at several levels when working with field instructors.

Recruitment

Research by Wasserman (1971) has shown that one of the greatest contributing factors to burnout is the discrepancy between initial expectations and the social demands of the role. Therefore, it is crucial for the fieldwork liaison to spend a substantial amount of time helping a potential field instructor to anticipate the energy investments and time commitments inherent in the role. Such expectations as weekly supervision, general availability, periodic written or oral student evaluations, attendance at field instructor meetings, and participation in curriculum committees are time consuming and must be balanced against other agency commitments which the social worker assumes. Demands on energy include such expectations as identifying appropriate and creative learning opportunities, familiarizing the student with agency and community resources, helping the student to make optimal use of supervision, and utilizing supervisory techniques that encourage the student to apply theory to the challenges of practice.

It is critical to discuss with potential field instructors their expectations of the fieldwork liaison and of the social work program generally. This is an ideal time to clarify issues such as handling unsatisfactory student performance, impact of the field evaluation on the student's grade, accessibility of the fieldwork liaison, use of campus facilities, and stipends or privileges accompanying field instructor status.

Inherent in recruitment is the notion of exploration and clarification. The end of this process should occur when mutual expectations have been discussed and mutual agreement has been reached. If either the fieldwork liaison or the potential field instructor has reservations about fulfilling the discussed expectations, it is important to be clear about such reservations. Assuming mutual interest in having the social worker as a field instructor, limitations of time or energy may be handled in a variety of ways: some tasks may be made optional (such as participation in curriculum committees); others may be shared with knowledgeable agency staff (such as orienting the student to the agency or community); and still others may be handled creatively rather than routinely (such as building in *sabbatical years* for fieldwork instructors who need respites rather than total relief from field instructor responsibilities). If clear understanding of handling limitations can be reached, then there is no reason not to welcome the field instructor into the role.

However, in some situations, even creative efforts cannot satisfy either the potential field instructor or the fieldwork liaison regarding the quality of a field placement. At such time, it is best to acknowledge with regret that a field placement with the social worker would probably be unfair to the social worker and to the student. The potential for burnout is initially too great if certain fieldwork deficits cannot be filled before the placement even begins.

Ongoing Field Placements

Indications of burnout by a field instructor may range from an overt acknowledgement of inability to carry out responsibilities, to more subtle indications of role overload such as cancelled supervisory sessions, failure to develop challenging learning experiences, superficial responses to students' requests for guidance, and inadequate input to student evaluations. In any case, when a fieldwork liaison suspects that a field instructor is experiencing burnout, a direct approach to the problem is warranted. Pines and Aronson (1981) suggest several major strategies for dealing with burnout: (1) becoming aware of the problem; (2) taking responsibility for doing something about it; (3) achieving some degree of cognitive clarity; and (4) developing new tools for coping and improving the range and quality of old tools. The fieldwork liaison's role in facilitating the field instructor's use of these strategies can help both of them come to terms with the extent to which existing pressures can be reduced or modified. Once certain modifications have been introduced, it may be possible for the field instructor to respond with more vitality to the needs of the social work student. The following strategies are ones that a fieldwork liaison may utilize to counteract the impact of burnout on field instructors.

Facilitating Awareness of the Problem: Awareness of the problem can be a logical outgrowth of a discussion between fieldwork liaison and field instructor as they explore concerns. The difficulties which precipitate such a discussion already have provided evidence of dysfunctional coping mechanisms. A first step toward more adequate coping is cognitive awareness that a problem exists. Rather than labeling the avoidance behaviors as the problem, the fieldwork liaison can be most supportive by identifying the problem as a function of the situation rather than as a function of the field instructor's personal inadequacy. Such awareness is likely to relieve the field instructor of feelings of guilt and, at the same time, stimulate efforts to take constructive action.

Encouraging the Field Instructor to Take Responsibility for Action: This is a difficult stage since, rather than demanding individual changes over which the field instructor may feel able to exert some control, the real need for change is at the organizational level.

If it is a situation problem, there is a temptation to feel that the organization should respond to it. However, given the propensity of the system toward maintaining homeostasis, it is unlikely to initiate changes simply because one person is experiencing difficulties. Therefore, the fieldwork liaison must assist and support the field instructor in identifying and taking specific actions that have the potential to result in real and concrete changes.

Achieving Cognitive Clarity: A person who experiences burnout usually cannot differentiate the things that can be changed from the things that cannot be changed. In fact, the persons most likely to experience burnout are those who assume that everything destructive and dehumanizing can be changed. Such people expend considerable energy confronting the stone walls of nonresponsive systems, ultimately feeling both hopeless and helpless in their inability to effect needed change. A fieldwork liaison often can help a field instructor to assess which aspects of the system are most likely to be responsive to efforts at change. Such cognitive clarity allows individuals to channel their energies where there will be the greatest likelihood of meaningful progress. Another aspect of cognitive clarity that warrants attention is the differentiation between the concrete demands of the work situation(s) and the demands field instructors place upon themselves, and that they sometimes erroneously attribute to their agency or to the social work program. Field instructors who hold higher expectations for themselves than anyone else holds for them actually have more control over their burnout than they may have acknowledged initially. Their choice becomes whether to modify the severity of their self-expectations in exchange for more flexibility in taking on desired tasks.

Developing Tools for Coping: In the process of reaching this step, some coping skills will have been developed already. However, ongoing learning involves the capacity to identify one's needs in specific situations. Perhaps the social work field instructor could benefit from learning some assertive skills which would enable him/her to be more straightforward in expressing needs; some group facilitation skills which could help in generating peer support for agency change; or some active listening skills to utilize in negotiating concerns with others in the work setting. Such communication skills can have several ameliorative effects: they can give the field instructor a sense of beginning confidence in responding in new ways to previously frustrating situations; they can reduce the sense of isolation that the burned out field instructor may be feeling as personal needs are communicated in the context of specific situations; and, perhaps most important, they can provide the field instructor with an increased sense of control in place of earlier feelings of helplessness.

If the fieldwork liaison offers to support the field instructor to combat burnout, it is likely that certain expectations of the social work program will be identified as sources of unwelcome stress. As these are identified, the fieldwork liaison must determine first whether the *perception* of the expectation is accurate and, if so, whether there is flexibility to modify such expectations in order to reduce the stress on the field instructor.

In addition to a reactive approach, the fieldwork liaison also should offer some proactive responses in an effort to replenish the diminishing energies of field instructors. Many field instructors would welcome opportunities to increase their knowledge and skill bases through programs sponsored by social work faculty. The opportunity to enroll in university courses; to invite faculty participation in agency in-service training; to request cooperative consultation; to have access to university library facilities; to be invited to preview films; to be informed of relevant guest speakers and colloquia on campus; or to meet periodically with other field instructors to address common needs all come under the general rubric of energy inputs. Such inputs can reduce the sense of isolation and uncertainty among field instructors at the same time that they refuel energy levels by providing new knowledge and skills.

PRELIMINARY FINDINGS

As part of an exploratory study on the impact of burnout on field instructors, questionnaires were mailed to fieldwork liaisons in a randomly selected sample of fifty accredited, undergraduate social work programs. Because only twenty questionnaires were completed and returned, the data can be viewed as providing information on selected experiences of the fieldwork liaison with burnout among their field instructors, rather than enabling broader generalizations.

With very few exceptions, fieldwork liaisons reported instances of burnout among field instructors in their programs. The percentages of field instructors who reported experience with burnout ranged from 0 to 50 percent, with a mean of 9 percent. Organizational problems were identified as overwhelmingly responsible for burnout in field instructors, with personal and health problems perceived as minor contributing factors. Such impressions lend credence to the notion that burnout occurs in a situational context, rather than stemming from personal inadequacies.

Further studies in this area could benefit from focusing on field instructors themselves. Social workers who resigned as field instructors because of burnout could provide valuable information about role shrinkage as a method of coping. Ongoing field instructors displaying behaviors associated with burnout could share their perspectives on desired changes. Long-term field instructors, who have balanced their educational and practitioner responsibilities successfully over the years, could be encouraged to share their strategies for maintaining a satisfying role performance. It is important to learn from persons who have avoided burnout as well as from those who are vulnerable to its impact.

SUMMARY

Viewing the person in the context of one's environment has long been a focus in social work. Now that the phenomenon of burnout can be identified as affecting some field instructors, it is especially crucial to appreciate the impact of the work environment on the adequacy with which social work field instructors balance their various professional roles. Role analysis and systems theory are both perspectives which conceptualize burnout as a product of role overload and organizational entropy. Thus, suggestions for reducing or preventing burnout must focus on the need for organizational responses that have the ultimate impact of replenishing diminished energy and clarifying realistic role expectations. Efforts which the fieldwork liaison can take to prevent or reduce burnout include careful assessment when recruiting field instructors; problem exploration; clarification; advocacy with ongoing field instructors; and a proactive approach to field work coordination which includes ample opportunities for field instructors to gain new professional knowledge, skills, and support from other field instructors.

NOTE

1. The term fieldwork liaison will be used when referring to the faculty person responsible for coordinating field placements.

REFERENCES

Ackerman, N. (1954). Systems concepts in casework theory and practice. *Social Casework*, *50*, 74-82.

Barrett, M. & McKelvey, J. (1980). Stresses and strains of the child care worker: Typologies for assessment. *Child Welfare*, *59*, 277-285.

Daley, M. (1979). Burnout: Smoldering problems in protective services. *Social Work*, *24*, 375-379.

Davis-Sacks, M.L., Jayaratne, S. & Wickess (1985). A comparison of the effects of social support on the incidence of burnout. *Social Work*, *3*, 240-244.

Freudenberger, H. (1977). Burnout: Occupational hazard of the child care worker. *Child Care Quarterly*, *6*, 90-99.

Harrison, D. W. (1980). Role strain and burnout in protective service workers. *Social Service Review*, *54*, 31-44.

Haynes, K. (1979). Job satisfaction of mid management social workers. *Administration in Social Work*, *3*, 207-217.

Janchill, M. P. (1969). Systems concepts in casework theory and practice. *Social Casework*, *50*, 74-82.

Jayaratne, S., Chess, W. & Kunkel, D. (1986). Burnout: Its impact on child welfare workers and their spouses. *Social Work*, *1*, 53-59.

Jayaratne, S., Tripodi, T. & Chess, W. (1983). Perceptions of emotional support, stress, and strain by male and female social workers. *Social Work Research and Abstracts*, *19*, 19-27.

Merton, R. (1957). *Social Theory and Social Structure*. Glencoe, IL: Free Press.

Perlman, H. (1962). Intake and some role considerations. In C. Kasius (Ed.). *Social Casework in the Fifties*. New York: Family Service Association of America.

Pines, A. & Aronson, E. (1981). *Burnout: From tedium to personal growth*. New York: Free Press.

Pines, A. & Kafry, D. (1978). Occupational tedium in the social services. *Social Work*, *6*, 499-507.

Pines, A. & Maslach, C. (1979). Characteristics of staff burnout in mental health settings. *Hospital and Community Psychiatry*, *29*, 233-237.

Wasserman, H. (1971). The professional social worker in a bureaucracy. *Social Work*, *1*, 89-95.

The MSW Supervisory Requirement in Field Instruction: Does it Make a Difference?

Bruce A. Thyer
Melvin Williams
J. P. Love
Karen M. Sowers-Hoag

ABSTRACT. In a retrospective review of social work students' evaluations of the quality of their field instruction supervision, it was found that MSW field instructors were not rated more highly than agency field instructors who did not possess an MSW degree. The sample consisted of 281 MSW students and 129 BSW students. The implications of these findings for social work education are discussed.

Field supervision is an integral part of the educational process for student social workers (Rotholz & Werk, 1984). Supervision serves as a primary method to teach practice knowledge and the effective and efficient delivery of service to clients (Munson, 1979). Field instruction supervisors are expected to teach student social workers how to understand and practice the art and science of professional social work and to serve as professional role models. Field instructors with a sound background in social work practice and the ability to create an environment which enhances the learning experiences of students provide a unique and essential component of professional social work education. The Council on Social Work Education's *Accreditation Standards and Procedures* clearly suggests that all social work interns receive supervision from a field instructor

---

The authors gratefully acknowledge the contributions of Reggie Blackstock in the design of the field instruction evaluation questionnaire.

© 1989 by The Haworth Press, Inc. All rights reserved.

who possesses a professional graduate degree from an accredited social work program (CSWE, 1984). The rationale for this standard is to ensure that the foundation, planning, teaching, and evaluation of the student's field instruction experience are focused on social work. Presumably, essential features of a professional *social work* education would be lost in the absence of MSW-supervised field instruction.

This guideline mandating supervision by an MSW has been implemented throughout virtually all accredited social work programs, and many writers in the area of social work field instruction support this mandate. For example, Wilson (1981) favorably observes that, "Most schools of social work require an MSW degree and two or more years of postmaster's experience (and/or ACSW certification) before one can become a field instructor" (p. 18).

Students and field instructors consistently report that the student/field instructor supervisory relationship is a pivotal factor in field instruction (Manis, 1979; Fortune et al., 1985). As Rosenblatt and Mayer (1975) have pointed out in their study of student views on field instruction, little has been achieved in the way of empirically-based research findings on the correlates of excellence in field instruction.

Research on field instruction has focused on the assessment of the intensity of the supervisory relationship (Rose, 1965; Kolevzon, 1979); instructor-student racial/ethnic combinations as they relate to quality of the field experience (Kolevzon, 1979; Ryan & Hendricks, 1987); supervisor-student gender combinations as they relate to the quality of field experiences (Thyer, Sowers-Hoag, & Love, 1986; Behling, Curtis, & Foster, 1982; Kolevzon, 1979); and the investigation of general factors that are associated with student satisfaction in the field (Raskin, 1982; Fortune et al., 1985).

Research on student satisfaction and the quality of field supervision has largely neglected the investigation of a critical variable in the field instruction process: Does it make a difference whether or not a field instructor possesses an MSW degree? One of the two previous studies which have examined this factor found that, of a sample of 170 undergraduate social work students, those students receiving supervision from a field instructor *without* an MSW were significantly more satisfied with the quality of their field experience compared to students receiving supervision from a field instructor *with* an MSW (Raskin, 1982). The second study of undergraduate BSW students (Smith & Baker, 1987) found that educational background (MSW, MA, BSW, BA) of the agency field supervisor did not significantly affect students' perceptions of the value of field instruction or of the quality of supervision received. Interestingly, however, agency field instructors with an MSW were perceived more favorably by field faculty than were their counterparts (MA, BA) from other disciplines in terms of the quality of their supervision and placement quality (Smith & Baker, this issue). Raskin (1982) suggests that, ". . . perhaps the field instructor's skills and abilities in technical, evaluation, and human relations areas are the key factors, rather than educational degree" (p. 52).

We conducted the following study, involving a large sample of both BSW and MSW students, to further investigate the relationship between the possession of an MSW by a field instructor and students' satisfaction with field instruction supervision.

METHOD

We retrospectively reviewed student evaluations of their field instruction experience, using a standardized questionnaire developed in the Office of Field Instruction at Florida State University, School of Social Work, and completed by all BSW and MSW students at the end of their concurrent or block placements. Part 1 provides demographic information about the student, field instructor, and agency. Part 2 consists of a standardized series of questions and rating scales on which the student evaluates the field instructor; Part 3 consists of questions and rating scales which the student uses to evaluate the agency as an internship training site. This evaluation questionnaire is identical to the one we employed in our previous study on the effect of student and field instructor gender combinations on field instruction quality (Thyer, Sowers-Hoag, & Love, 1986).

The field instructor evaluation component (Part 2) consists of 13 items which are rated by the student on a six point scale. Potential scores range from 13 to 78, and higher scores reflect a more favorable rating. These questions are depicted in Table 1.

Table 1

Questions and Rating Scale Used by Students to Evaluate

Their Field Instructor

In your opinion, how well did your Field Instructor:	Extremely Well			Not very Well	
1. Help you feel comfortable with your work?	6	5	4	3	2	1
2. Establish a comfortable working relationship with you?	6	5	4	3	2	1
3. Give you the amount of time you felt you needed?	6	5	4	3	2	1
4. Assist you in learning and developing work skills and techniques?	6	5	4	3	2	1

5. Help you integrate classroom learning with field practice?   6 5 4 3 2 1

6. Plan your orientation to the agency?   6 5 4 3 2 1

7. Offer constructive criticism?   6 5 4 3 2 1

8. Listen to your points of view?   6 5 4 3 2 1

9. Provide support when needed?   6 5 4 3 2 1

10. Provide regularly scheduled conference times?   6 5 4 3 2 1

11. Organize your learning experience?   6 5 4 3 2 1

12. Provide help in times of crisis?   6 5 4 3 2 1

13. Assist you in learning about and working with minority groups served by the agency?   6 5 4 3 2 1

The individual student's total score on these questions pertaining to their evaluation of the field instructor served as the dependent variable in the present study. Field instructor possession of an MSW or non-MSW graduate degree served as the independent variable. Evaluations were obtained from 410 students (281 MSW students, 129 BSW; 336 female students, 74 male students). Two hundred and ninety-nine of these students received daily supervision from a field instructor who possessed an MSW, while the remaining 111 students received agency supervision from a field instructor with a master's or doctorate in another human service profession. These latter students did have periodic conferences during their internship with faculty who have an MSW, in accordance with CSWE accreditation standards, but completed Part 2 of their field evaluation form with respect to their non-MSW agency supervisor.

Placements involved approximately 65 percent of students in public agencies, 3 percent in private not-for-profit agencies, and the rest in sectarian, for-profit, and other agencies. In terms of client age groups, 60 percent of the students worked primarily with children and youth, 10 percent worked with young adults, and the rest worked with middle-aged adults, the elderly, or with a mixture of age groups. Fields of practice included child welfare, mental health, developmental disabilities, aging, health, school social work, and substance abuse. While no systematic comparative data are available, we believe that the range of agencies and clientele in the present study is broadly representative of social work practice in general.

RESULTS

The 299 students interning with an MSW supervisor rated the quality of their field instruction received from this person at a mean score of 66.51 (s.d. = 10.11). The 111 students receiving agency supervision from a field instructor who did not have an MSW rated the quality of their supervision at a mean score of 65.75 (s.d. = 9.79). This difference failed to exceed chance expectations [$t(408) = .68$, $p < .05$], suggesting that there are no meaningful differences in the quality of field instruction supervision as perceived by the two groups.

DISCUSSION

Despite the importance in the social work literature of the educational background of the agency field supervisor, the results of our study indicate that educational background had little bearing on student satisfaction with field instruction supervision. There are several possible explanations for our results. First, it may be that the CSWE accreditation standard which mandates field supervision by an MSW is not educationally justifiable. This interpretation does not deny the possible usefulness of the MSW supervisory requirement for purposes of professional socialization, or other more subtle aspects of the educational process, but such a contention would require empirical support in its own right. A second possible interpretation of our results is that our instrument used to evaluate field instruction may be insensitive to the educational processes at work in the agency settings. This may be valid; however, until useful measures of the field instruction process become widely accepted in social work education, individual schools of social work will rely upon idiosyncratically developed methods of evaluation.

A major limitation of this study is that the measures of student perception are potentially distorted and subject to a "halo" effect. Halo effect is the tendency for a respondent to rate an object in the constant direction of a general impression of the object and thus poses a threat to the validity of the study. A second limitation of this study is the use of a sample drawn from only one school of social work. However, it should be noted that the only two previous empirical studies on this topic also involved samples of students from a single school and sampled far fewer subjects. These earlier studies yielded similar findings and are supportive of the results of this study.

In summary, the three published studies to date that have empirically examined the validity of requiring field instructors of social work students to possess an MSW have found that no meaningful differences exist in favor of MSW, as opposed to non-MSW, supervision. Although the profession may continue to mandate such a requirement for field instructors, it is important to realize that no empirical evidence exists to justify this requirement.

REFERENCES

Behling, J., Curtis, C., & Foster, S. A. (1982). Impact of sex-role combinations on student performance in field instruction. *Journal of Social Work Education*, *18*(2), 93-97.

Council on Social Work Education. (1984). *Accreditation standards and procedures for master's degree and baccalaureate degree programs in social work education*. New York: Author.

Fortune, A. E., Feathers, C., Rook, S. R., Scrimenti, R. M., Smollen, P., Stemerman, B., & Tucker, E. L. (1985). Student satisfaction with field placement. *Journal of Social Work Education*, *21*(3), 92-104.

Kolevzon, M. S. (1979). Evaluating the supervisory relationship in field placements. *Social Work*, *24*, 241-244.

Manis, F. (1979). *Openness in social work field instruction: Stance and form guidelines*. California: Kimberly Press.

Munson, C. E. (Ed.). (1979). *Social work supervision*. New York: Free Press.

Raskin, M. S. (1982). Factors associated with student satisfaction in undergraduate social work field placements. *Arete*, *7*(1), 44-54.

Rose, S. (1965). Students view their supervision: A scale analysis. *Social Work*, *10*, 90-96.

Rosenblatt, A., & Mayer, J. E. (1975). Objectionable supervisory styles: Student views. *Social Work*, *20*, 184-188.

Rotholz, T., & Werk, A. (1984). Student supervision: An educational process. In C. E. Munson (Ed.). *Supervising student internships in human services* (pp. 15-27). New York: The Haworth Press, Inc.

Ryan, A. S., & Hendricks, C. O. (1987, March). *The challenge of ethnic-sensitive field instruction*. Paper presented at the annual program meeting of the Council on Social Work Education, St. Louis, MO.

Smith, S. L., & Baker, D. R. (this issue). The relationship between educational background of field instructors and the quality of supervision. In M. S. Raskin (Ed.). *Empirical studies in field instruction* (257-270). New York: The Haworth Press, Inc.

Thyer, B. A., Sowers-Hoag, K. M., & Love, J. P. (1986). The influence of field instructor-student gender combinations on student perceptions of field instruction quality. *Arete*, *11*(2), 25-30.

Wilson, S. (1981). *Field instruction: Techniques for supervisors*. New York: Free Press.

The Relationship Between Educational Background of Field Instructors and the Quality of Supervision

Susan L. Smith
Donald R. Baker

ABSTRACT. This study explores the relationship between the field supervisor's educational background (MSW or master's in related field; BSW or bachelor's in related field) and the quality of supervision and field placement as perceived by social work faculty and students. Ratings of supervision by both field faculty and student interns were employed in a multivariate analysis. Results show that none of the student ratings were significantly related to the supervisor's educational background. Seven of nine items rated by faculty were significantly related to the supervisor's educational background.

The social work field has discussed for decades the desired qualifications of agency field instructors. The MSW degree traditionally has been recognized by social work educators and the Council on Social Work Education as the most desirable educational background for agency field instructors. During the 1960s, there was increased emphasis on using nontraditional settings for student placements. This led to greater use of field instructors from various educational backgrounds, often with bachelor's degree only and with other than a social work education. In these situations, a member of the school faculty theoretically would supplement the student's field supervision to assure that a social work focus was maintained.

© 1989 by The Haworth Press, Inc. All rights reserved.

If the field instructor does not have a social work degree, the current accreditation standards for undergraduate programs mandate that the field faculty member must be responsible for assuring the maintenance of a social work focus within the student's supervision and field experience (CSWE, 1981). This recent standard no longer distinguishes between the BSW and MSW degree for field instructors, even though many programs still require the MSW degree for their field instructors. The connection between specific educational credentials of the field instructor and quality of field supervision continues to be debated; to date, this issue has not been resolved.

This study will explore the overall quality of field learning experiences and supervision, and specific aspects of supervision provided by field instructors with an MSW, a master's degree in a related field, BSW, or bachelor's degree in a related field. It is important to recognize that possession of an MSW is not a sufficient qualification for a field instructor. The many prerequisites for performing as a competent field supervisor are enumerated and discussed by Wilson (1981). The analysis reported in the present study will provide some basis for ascertaining whether MSWs are perceived as superior field instructors by field faculty and student interns.

CONCEPTUAL MODEL

Differences in supervision by field instructors with various educational backgrounds will be explored in relation to the knowledge/values/skills paradigm of competency-based social work. Many aspects of knowledge are essential to effective field supervision: knowledge about normal and abnormal physical and psychosocial functioning, practice theories and methods, service delivery systems, and the process of supervision. One rationale for the utilization of MSW supervision in field instruction is that the social work knowledge base can be transferred to the student via an apprentice model of professional education. An implicit assumption is that MSWs have more knowledge and skills than BSWs and, because of extensive exposure to the person-environment blend of theory and practice knowledge, can better socialize and train field students in those aspects of practice that distinguish social work from other helping professions.

These assumptions, characteristic of the "uniformity myth" as it is termed in research on the helping process, are rather tenuous given the wide variance in knowledge content received by students in graduate social work training and the rapid evolution of practice knowledge and skill over the past twenty years. It is possible that there is considerable discontinuity in knowledge and skill base between the MSW schooled in the heavily psychoanalytic era of social work practice and the MSW trained in the more recent behavioral and task-centered practice models. Similarly, given the current emphasis on generalist models within undergraduate education, BSW practitioners can be assumed to possess a different skill and knowledge base than the MSW, but not necessarily less knowledge and skill. Moreover, a recent survey of supervision in social work practice suggests that many supervisors lack formal training in supervision and tend to model their supervisory behavior on the type of supervision they received in their field experiences (Munson, 1981).

An important consideration in relation to knowledge/value/skill competencies of undergraduate field instructors is that they be familiar with the role of BSWs in social work practice and the focus of the BSW curriculum. Wilson (1981) points out the negative consequences of placing BSW students in agencies that employ only MSWs — the student has no appropriate role models. When a field instructor believes that one degree is superior to another, it can be counterproductive to the learning experiences and quality of supervision received by the student.

Other helping professions such as counseling or psychology share many common values with social work. These include human dignity, self-determination, and confidentiality. However, it seems that social work has maintained the strongest commitment to social justice and advocacy for the poor and minority groups. While it is likely that social work field instructors would most closely personify social work values, the profession does not have a monopoly on social consciousness. Other professionals can facilitate the socialization and training of social work students. At a minimum, this is a question that merits research, and is the focus of the present study.

Skill level differences between the BSW and MSW practitioner, and between the social work trained and untrained supervisor, also may have implications for the level of supervision provided to field students. A study by Shulman (1981), in which the skill profile of MSWs and BSWs was compared across 27 specific interviewing skills, found that BSW practitioners were rated higher in 21 skills while the MSWs were rated higher in six skills. Due to the small sample sizes, the generalizability of these findings is limited.

Shulman (1982) did not find an expected relationship between supervisor education (MSW, BSW, and other degrees) and worker perceptions of supervisor skill, the working relationship, or the supervisor's helpfulness. In explaining this absence of relationship, Shulman indicated problems with the methodology employed and the difficulties in defining educational and training-related variables. A need for more study of the differential impact of supervisor education was indicated.

It would seem that the specific skills and methods of social work field instructors would be more complementary to the training of social work students than the skill orientation of non-social work trained persons. However, as with other dimensions of competency, this would vary with the individuals' educational background and professional development, as indicated by Shulman (1982).

METHOD

Field faculty and students completed an eight item questionnaire evaluating selected aspects of agency supervision and overall quality of the placement. They also completed a fifteen item questionnaire reflecting different learning experiences expected to be provided within the field placement at both mid-placement and final student evaluation periods. Supervision items are presented in Figure 1 and experiential items are presented in Figure 2. Data were analyzed to determine the extent to which ratings by field faculty and students of supervision and placement were associated with the level of the supervisor's educational background.

FIGURE 1. Learning Experience Items

Assessment of situations to determine existence of needs or problems.
Establish with the client system goals for intervention.
Continuing contacts with client system to accomplish goals.
Ability to work with a variety of clients and problem situations.
Working with persons in crisis situations.
Completion of interventive process from initial contact through termination.
Work with problem-solving or therapeutic groups.
Work with groups in an educational, recreational, or other role.
Collaborate with persons from other professions.
Make referrals to, or work with, other community agencies.
Become familiar with administrative functions within your agency.
Participate in public relations, funding, or other community-related activities.
Participate in research endeavors.
Participate in agency staffings and/or professional workshops.
Indepth work with complex problem situations.

FIGURE 2. Supervision Items

How would you evaluate the field instructor's knowledge of practice methods?

To what extent was the emphasis in choosing learning assignments based on your learning needs rather than the agency's manpower needs?

Was the field instructor accessible and available to give the student guidance on a daily basis?

Did the student have regular weekly conferences with the field instructor for supervision?

To what extent did the field instructor give the student feedback related to developing the student's interviewing/communication skills and assisting him/her in skill development (process supervision)?

How comfortable do you think the student was with the style of supervision he/she received from the field instructor?

Overall, how would you evaluate the quality of supervision which the student received from this field instructor?

Description of Faculty and Students

The field faculty utilized to rate supervisors and placements comprised all members of the social work program at Illinois State University (ISU) and possessed MSW degrees. The agency field instructors evaluated in the present study participated from one to three years as a field instructor and supervised from four to seven of the surveyed students over the study period. All students were senior social work majors within the ISU social work program.

Twenty-nine different agencies were employed in the present study. One to two students were placed at each agency within any given field sequence. With multiple placements over the three year study period, agency supervisors received ratings from two students on the average; a range of one to seven students provided ratings for each supervisor.

Analytical Procedures

All field faculty and students participating in the study were asked to rate various supervisor attributes and behaviors. They also were asked to rate the overall quality of the placement and supervision provided, and the extent to which various learning experiences were offered. All supervision-related items were rated on a five point scale with a range of 0 to 4, higher values representing more favorable impressions. In addition to the seven supervisory items, fifteen items reflecting different types of field experiences were rated on a five point scale ranging from "no experience" to "frequent experience." The ratings of these items were summed to yield a single variable reflecting the overall extent to which a variety of experiences were provided within the field placement setting. Analysis of the item-total correlations was performed with the reliability procedure of SPSSX (1983). A Cronbachs Alpha of .74 was obtained for the experience scale, indicating adequate internal consistency.

Ratings were completed by faculty and students at the end of the first semester of placement and at the end of the second semester of placement. Each first and second semester rating was averaged to yield one rating of each item for each field placement. To simplify data analysis, only complete sets of observations were employed for each rater. Cases were deleted if there were one or more missing values. Although there were 144 student placements during the study period, complete data were available for 68 placements only.

Supervision variables were analyzed in two separate groups—

field faculty and student interns. A multivariate analysis of variance was used to deal with the large number of supervision variables employed in the present study. Wilke's Lambda and its associated F test indicate whether there is an overall relationship between the supervisor's educational background and the supervision-related items. Since the supervisor's educational background was found to be statistically significant, a univariate analysis of variance was performed on each supervision variable or item. Post hoc comparisons between the four levels of supervisor education were assessed by the Scheffe test (Namboodiri, Carta & Blalock, 1978), a relatively conservative approach to the comparison of multiple means that indicates which levels of supervisor education are producing the effect.

Data Limitations

A primary limitation of this research is the small number of the field instructors at the bachelor's level who where included in the sample. This limits the generalizability of the data, particularly as it relates to field instructors with the BSW. Also, some of the differences may relate to certain limitations of the settings in which BSWs functioned as field instructors. In this study, these settings were primarily outreach and referral types of programs or nursing home placements—settings in which students were somewhat limited in their ability to assume a broad range of interventive roles. In most settings in which both BSWs and MSWs were employed, the MSWs served as field instructors. Also, the BSW field instructors evaluated in this study generally were much younger and less experienced than the MSW field instructors. These factors limit comparison of the two groups based on the present data and should be taken into consideration in examining the data presented in this study.

RESULTS

The results of the multivariate analysis of variance was significant for faculty ratings, F (df = 27, 129) = 3.24, $p < .001$, but not for the student intern ratings. The F-ratios from the univariate analysis of variance for faculty and student ratings are reported in Table 1. The

Table 1

F-Ratios Summarizing Analysis of Variance Results For Relationship

of Ratings of Supervisor and Placement with Supervisory

Educational Background

Items	Faculty	Students
Knowledge	11.55**	2.67
Assignments	13.81**	2.73
Available Daily	6.22**	2.44
Weekly Conference	12.08**	1.80
Process Supervision	6.41**	.36
Student Comfort	1.96	.41
Experiences Provided	2.31	.89
Quality of Supervision	13.93**	.73
Quality of Placement	5.35*	1.38

*   p < .01

** p < .001

supervisor's educational background was significantly related to seven of nine items rated by the faculty. The two items not significantly associated with supervisor educational background are the variety of field experiences provided to the student and the ratings of student comfort. None of the student ratings were significantly related to the supervisor's educational background.

As can be seen in Figure 3, the MSW supervisors performed better than other groups on all field faculty ratings of supervision. The general pattern of group differences indicates that MSW supervisors were generally viewed in a more positive light than supervisors from other educational levels. The Scheffe tests indicate an absence of statistical differences between the MSW- and MA-level supervisors. Most of the differences occurred in the comparison of

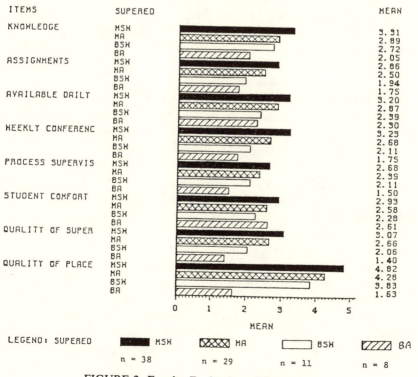

FIGURE 3. Faculty Evaluation of Supervision

the BA- level supervisor to the MSW- and MA-level supervisors. Significant differences for these categories of educational background occurred for ratings of the practice knowledge of supervisors, their emphasis on student needs in the selection of learning tasks, the use of weekly conferences, the use of process supervision, and the quality of both supervision and agency placement.

Fewer differences were found between the BSW-level supervisors and other educational groups. While there were no differences between the BSW- and MA-level supervisor on any of the items, there were differences between the BSW supervisors and the MSW supervisors on daily availability for conferences, their emphasis on student needs in the selection of learning tasks, and the overall quality of supervision provided.

Although MSW supervisors generally are perceived more favorably by field faculty, the absence of statistically significant differences between the MSW- and MA-level supervisor indicates a fairly high degree of substitutability between these two groups as undergraduate social work field supervisors. The general lack of difference between MA and BSW supervisors indicates that there also may be some substitutability for the BSW supervisor as well.

These findings suggest that individuals possessing a BA from a non-social work area might not be adequate choices as supervisors, at least from the perspective of the field faculty. The lack of significant differences between MSW and MA supervisors indicates that there may be some substitutability of individuals from either background as field supervisors. Although a few differences in rated items did occur between the BSW and MSW, the lack of significant differences in the ratings of BSW and MA supervisors suggests that individuals with a BSW also may be somewhat substitutable for the MSW supervisor.

Student ratings are reported in Figure 4. As indicated by the outcome of the multivariate analysis of variance for student intern ratings, there were few, if any, differences in ratings associated with the supervisor's educational background. While the pattern of mean differences indicated in Figure 4 parallels the results obtained for the field faculty ratings, the absence of any significant difference obviates a discussion of student ratings of supervision as a function of supervisor educational background.

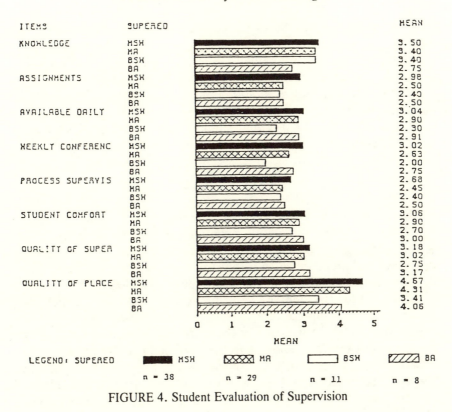

FIGURE 4. Student Evaluation of Supervision

It is possible that the failure to observe a significant relationship between supervisor educational background and student ratings, compared to the strong association obtained when field faculty ratings are considered, may reflect differences in the perspectives of faculty and students. Field faculty have more experience in making the judgements required of the study task. Students, on the other hand, are more in the position of naive participant observers whose judgements may be open to different sources of bias than the field faculty employed in this study. Another analysis of the data from the present study (Baker & Smith, 1986) suggests that student interns and field faculty differ in the importance they give to items involving supervisory judgement and placement quality, and differ in their perceptions of the extent of occurrence of various types of experience.

In future attempts to evaluate supervisor performance in social work, the potential sources of bias involved in using student versus faculty as raters or judges should be taken into account. The results of the present study and the analysis reported in Baker and Smith (1986) indicate that faculty and student ratings of supervision can provide distinct and different views of the supervisory process.

DISCUSSION

The results of this research have implications for the selection and training of field instructors for undergraduate social work education. Findings support selection of field instructors with the MSW whenever possible, but also allow for selective usage of field instructors with a BSW or a master's degree in a related field. The use of persons with BA degrees from other areas as field instructors, however, is not supported.

The findings help to identify the limitations of field instructors (from various educational backgrounds) which need to be strengthened through training offered by the university. For example, the lowest rated aspect of supervision in this study is the provision of process supervision. Systematic feedback concerning student skill acquisition is stressed in process forms of supervision. This feedback is important in both student and faculty judgements of supervision quality and perceptions of student comfort with the supervisor (Baker & Smith, 1986). Supervisors from every educational background can utilize process supervision to increase student skills and to reduce student uncertainty regarding the outcomes they are achieving within the field experience. Unfortunately, the present study suggests that supervisors do not utilize process supervision to a great extent regardless of their educational background.

Specific strategies for strengthening process supervision among all field instructors, and especially non-MSW field instructors, may have a positive impact on several other aspects of supervision. In order to give students feedback on skill development and to assist them in planning for the remediation of specific skill deficits, a field instructor would need to have regular conferences in which the "process" aspects of the student's work are discussed and plans for future improvement are made. Process supervision also necessitates that field instructors observe students in interactions or in other ways, such as tapings or process recordings, to directly observe and evaluate the student's actual level of functioning.

Some possible strategies to strengthen process supervision among field instructors include offering training workshops in interview training (using members of the methods faculty to provide for continuity of the learning experience) and specific evaluations of interviewing skills in the evaluation conferences. Training workshops on the teaching of interviewing skills in the field encourage field instructors to devote attention to "process" areas in student supervision. By becoming more familiar with the specific skills taught in the methods curriculum and the learning process involved in modeling, role-playing, and audio or videotape feedback, field instructors can begin to generalize some of this teaching process to the field setting. Discussion about general areas of difficulty for beginning field students and how to provide constructive feedback may help educate field instructors with the role and function of process supervision in social work. In addition, if specific evaluation of student's interviewing/interpersonal skills is solicited from the field instructor during the evaluation conference, more investment of the field instructor may be focused on these skills. When field instructors report that they really have no basis for evaluating such skills, planning for more development in this area in the future may be initiated.

An additional strategy to facilitate the use of process supervision might include formalizing existing mechanisms for the assessment of student interviewing performance throughout the methods/field curriculum. For example, tapings of student performance including written assessments of strengths and weaknesses could be required. The use of these assessments in early planning sessions with students and field instructors that focus on individual student learning needs would involve field instructors in ongoing evaluation of student performance and planning for future growth.

REFERENCES

Council on Social Work Education. (1984). *Handbook of accreditation standards and procedures*. New York: Author.

Judah, E. H. (1979). Values: The uncertain component in social work. *Journal of Education for Social Work, 15*(2), 79-86.

Kadushin, A. (1976). *Supervision in social work*. New York: Columbia University Press.

Manis, F. (1979). *Openness in social work field instruction: Stance and form guidelines*. California: Kimberly Press, Inc.

Munson, C. E. (1981). Style and structure in supervision. *Journal of Education for Social Work, 17*(1), 65-72.

Namboodiri, N., Carter, L., & Blalock, H. (1975). *Applied multivariate analysis and experimental design*. New York: McGraw-Hill.

Shulman, L. (1981). *Identifying, measuring, and teaching helping skills*. New York: Council on Social Work Education.

Shulman, L. (1982). *Skills of supervision and staff management*. Illinois: F. E. Peacock.

Siporin, M. (1982). The process of field instruction. In B. W. Sheafor & L. E. Jenkins (Eds.). *Quality field instruction in social work* (pp. 175-194). New York: Longman.

Smith, S. L., & Baker, D. R. (1986). *A comparison of field faculty and student intern perceptions of selected aspects of supervision*. Paper presented at the Annual Program Meeting of the Council on Social Work Education, Miami, FL.

SPSSX Users guide. New York: McGraw-Hill.

Wijnberg, M. H., & Schwartz M. C. (1977). Models of student supervision: The apprentice, growth, and role systems models. *Journal of Education for Social Work, 13*(3), 107-113.

Wilson, S. J. (1981). *Field instruction: Techniques for supervisors*. New York: Free Press.

A Comparison of Beliefs About Student Supervision Between Micro and Macro Practitioners

Julianne Wayne

ABSTRACT. This study explores the views held by supervisors of micro and macro practice on the supervisory process for social work students. Data were gathered through in-person interviews with 40 supervisors of each group drawn from 2 schools of social work. Findings indicate that many currently accepted beliefs about, and approaches toward, supervision are less applicable for education of macro than micro practitioners, although social work educators believe them to be appropriate for all social work education.

The generally accepted principles and practices of educationally-focused social work supervision have grown from an approach originally developed for the education and training of direct service practitioners. Early formulations of social work supervision borrowed heavily from the theoretical foundations and methods of the casework practice it sought to enhance. Throughout the decade, the conceptual framework for social work supervision broadened to incorporate knowledge from the social science arena, but the major components of supervision remain as they were in the early 1900s. The case record endures as the principle vehicle of supervision and the one-to-one conference as its principle structure (Kadushin, 1976).

Although the particular social work method taught to students will influence the content or curriculum of supervision, the supervisory process and related procedures are, for the most part, generic.

A national survey of directors of field instruction in Master's degree level social work programs in 1982 reveals that this group tends to judge field instructors of macro practice as inferior supervisors

© 1989 by The Haworth Press, Inc. All rights reserved.

271

when compared with field instructors of micro practice (Wayne, 1982). The directors believed that:

> supervisors of macro practice give their students less time than do supervisors of micro practice, offer less structured supervision than do supervisors of micro practice, offer apprenticeship training while supervisors of micro practice offer instructional supervision, and, unlike supervisors of micro practice, don't establish educational objectives for their students.

The literature on supervision documents that other social work educators share some of these perceptions (Murphy, 1957; Rothman & Jones, 1971). The judgment that macro supervisors are inferior to their micro counterparts, however, results from measuring all supervisors against a single standard, a standard that may be more applicable to education for micro than macro practice.

The purpose of this study is to learn whether or not these two groups of field instructors share similar attitudes towards and beliefs about student supervision. Since there is little literature by macro practitioners on the subject, their responses provide new and important information to consider.

HYPOTHESES

The following hypotheses are tested in this study.

1. Supervisors of micro practice have greater interest in supervision as a professional activity and greater motivation to gain expertise in its practice than do supervisors of macro practice.

A rationale for this hypothesis lies in the examination of each group's career ladder. Kadushin (1976) writes:

> . . . community organizers often work in agencies with limited staff or are members of a small specialized unit in large agencies. In either case, there is no elaborate hierarchal structure which includes supervisory personnel. (p. 15)

Because of their different work settings, Kadushin suggests that macro practitioners are less likely to aspire to supervisory positions than are micro supervisors.

2. Supervisors of micro practice more strongly adhere to generally accepted supervisory practices than do supervisors of macro practice (e.g., the regularly scheduled weekly conference and the use of the process recording).

This hypothesis is based on the recognition that the regularly scheduled one-to-one supervisory conference is consistent with the widely used format for clinical practice (i.e., the weekly interview between client and micro practitioner). The work schedule of macro practitioners, however, is less regular or predictable. A regular conference schedule may be out of "sync" with the work patterns of macro practitioners.

Process recordings are valued because they inform the supervisor about the student's practice and thus protect clients. They also provide material useful for educational assessment of the student.

Rothman and Jones (1971) note, however, that:

> Recording in community organization has remained indeterminate, problematic, and/or neglected through the years. Because of the variability of the work unit, it has been difficult to standardize the recording procedures. (p. 19)

Miller (1974) refers to the less intensive use of process recordings by community organizers. She explains it (along with the less intensive attention to supervision in general) in terms of the "relative visibility" of service and the power of the client, which reduce the need for process recordings as a protection for clients against poor practice (p. 1498).

Thus, it can be expected that the two groups of field instructors would use recordings differently.

3. Supervisors of macro practice believe in establishing a more egalitarian relationship with students and place greater value on peer learning for their students than do supervisors of micro practice.

The quality of relationships experienced by a social worker in his/her own education and practice is likely to be reflected in the relationship encouraged by the worker when instructing others.

Grosser (1976) points out that, in contrast to the micro practitioner, the macro practitioner does not necessarily deal with an impaired or "helpless" clientele. He advocates a point of view in which the client and nonclient are different but equal and share planning and other processes in order to bring about changes in the social systems of which they are both a part. This approach suggests an attitude of greater equality in professional relationships between macro practitioners and consumers of their service than may be expected between micro practitioners and their clients. It is possible that these attitudes may be transferred to the supervisor-student relationship.

Kadushin (1976) offers another perspective that could influence the supervisory relationship. He states:

> Of all the specialized subgroups in social work, community organizers feel most strongly about the need for worker autonomy. Supervision suggests a subservience that runs counter to this strong value. (p. 15)

Kadushin (1976) asserts that the community organizer's need for autonomy develops from the nature of his/her work, which he describes as usually diffuse and with amorphous goals — it "requires a great measure of the on-the-job autonomy in dealing with the demands of a non-standardized situation" (p. 15).

This need for professional autonomy could also encourage the macro practitioner to foster independence in his/her students through a relationship that is less controlling and more egalitarian, and where the supervisor is less central to the learning experience and greater use of peer learning is encouraged.

4. Supervisors of micro practice more highly rate "in touch with feelings" as a desirable trait in students than do supervisors of macro practice.

This hypothesis is based on the observation that the study of, and attention to, affect and emotion are more central to the theories that inform clinical practice than those that inform community organizing, administration, and social planning. It is believed that the degree of focus on this area would be transferred respectively to each group's supervisory practice.

METHODOLOGY

The researcher conducted face-to-face interviews with eighty (80) field instructors of Master's degree social work students. All of the field instructors had MSW degrees. The instructors were divided evenly between new (2 years or less) and experienced (3 years or more) supervisors of micro and of macro practice. The sample was drawn evenly from the Boston College (N = 40) and University of Connecticut Schools of Social Work (N = 40) since, aside from Boston University (where the researcher held the position of Director of Field Education), they are the only schools within commuting distance of the interviewer that offer majors in both micro and macro practice. Within the micro track, Boston College offers a casework major only (see Table 1), while the University of Connecticut offers a major in groupwork as well (see Table 2). Since the opportunity existed to explore differences within micro practice, the micro sample from the University of Connecticut was divided evenly to represent each of these methods (casework and groupwork). Each item is tested for differences between these micro sub-groups. Within the macro track, Boston College offers a combined community organization/social planning and a separate administration major. The University of Connecticut offers three separate majors in community organization, social planning, and administration. Representation was sought from all these groups of macro practice, although the macro pool was too small to permit an even distribution across these sub-groups.

Each hypothesis also is tested for differences between groups defined according to various combinations of the supervisor's own major method track as an MSW student and the method track for which he/she is supervising a student. Since only one supervisor crossed from a macro to a micro practice track, the sample is too small to test for the effect of movement in this direction. Three subjects had studied to be generalists (with no diversion into micro or macro tracks) and are, therefore, excluded from these tests. The groups compared in this aspect of the study are as follows:

Table 1

Sample From Boston College Graduate School of Social Work

Respondents	Micro Practice	Macro Practice		Total
	Casework	Comm. Org./ Soc. Plan.	Admin.	
New Supervisors	10	6	4	20
Experienced Supervisors	10	5	5	20
	20	11	9	40

Table 2

Sample From University of Connecticut School of Social Work

| Respondents | Micro Practice | | Macro Practice | | | |
	Casework	Group Work	Comm. Org.	Admin.	Soc. Plan.	Total
New Supervisors	5	5	3	5	2	20
Experienced Supervisors	5	5	2	5	3	20
	10	10	5	10	5	40

- Group A — Supervisors who majored in a micro method or track and are supervising a micro method, $N = 37$.
- Group B — Supervisors who majored in a micro track or method and are supervising for a macro method, $N = 20$.
- Group C — Supervisors who majored in a macro method or track and are supervising for a macro method, $N = 19$.

There is a heavy cross-over of micro majors to macro supervision, especially in administration (13 out of 19 administration students are supervised by supervisors who had majored in micro practice). Many micro practitioners are promoted to administrative positions in their agencies and are then asked to supervise administration and other macro method majors. It is very rare for a macro major to move into micro practice.

Each item is tested for differences between age groups and gender, and for differences between schools of social work. The sample includes 43 male (54 percent) and 37 female (46 percent) subjects. As a profession, social work is numerically dominated by female caseworkers. However, the pool of groupwork and macro supervisors for this study (both of which are minority groups within the profession) was comprised of more males than females. The predominance of males in this study is a result of using a stratified rather than a representative sample of the profession.

Micro subjects range in age from 27 to 61 years and macro subjects range from 28 to 56 years of age. Seventeen (42.5 percent) of the micro and 26 (65.0 percent) of the macro supervisors ranged from 35 to 50 years of age. More micro than macro supervisors continue supervising students throughout their careers. The heaviest concentration of macro supervisors falls into what are usually considered the middle years of a professional career (ages 35 through 50), while slightly more than half of the micro supervisors (57.5 percent) are in their younger and older years.

Selection Process

The directors of field education at each of the schools provided master lists of student placements. These contained the names of the students, their major method, first or second year status, agency placement, and the names of their field instructor and faculty advisor.

The field instructors selected to be interviewed were in agencies throughout New England that required the least distant travel. No more than two field instructors from a single agency were selected. This was to control for the possible effect of the professional culture within an agency on attitudes and approaches towards supervision.

Each field instructor was mailed a letter in which the researcher introduced herself, explained the research project, and indicated she would telephone to set up an appointment. The potential subjects were further screened over the telephone to be sure they held a Master of Social Work degree. Two people declined to participate, offering busy schedules as the reason. Those field instructors with degrees in related fields almost consistently expressed disappointment that they did not qualify for the study.

Analysis of Data

The open-ended questions of the interview schedule were tape-recorded with the respondents' permission. The research assistant and researcher coded responses independently. In instances of disagreement between the two, a third listener was called upon. The inter-rater reliability for the open-ended questions was greater than 95 percent.

The methods of statistical analyses utilized were t tests, one-way analyses of variance, and chi squares. For all analyses, the .05 level of significance was utilized in hypothesis testing.

FINDINGS

The Interest and Motivation Factor in the Supervisory Process

It is hypothesized that supervisors of micro practice feel greater interest in supervision as a professional activity and greater motivation to gain expertise in its practice than do supervisors of macro practice.

In order to test this hypothesis and its underlying assumptions, the interview schedule contained the following questions to be answered on a five point rating scale — (0) not at all, (1) somewhat, (2) moderately, (3) very, and (4) extremely:

1. How would you rate your motivation to gain skills in educational supervision as compared to other professional skills?
2. How helpful to your career advancement is the acquisition of educational supervisory skills as compared to other skills?
3. How likely are you to read literature on educational supervision as compared to other professional literature?
4. How motivated would you be to take a course on "Supervision"?
5. How motivated would you be to take a course on "Supervision for Macro Practice"?
6. How motivated would you be to take a course on "Supervision for Micro Practice"?

The results are summarized in Table 3.

Supervisors of micro practice express a significantly greater motivation to gain supervisory skill, likelihood of reading supervisory literature, and motivation to take a course on "Supervision" and "Supervision of Micro Practice" than macro supervisors. The latter become significantly more motivated to take a course in supervision when it is designated as being focused specifically on macro practice.

Supervisors of micro and macro practice do not differ significantly in their belief about the importance of supervision skills for their career advancement. Significant differences, however, do appear among all groups when they are analyzed according to whether they cross practice tracks. The mean rating of the importance of supervision skills for career advancement was 2.30 for those who stayed in micro practice (Group A), 1.40 for those who crossed into macro from micro practice (Group B), and 2.95 for those who stayed in macro practice (Group C).

Those who majored and are supervising in macro practice believe most strongly that supervision skills will be helpful to their career advancement. Those who majored in micro practice and are supervising in macro practice believe this least strongly.

Supervisors were asked, "Does your agency encourage, discourage, or remain neutral about your supervising a student?" Significantly more supervisors of micro (32 or 80 percent) than macro practice (20 or 50 percent) reported their agency as encouraging their supervisory activity ($x^2 = 7.91$, p = .0049). Seven (17 percent) of micro and 16 (40 percent) of macro supervisors reported their agencies as remaining neutral. Without agency encouragement for their work with students, supervisors report little or no relief from other responsibilities. For these practitioners, supervising becomes a volunteer "overload" activity. Supervisors were asked, "Which of your present assignments do you find most interesting?" The results are described in Table 4.

Significantly greater numbers of micro (32 percent) than macro (5 percent) supervisors find supervising a student to be the most interesting of their assignments ($x^2 = 9.93$, p = .0016). Eighty percent of macro supervisors find their macro practice to be the most interesting of their assignments, while 42.5 percent of the micro supervisors find their micro practice to be the most interesting of their assignments. The difference between the two groups becomes even more striking when the "supervising students" and "other teaching" categories are combined. In that case, 19 out of 40 (50 percent) micro supervisors and 3 out of 40 (8 percent) macro supervisors express greatest interest in a teaching-related activity.

Although the data support the hypotheses that supervisors of micro practice feel greater interest in supervision as a professional activity and a greater motivation to gain expertise in its practice, over two-thirds of each group (31 micro supervisors and 27 macro supervisors) indicate feeling positively about supervising students. Approximately 88 percent of both groups (35 micro supervisors and 34 macro supervisors) plan to continue supervising students in the future.

The Supervisory Process

It is hypothesized that supervisors of micro practice more strongly adhere to generally accepted supervisory practices than do supervisors of macro practice (e.g., the regularly scheduled weekly conference and the use of process recording).

When asked about scheduling a regular weekly time slot for a supervisory conference and regularly requiring written material from students for teaching purposes, the responses were as shown in Table 5.

Table 3

Comparative Ratings of Motivation Factor

In Supervisory Process

	Micro Supervisor (N=40)		Macro Supervisor (N=40)		2 Tail Prob.
	Mean	SD	Mean	SD	
Motivation to gain supervisory skills	2.73	.75	2.18	.93	.005
Helpfulness of supervisory skills to career advancement	2.33	.997	2.18	1.357	.575

Likelihood of reading supervisory literature	2.00	1.01	1.20	1.11	.001
Motivation to take a course in Supervision	2.38	1.17	1.35	1.21	.000
Motivation to take a course in micro supervision	2.38	1.314	.58	.903	.000
Motivation to take a course in macro supervision	1.40	1.516	1.90	1.37	.126

Table 4

Most Interesting Assignments

Responses	Micro Supervisors	Macro Supervisors	Total
Supervising Students	13	2	15
Other Teaching/ Consulting or Supervisory Assignments	6	1	7
Micro Practice	17	5	22
Macro Practice	3	32	35
Cannot Choose	1	0	1
	40	40	80

Table 5

Conference Scheduling and Use of Materials

Responses	Micro Supervisors (N=40) Responding Yes	Macro Supervisors (N=40) Responding Yes	X^2	Prob.
Regularly Schedule Supervisory Conferences	39	32	4.51	.033
Regularly Require Written Material for Teaching Purposes	38	16	27.58	.001

Significantly greater numbers of micro than macro supervisors schedule regular weekly conferences with students and regularly require written material from them for teaching purposes. The hypotheses are supported by the data.

Although they structure their time with students differently than each other, there is no significant difference between groups in the amount of supervisory time they offer. Micro supervisors report spending a mean of 100.13 minutes each week with students, and macro supervisors report spending a mean of 99.23 minutes each week with students.

When asked about the purpose of the students' written material (whether regularly required or not), three macro supervisors indicated they did not use written material at all.

The data reveal that when students' written material is used for teaching purposes, supervisors of micro and macro practice differ significantly in identifying the purpose(s) for the material (see Table 6). Micro supervisors tend to use written materials (usually process recordings) to be aware of what their student is doing, to encourage the student to conceptualize practice, to create a framework for conferences, and to help assess the student's progress. Macro supervisors tend to use written materials to help students plan ahead (rather than analyze past practice) and as actual products (e.g., budgets, grant proposals, and media releases).

The Supervisory Relationship

It is hypothesized that supervisors of macro practice believe in establishing a more egalitarian relationship with students than do supervisors of micro practice, and that supervisors of macro practice place greater value on peer learning for their students than do supervisors of micro practice.

To test these hypotheses, respondents were asked their reaction to the notion of a student and supervisor entering into a friendship outside the supervisory relationship. A response of either "no threat to" or "could enhance the supervisory relationship" is to be interpreted as more supportive of an egalitarian relationship with students than a negative response to the notion of friendship.

The results reveal that micro and macro supervisors tend to hold different views on this matter. Nine supervisors of micro practice (25 percent) and 17 supervisors of macro practice (45 percent) believe a friendship with a student would present no problem and could possibly enhance the supervisory relationship (x^2 = 3.52, p = .0608).

There are significant differences, however, between groups according to their own major method (x^2 = 9.43, p = .0089). Fourteen out of 57 supervisors (25 percent) who majored in micro practice, as compared to 12 out of 19 supervisors (63 percent) of those who majored in macro practice, believe a student-supervisor friendship would either pose no threat to, or could possibly enhance, the supervisory relationship.

Another question asks, "When deciding upon assignments for your student, and in case of disagreement between you and your student, who should have the final decision-making power?" The response of "student" is interpreted as more supportive of an egalitarian relationship with students than the response of "supervisor." (This question was added after the interview process had begun. The original question was, "How do you decide upon student assignments?" This question was too unstructured to elicit helpful data to test this hypothesis. Hence, there are 18 missing responses to this question.)

Significantly greater numbers of macro (88 percent) than micro (19 percent) supervisors believe the supervisor should have the final say about student assignments (x^2 = 4.93, p = .0264). Although macro practitioners feel more positively about a friendship with students outside of the supervisory relationship, as a group they are more ready than the micro supervisors to exert their authority within the supervisory relationship.

Another question asks respondents to rate the value of peers as an educational resource for most students, using a five point scale ranging from no value (0) to extremely valuable (4).

Both groups consider "peers" to be a very valuable resource for professional education. Micro supervisors responded with a mean score of 3.03 and macro supervisors with a mean score of 2.87 (p = .407). Supervisors who majored in micro practice rate peers as a resource for education significantly higher (mean = 3.09) than do supervisors who majored in macro practice (mean = 2.56), re-

Table 6

Differential Use of Students' Written Material

Responses	Micro Supervisors (N=40) Responding Yes	Macro Supervisors (N=37) Responding Yes	X^2	Prob
Informs Me of What Student is Doing	16	4	8.15	.0043
Encourages Student To Conceptualize From Practice	20	8	0.69	.0097

Makes Student Plan Ahead	4	14	8.32	.0039
Creates Framework for Conferences	12	2	7.82	.0052
Actual Product Student Needs, e.g., Budget, Grant Proposal	2	24	30.80	.0000
Evaluation Tool To Help Assess Student's Progress	18	3	13.19	.0003

gardless of the method for which they are supervising. There is no significant difference between supervisors who majored in micro practice and who are supervising for micro or macro practice. The data do not support the hypothesis that supervisors of macro practice value peers as an educational resource more highly than do supervisors of micro practice. In fact, it tends to support the opposite conclusion.

The Value of Learner Characteristics

In order to learn more about each group's beliefs about the learning process, respondents were asked to rate each of several traits or characteristics according to their importance in the make-up of a good student. A five point scale from (0) not important to (4) extremely important was used to rate the following student characteristics:

- a. intelligent
- b. can take direction
- c. stimulating to supervise
- d. creative
- e. independent
- f. sense of humor
- g. prepared for conferences
- h. in touch with feelings
- i. curious
- j. thinks critically
- k. can take criticism

It is hypothesized that supervisors of micro practice and related client orientation would rate "in touch with feelings" more highly than would supervisors of macro practice.

Supervisors of micro practice rate "in touch with feelings" as a desirable trait of students significantly higher (mean = 3.65) than do supervisors of macro practice (mean = 3.03, p = .001) (see Table 7). However, both groups rate it between very and extremely important. The difference between these groups widens when analyzed according to those who crossed practice tracks and those who didn't. The mean of those who stayed in micro practice is 3.65, the

Table 7

Selection of the Single Most Important Student Trait

Responses	Micro Supervisors (N=40) Responding Yes	Macro Supervisors (N=40) Responding Yes	X^2	Prob.
In Touch With Feelings	14	5	5.59	.0181
Thinks Critically	5	12	3.66	.0557

mean of those who crossed practice tracks from micro to macro is 3.20, and the mean of those who stayed in macro practice is 2.79. The one-way ANOVA and analyses of differences between each set of sub-groups reveal that, although each sub-group differs significantly from the other, the greatest differences lie between those who majored in micro practice and those who majored in macro practice.

After rating each of the items on this question, subjects are asked to select which of the traits they believe is the single most important. Micro supervisors selected "in touch with feelings" more than any response, while macro supervisors selected "thinks critically."

Significantly greater numbers of micro than macro supervisors select "in touch with feelings" as the most important trait in the make-up of a good student. More macro than micro supervisors appear to select "thinks critically" as the single most important trait in the make-up of a good student. When asked to rate the importance of "thinks critically" on a scale of zero to four, however, there is no significant difference between micro and macro supervisors. Both groups rate it highly (mean score of 3.4). The difference between the groups appears when subjects are asked to select the single most important trait.

SUMMARY OF FINDINGS

1. Supervisors of micro practice have greater interest in supervision as a professional activity and greater motivation to gain expertise in its practice than do supervisors of macro practice. The original hypothesis is supported by the data.

2. Supervisors of micro practice adhere more strongly to generally accepted supervisory practices than do supervisors of macro practice (e.g., the regularly scheduled weekly conference and the use of the process recording). The original hypothesis is supported by the data.

3. Supervisors of micro practice believe in establishing a more egalitarian relationship with students than do supervisors of macro practice. Supervisors who majored in micro practice place greater value on peer learning for their students than do supervisors who majored in macro practice. The findings do not support the original hypothesis.

4. Supervisors of micro practice rate "in touch with feelings" more highly as a desirable trait in students than do supervisors of macro practice.

The original hypothesis is supported by the data.

DISCUSSION

The Motivation and Interest Factor in Student Supervision

Although the results reveal that the vast majority of all supervisors react positively to supervising a student and plan to continue doing so, supervisors of micro practice express a greater motivation towards, and interest in, this activity than do supervisors of macro practice. They are more likely to read supervision literature, take a supervision course, and rate student supervision as the most interesting of all their assignments.

Within the sub-groups of macro supervisors, those who first studied and engaged in micro practice rate the helpfulness of supervisory skills to career advancement significantly lower than those who majored and also are supervising in macro practice. Interestingly, the move from micro to macro practice usually reflects a promotion to a supervisory position within an agency. It appears that this group either believes career advancement did not result from supervisory skills or that such skills will affect careers only minimally, if at all, in the future.

The goals and interests of the social work therapist resemble the goals and interests of the educator. By fostering psychosocial and intellectual development, both groups of professionals seek to help individuals function to the best of their ability within their social environment. Half of the micro practitioners find their teaching-related responsibilities to be of greatest interest to them.

Education for social work is dependent on this interest in teaching and the voluntarism of agency-employed professionals working as student supervisors. Until now, social work educators have operated as if this strong interest in student supervision runs evenly through the entire profession. The data in this study indicate otherwise. In contrast to 50 percent of micro supervisors, only 8 percent of macro supervisors choose a teaching-related responsibility as their most interesting assignment.

When planning for field education, it is important to consider that only 50 percent of macro supervisors compared to 80 percent of micro supervisors perceive their agencies as encouraging their supervision of students. The remaining supervisors, for the most part, perceive their agencies as neutral on the subject. This could mean that large numbers of macro supervisors get little relief from other assignments when taking on a student, or they get few rewards for their efforts within their agencies. Macro supervisors may need more support from schools of social work than their micro counterparts.

This discussion raises new questions. Are supervisors' perceptions about agency support accurate? Do agencies have a double standard for supervision for micro and macro practice? In any case, it can be concluded that student supervision is more central to the micro professional culture than to the macro.

Both groups of supervisors perceive supervision courses to be focused on supervision for micro practice. Micro supervisors express equal motivation to take a course on general supervision and supervision for micro practice, while macro supervisors express a significantly greater motivation to take a course on supervision for macro practice than on general supervision, although this interest is still below that of micro supervisors. As noted earlier, supervision theories and practices developed from the casework method. The lesser interest in supervision by macro practitioners may be reinforced by the limited attention given them by experts in supervision. Macro supervisors have yet to do their own writing on the subject.

The Supervisory Process

As predicted, supervisors of micro and macro practice supervise students differently.

Both groups spend approximately one hour and forty minutes in supervision with students each week. This amount of time is consistent with the standard set by most schools of social work. Significantly greater numbers of micro supervisors do so through a regularly scheduled weekly conference. This may result from the very nature of macro practice which provides other contexts for learning-teaching transactions. Many of these could be formalized as supplements to, or even substitutes for, the supervisory conference. For example, while micro supervisors need to resort to videotape and one-way mirrors to observe their students' practice, macro supervisors and students frequently have opportunities to observe each other in practice first-hand. Specialized teaching techniques could be identified and developed for these and other situations which would reduce the reliance on the traditional and conventional weekly conference.

The other finding of note is that significantly greater numbers of micro supervisors regularly require students' written material for educational purposes. The use of the material by the two groups of supervisors, whether regularly required or not, is for very different purposes. Micro supervisors use material to provide a framework for conferences, to inform them of what their students are doing, to help students conceptualize from practice, and to help assess their progress. Macro supervisors use written material to help students plan future strategies and also because it frequently is a needed product (e.g., a budget, a proposal, or a media release).

Micro supervisors use process recordings to teach and evaluate the student through the analysis of the processes in which they have engaged with the client. Macro supervisors use written material to teach students how to plan for a clearly defined result. An integrated model of supervision would borrow from both perspectives and enrich each approach. Goal formulation for each client encounter is often given short shrift in clinical practice (a behaviorist approach excepted) as is a systematic retrospective analysis of student behaviors in macro practice. This process versus product (or results) orientation may be inhibiting each group from developing more effective teaching processes and tools.

The Supervisory Relationship

Contrary to widespread beliefs, the results of this study challenge the impression of many that macro supervisors exercise a more egalitarian approach to supervision than do micro supervisors. Studied out of context, some data could be interpreted as supportive of that hypothesis. For example, in contrast to supervisors of micro practice, supervisors of macro practice tend to believe a student-supervisor friendship outside of the supervisory relationship would either not hurt or could enhance the supervisory relationship. Significantly greater numbers of those who majored and are supervising in macro practice than those who majored in micro practice believe this to be true.

The results also reveal, however, that although the majority of both groups believe the supervisor rather than the student should have the last word in determining student assignments, significantly greater numbers of macro than micro supervisors express this view. Additionally, those who majored and are supervising in macro practice also rate the value of peers as an educational resource significantly lower than do those who majored in micro practice.

On the surface, the indication of greater acceptance of friendship with students by macro supervisors appears to suggest an egalitarian approach to supervision. It may instead only reflect an informal rather than a democratic, professional sub-culture. In spite of collegial appearances, macro supervisors are more ready than micro to exert their authority over students in the selection of student assignments, an important aspect of the total agency experience.

The Value of Learner Characteristics

It has been hypothesized that macro supervisors assign greater importance to the cognitive rather than affective aspects of the educational experience. Supervisors of micro practice do indeed rate "in touch with feelings" significantly higher than do supervisors of macro practice as a desirable trait in students; micro supervisors select it as the single most important trait in the make up of a good student. Supervisors of macro practice tend to select "thinks critically" as the single most important trait; both groups, however, rate it equally when it does not compete with other traits as the most important.

The data indicate that micro supervisors consider the student's ability to deal with feelings as the priority, although they believe that both the cognitive and affective aspects of the social work education process are important. This is consistent with widespread clinical practice that seeks to help clients recognize the relationships between their emotions and their behaviors. In order to be effective, the student social worker is expected to have this ability.

In contrast, there is a tendency for greater numbers of macro than micro supervisors to select "critical thinking" as the most important student trait and to rate "in touch with feelings" significantly lower than do micro supervisors, even when this choice does not compete with other traits. This is consistent with the macro supervisor's emphasis in the supervisory process on developing intervention strategies rather than analyzing the nuances and subtleties of interpersonal relations and intrapsychic dynamics.

CONCLUSION

The findings of this study indicate that many currently accepted beliefs about, and approaches toward, student supervision are less applicable for the education of macro than micro practitioners, although most social work educators believe them to be appropriate for all social work education. It is admittedly difficult to break with established tradition. Yet, a re-examination of old assumptions can stimulate thoughts about new possibilities for the macro practitioner, a minority sub-group within the social work profession.

REFERENCES

Grosser, C.F. (1976). *New directions in community organization: From enabling to advocacy*. New York: Praeger.

Kadushin, A. (1976). *Supervision in social work*. New York: Columbia University Press.

Miller, I. (1974). Supervision in social work. *Encyclopedia of social work*, (pp. 1494-1501), *16*, Washington, D.C.: N.A.S.W.

Murphy, C.G. (1957). Community organization for social welfare. *Social work year book*. New York: National Association of Social Workers.

Rothman, J., & Jones, W.C. (1971). *A new look at field instruction: Education for application of practice skills in community organizing and social planning*. New York: Association Press & Council on Social Work Education.

Wayne, J. (1982). *A survey of field instruction: Department directors' views of supervisors of micro and macro practice*. Unpublished paper, Boston University School of Social Work.

PART IV:
STUDENTS: STRESS, SATISFACTION, AND SUCCESS IN FIELD PLACEMENT

Introduction

The papers in Part IV provide information about stress, satisfaction, and performance of students in field placement. A survey instrument was developed by the majority of authors and utilized as the primary research tool. Linda I. May and Allie C. Kilpatrick's paper, *"Stress of Self-Awareness in Clinical Practice: Are Students Prepared?"*, asked directors of field instruction to provide strategies that are used in their schools to prepare MSW students for stress that results from self-awareness in field placement. The field instructor was identified as the most important person to help the student with stress related to self-awareness; the educational advisor was next in importance. A large majority of the respondents felt that preparing students for stress was the school's responsibility, but little was being done in a formal way to help students. This study identifies the various mechanisms schools have established to assist students with stress. Further research is needed which will assess how these methods are implemented and which, if any, lead to a reduction of stress.

In an earlier section, Wayne, Skolnik, and Raskin compared the perceptions of Canadian and U.S. directors of field instruction. There seemed to be commonality of concerns with regard to field

© 1989 by The Haworth Press, Inc. All rights reserved.   *299*

instruction and its place in the social work curriculum. In this section, Nai-ming Tsang provides insights into "Factors Associated with Fieldwork Performance in a Social Work Course in Hong Kong." He cautions that cross-cultural comparisons should not be made until additional studies that utilize a similar research design are carried out. It will become evident from the studies in Part IV that similar factors and questions are addressed by researchers in the U.S. who often arrive at similar results.

The factors that were studied by Tsang explained 24.4 percent of the variation in students' fieldwork performance (as measured by grades). These factors include: academic grades; sex of the student; social work related experience; and highest academic qualification prior to entering the school. The study predicts the type of student in Hong Kong that will be successful in both fieldwork and in overall performance: a female who passed the School Certificate Examination (minimum qualifications), who has three years of social work related experience and two years of volunteer work experience, and who is not being sent to school by a sponsoring agency.

The next two studies examine the factors associated with student satisfaction in field placement. Raskin surveys undergraduate students in ten accredited undergraduate programs in Virginia ("Factors Associated with Student Satisfaction in Undergraduate Social Work Field Placements"). Fortune et al. surveyed students in one graduate school in Virginia ("Student Satisfaction with Field Placement"). Fortune et al. do not replicate Raskin's earlier study, but many of the same variables are considered and similar statistical tests are carried out.

The findings from both studies show that: (1) Student Characteristics (e.g., age, marital status, sex, previous volunteer/paid experience) are not associated with student satisfaction in field placement; (2) Relevant (New) Learning is the major factor that contributes to student satisfaction; (3) Variety of Tasks is associated with satisfaction; and (4) Agency Climate does not have a significant impact on satisfaction.

Fortune et al. found a stronger association between supervisory variables and satisfaction than was found in the Raskin study. Only 13.7 percent of the variance of Overall Student Satisfaction was explained by supervisory variables in Raskin's study. The supervisor may have some impact on student satisfaction, but this is not the sole or even major factor related to student satisfaction. When this result is combined with findings described earlier by Thyer et al. (Part III) and Smith and Baker (Part III), it becomes clear that the role, academic degree, and influence of the field instructor on student learning require additional research attention. Perhaps the structure of social work supervision, the placement process, CSWE accreditation standards, and existing models of field instruction have placed too much emphasis on the field instructor.

The challenge for future researchers is to utilize the results from beginning empirical studies as a springboard for posing more sophisticated questions and using more advanced analytical techniques. An additional challenge will require educational institutions, agencies, students, and field directors to be risk-takers and to use the knowledge that is becoming available about field instruction. This may necessitate leadership on the part of the Council on Social Work Education to encourage innovations, sponsor research, and promote field instruction as an equal partner in the social work curriculum. It also may require a willingness to give up some of the misconceptions and myths that have allowed us to continue without much creative change in the last century. A new Century of Progress will hopefully see first-class status for curriculum, personnel, and research in field instruction.

Stress of Self-Awareness in Clinical Practice: Are Students Prepared?

Linda I. May
Allie C. Kilpatrick

ABSTRACT. What is the position of schools of social work on the preparation of MSW students for the stress that may accompany self-awareness in clinical practice? Directors of Field Instruction at eighty-nine MSW programs throughout the United States were surveyed on this and related questions. The results are presented in this article.

A caseworker must have self-awareness. Without a knowledge of his own pet hates, his biases, he may easily distort his picture of the client's personality and betray the reality of the client's situation. Self-awareness is not easy to acquire, and when acquired is often painful. But it is essential that the worker have it. (Nichols, 1970, p. 157)

Statements similar to the preceding can be found throughout the literature on social work education. The educational process can be stress-producing, and much of this stress relates to the self-awareness which occurs when students begin clinical work. However, little has been written on the role of schools of social work in facilitating and helping students to cope with this sometimes stressful process and in using it positively and constructively.

A study was conducted to answer the following question: What is the position of schools of social work in the United States on the preparation of MSW students for the stress that may accompany self-awareness when they begin clinical practice? Following a re-

© 1989 by The Haworth Press, Inc. All rights reserved.

303

view of related literature, this study will be described and discussed.

REVIEW OF RELATED LITERATURE

The literature on stress in social workers and social work students is sparse. As helping professionals, social workers also can learn from reports about the stress which occurs in the training of physicians. Although there are many differences between stress in social work and medical training, there also exist some significant similarities.

Stress in Social Work Students and Social Workers

In a survey of graduate social work students, Munson (1984) measured levels of stress associated with classroom work and field practice. Fifty percent of the participating students experienced some stress, most of which was related to classroom work rather than field work. Although the symptoms reported indicated generally low levels of stress, Munson suggested that schools of social work take a more active role in assisting students who experience "inordinate amounts of stress." He further indicated that supervision may play a major part in alleviating and/or preventing high levels of stress, and that supervision may account for the low levels of stress reported in field placement assignments.

In 1974, Mayer and Rosenblatt identified sources of stress related to interactions with clients. These included (1) the desire to develop *amicable* relationships with clients; (2) the setting of goals which may be unattainable in the absence of adequate resources; and (3) the setting of high, unrealistic standards for oneself and the tendency to blame oneself when goals are not met. They suggested that by observing more experienced practitioners, students could develop more realistic expectations of the casework process and, subsequently, reduce the stress associated with the process.

Barnat (1973) outlined aspects of anxiety in first-year social work students. These included (1) the myth of therapy as a string of peak experiences; (2) the student's conscious or unconscious inhibition about invading privacy; and (3) the student's conflict with authority. Barnat stated that one of the most helpful components of the supervisory relationship in resolving anxiety was nonjudgmental authoritativeness on the part of the supervisor.

Pines and Kafry (1978) surveyed 129 social service workers who attended a workshop on burnout. Eleven percent of their respondents experienced "tedium in its most extreme form." They speculated that the characteristics that attract people to social service professions also make them more vulnerable to professional pressures and burnout. Pines and Kafry suggest that, while social service workers are likely to be sensitive and responsive to the needs of others, professionals are not getting the support and sensitivity they need from others.

Stress in Medical Students

As indicated earlier, social workers and social work students often experience stress related to their direct contact with clients or patients, and to other aspects of the educational process. Similarly, medical students have been found to experience various stages and types of stress.

Gaensbauer and Mizner (1980) identified sources of stress related to developmental stages in medical education. First year stress was related to the complexity and quantity of classroom material. In the second and third years, where students are exposed to increasingly intense clinical problems, stress was related to the students' commitment to the profession, death issues, and the intensity of interactions with patients and other staff. Fourth year anxiety revolved around the ability to perform as a doctor after graduation, as well as around the process of ending a phase of one's life. The authors suggested a number of methods by which medical schools can help students cope with stress, including the use of advisors, peer counselors, "rap" groups, and small group discussions.

Sacks et al. (1980) reported on the psychiatric problems of third year medical students. They postulated that intense patient contact can trigger closeness and intimacy issues, sometimes resulting in a crisis for the student. Their case studies illustrated situations in which the problems of patients triggered unconscious conflicts in students, including sibling rivalry, anger at maternal deprivation, and unresolved sexual issues. The authors emphasized the need to determine whether the difficulties set off by client problems were related to the phase of the student's education or were indications of a more serious pathology, and to deal with these conflicts adequately in treatment or supervision to prevent their recurrence.

Marital status was found to have an effect on stress levels in a study of medical students (Coombs & Fawzy, 1982). In this study, unmarried students reportedly experienced more stress in medical school than did married students. The authors believed that these results support the hypothesis that emotional support from a spouse offsets daily tensions which might be experienced.

Self-Awareness and Related Student Issues

In exploring the nature of stress in students, it becomes clear that much of this stress, especially in the clinical phase of education, can stem from the awareness of personal limits and unresolved conflicts, and the unlikelihood of reaching unrealistically high goals that have been set. Keeping this in mind, this review looks at the observations of several authors on the importance of self-awareness in social workers and the potential stress that can be triggered by the development of self-awareness in social work students.

Hamilton (1954) states that self-awareness, while not the major goal of professional education, is necessary in the development of a helping professional and is a by-product of learning essential subject matter. She discusses three levels of self-awareness which are experienced by social work students. The first involves a shift from a general desire to help others to a clearer identification of oneself as a professional. The second involves greater insight into one's own personality and how it affects performance with clients. The third involves an awareness that not every problem or symptom has been studied, along with the continuing awareness that there are some unresolved conflicts that may affect performance. The second level, which can produce anxiety, must be worked through before level three can be reached.

Lammert (1986) contends that heightened self-awareness in the therapist leads to greater empathy with the client. She indicates that developing self-awareness is a difficult task, but that self-awareness can be learned through such methods as supervision, T-groups, and "awareness training."

Three authors discuss the importance of self-awareness as it relates to the supervisory process. Davenport (1984) states, "As a clinical social worker and an educator, I believe that whatever of my own madness is not acknowledged remains to poison my work and my life" (p. 347). She describes a post-MSW training program in which the focus is to allow psychotherapists to explore their inner selves for the purpose of providing better services to clients. Davenport discusses the stress of this program and explains that strict criteria and an in-depth screening process are used to determine the readiness of each applicant. Before entering the program, participants are aware of the intensity and nature of the work. Individual and group supervision are used. Supervisors and interns are expected to be open to the exploration of the effect of their own personality and character on their work with clients.

Atwood (1986) also explores issues related to self-awareness in the supervisor. She reviews academic theories of self-awareness and examines the factors and methods for influencing and developing self-awareness in supervision. She states that, by examining their own motivations, "supervisors not only allow themselves to become psychologically more self-aware but also learn to become more effective . . ."(p. 95).

Spira (1986) reports on the experiences of MSWs in agencies and under private supervision. Her subjects indicate that they value the development of self-awareness in supervision and see this as fostering growth. MSWs under private supervisors more often reported satisfaction with this aspect of supervision. Subjects perceived this aspect of supervision negatively when they felt that the supervisor was being critical, or when they did not feel that they received support in dealing with their evolving self-awareness.

Reid (1977) discusses the feelings, values, and unresolved conflicts that often are experienced by social workers when they are working with clients. He discusses the importance of being aware of these conflicts and feelings, and the part this awareness plays in preventing these feelings from interfering with the therapeutic process. In learning to use this understanding of themselves more effectively with clients, students or beginning clinicians may need the help of a supervisor, consultant, or therapist.

Pascoe (1975) believes that personal growth is important in social work students. He hopes that schools will take responsibility for creating an educational structure that fosters growth of students, both emotionally and intellectually, and that facilitates management of the emotional pain that may accompany such growth.

Methods of Coping with Stress

In addition to the methods discussed previously, a variety of other suggestions have been made in the literature regarding ways to handle the anxiety, stress, or emotional pain that may accompany self-awareness and personal growth in social work students. Some deal specifically with the stress accompanying self-awareness. Others deal with more general anxiety and areas of growth in students.

Kagwa (1976) uses discussion of racial issues in the classroom to heighten self-awareness of students' own feelings about such issues. She says that students may later experience stresses in working with clients if they lack awareness and clarification of the conflictual feelings that may exist.

Balgopal (1974) describes a model of sensitivity training which increases self-awareness and helps students in handling stresses they experience during their social work education. According to Balgopal, sensitivity training can give students peer group support, a chance to voice emotional struggles in coping with their new roles, and an awareness of their feelings and how to control them in working with others.

In working with students as a field instructor, Schwartz (1978) used an exercise to help the students with countertransference — "the therapist's conscious or unconscious emotional reactions to a patient" (p. 204). Through the use of role-play, she helped students to be aware of feelings that were aroused by clients. Using this process, students were able to perform more effectively with clients.

Beck (1976) and Nichols (1968) have written about counseling or therapy for the clinical student. Beck (1976) says that the initial involvement of social work students with clients' problems stirs up and increases, rather than resolves, unconscious anxieties and conflicts. She describes a referral service developed specifically to meet the needs of social work students who wish to explore these types of issues through therapy. Students surveyed indicated that they sought therapeutic help for difficulties in relationships, alleviation of anxiety experienced in field and academic work, and improvement in clinical functioning.

Nichols (1968) describes another type of treatment program for clinical students. This program involves trainees in marital therapy who are required to undergo personal therapy. The therapy is growth-oriented and focuses on helping trainees with feelings that might be stirred up by clients and blocks that may occur due to these feelings.

DEFINITION OF TERMS

It is important to understand the meaning of terms as they are used in this study. The terms primarily used are *stress*, *self-awareness*, and *stress of self-awareness*. They are defined as follows. Stress, according to Selye (1978), is "the nonspecific response of the body to any demand, whether it is caused by, or results in, pleasant or unpleasant conditions" (p. 74). Rahe and Holmes (1967) refer to stress as the physical or emotional adaptation to life events or changes, pleasant or unpleasant, which require some adjustment from one's previous manner of functioning. For the purposes of this study, stress is defined as the student's need for such adaptation when faced with a growing awareness of personal limits and unresolved conflicts.

Self-awareness was defined by Bruck (1963) as "the student's conscious recognition of his own motivations, feelings, and behavior" (p. 126). When social work students begin working with clients, they often realize that they have more unresolved emotional conflicts than they had previously thought. As they continue working with clients, students become more aware of such issues and the need to resolve them in order to work more effectively with clients. In this study, self-awareness refers to the recognition of these conflicts and the need for change or resolution.

The process of becoming more self-aware, along with its accompanying recognition of a need for change, is a source of potential stress for social work students. In working with clients, students experience a stressor (becoming self-aware) which requires some adjustment or adaptation. This combination of self-awareness and the student's reaction or adjustment to it is referred to in this study as *stress of self-awareness*.

METHODOLOGY

A survey was used to study the preparation of MSW students for the stress of self-awareness in clinical practice. The population consisted of the eighty-nine schools of social work having MSW programs and accreditation by the Council on Social Work Education (CSWE, 1981). A questionnaire was mailed to the Director of Field Instruction at each of the schools. Included with each questionnaire was a self-addressed return envelope and an explanatory cover letter. Through the use of code numbers on the questionnaires, those who did not respond by the first deadline were sent a second mailing.

The self-administered questionnaire was designed by the authors to determine which strategies are used in schools of social work to prepare MSW students for the stress of self-awareness before they enter field placements, and to help them with this stress while they are in placements. Fifteen strategies for dealing with this issue were presented in the questionnaire. Respondents were asked to indicate the position of their schools on each strategy on a continuum ranging from "require" to "never used." The study also sought to determine strategies that are being used other than those on the questionnaire, suggested strategies, and addressed attitudes about the involvement of schools in this issue. Demographic information also was requested. The instrument was pretested and revised before being administered.

FINDINGS

Insight into the current preparation of MSW students for the potential stress of self-awareness can be gained from the information gathered in this study. Seventy-five percent of the questionnaires were completed and returned, and all geographic regions of the United States were represented by the respondents.

Positions on Strategies

The results of the study indicated that very few strategies for dealing with stress of self-awareness are required by schools of social work, while many are never used by a majority of schools (see Table 1). Most are not discouraged, however, and only a few are never required.

More specifically, a majority (59 percent) of participating schools required strategy M, having students deal with stress of self-awareness with their field instructors while in field placements. Over one-third of the participating schools required classroom material on this topic before and during placements, and video feedback of role-played interviews before entering placements was required by 20 percent of the schools.

Three strategies were not required by any of the respondents. These included having preadmission students meet with students currently in placements (Strategy A), having students seek therapy before entering placements (Strategy N), and having students seek therapy while in placements (Strategy O).

Six strategies listed on the questionnaire were listed as never used by at least half of the responding schools. These included stress reduction workshops for students before entering placement (78 percent); stress reduction workshops for students in placements (64 percent); faculty-led groups dealing with this issue before entering placements (64 percent); student-led groups dealing with this issue before entering placements (56 percent); therapy for students before entering placements (53 percent); and preadmission students meeting with students currently in placements to discuss this issue (50 percent).

None of the listed strategies were discouraged by more than three percent of the schools, and most were not discouraged by any schools. The strategies that were most often encouraged included video feedback of interviews with clients while in placements (42 percent); beginning students meeting with students currently in placements to discuss this and other aspects of clinical practice (33 percent); classroom material on the stress of self-awareness during placement (31 percent); students dealing with stress of self-awareness with their field instructors while in placements (28 percent); and preadmission students meeting with students currently in placements to discuss this and other aspects of clinical practice (26 percent).

Half of the schools were neutral on students seeking therapy while in placement. Other strategies which were not consistently

Table 1

Positions of Schools on Listed Strategies *

Strategy	Required	Encouraged	No Encouragement or discouragement	Discouraged	Never used	No answer
A 0%	26%	20%	2%	50%	2%	
B 6	33	38	0	20	3	
C 38	22	20	0	17	3	
D 43	31	19	0	5	2	
E 3	6	11	0	78	2	
F 3	9	19	2	64	3	
G 20	25	17	0	36	2	
H 5	42	36	0	14	3	
I 6	11	24	0	56	3	
J 9	20	26	0	43	2	
K 0	13	11	0	64	3	
L 13	8	28	0	48	3	
M 59	28	6	0	5	2	
N 0	3	39	2	53	3	
O 0	5	50	3	38	4	

* The strategies are listed on following page.

Table 1 (Continued)
Strategies Listed on Questionnaire

A. During the admission process, prospective students meet with students currently in placement to discuss various aspects of clinical practice, including the stress of self-awareness.

B. Beginning students (pre-placement) meet with students currently in placement to discuss various aspects of clinical practice, including the stress of self-awareness.

C. The issue of stress of self-awareness in clinical practice is covered in classroom material before students enter practicum.

D. The issue of stress of self-awareness in clinical practice is covered in classroom material while students are in practicum.

E. Students attend stress reduction workshops before entering practicum.

F. Students attend stress reduction workshops while in practicum.

G. Students receive video feedback of role-played interviews in the classroom before entering practicum.

H. Students receive video feedback of interviews with clients while in practicum.

I. Students confront the issue of stress of self-awareness in peer (student-led) groups before entering practicum.

J. Students confront the issue of stress of self-awareness in peer (student-led) groups while in practicum.

K. Students confront the issue of stress of self-awareness in faculty-led groups (other than classes) before entering practicum.

L. Students confront the issue of stress of self-awareness in faculty-led groups (other than classes) while in practicum.

M. Students deal with the stress of self-awareness with the field instructor while in practicum.

N. Students seek therapy before entering practicum.

O. Students seek therapy while in practicum.

encouraged or discouraged by a significant number of schools include having students seek therapy before entering placement (39 percent); having beginning students meet with students currently in placement to discuss this and other aspects of clinical practice (39 percent); giving video feedback on interviews with clients during placement (36 percent); having faculty-led groups to deal with this issue while in placement (28 percent); and having student-led groups to deal with this issue while in placement (26 percent). Some of these same strategies also were encouraged by a significant number of other schools. The exception is that of students seeking therapy both before and during placement, almost unanimously listed in either the "never used" or "no consistent encouragement or discouragement" category.

A complete listing of the strategies, positions, and percentages of respondents for each position can be found in Table 1.

Other Strategies Used

Several strategies other than those listed on the questionnaire were used by responding schools. Individual advisement with faculty advisors and with field liaisons was most frequently mentioned. Other methods included intensive orientation sessions before entering field placements; role-playing; clarification of values; guest speakers; process recording; having students write self-profiles; and pre-placement interviews.

Strategies used by individual faculty members included support groups, individual advisement, and role-playing. Others included stress management seminars, faculty advisor seminars, measuring students' self-esteem before and after their social work education, and recommending that students seek therapy. One respondent commented that all of the listed strategies were used at one time or another by individual faculty members, although none were required by school policy. Another reported that, while graduate students had no specific methods for dealing with the stress of self-awareness, BSW students were required to devise, implement, and evaluate a "strategy for managing stress related to professional life."

Suggested Strategies

Respondents suggested various methods to be used in helping students with the possible stress of self-awareness. The most common suggestion was to provide seminars for field instructors in which this topic is addressed. Also suggested were such methods as having a buddy system in which first- and second-year students would be paired up; having a close advising relationship; having a support system for field faculty; dealing with this issue specifically rather than with stress in general; and simply informing students of the issue. One respondent suggested not "overdoing it," saying that this issue is important, "but it is not where we begin."

Attitudes

Seventy-eight percent of the respondents felt that schools of social work should take responsibility for preparing MSW students for the possible emotional stress they may encounter as a result of the self-awareness process. About 5 percent of the respondents said that this was not the schools' responsibility. Of those who said that preparing students for stress was the schools' responsibility, 57 percent thought that this preparation should be done both before and during a student's placement. Twenty-one percent felt that preparation should be done during placement only, 13 percent before placement only, and 9 percent before admission.

The field instructor was listed by two-thirds of the respondents as the most important person in helping students with the potential stress of self-awareness. The educational advisor was next in importance, followed by the field liaison and the practice course instructor.

The implications of these findings are discussed in the following section. Limitations of the study and suggestions for further research also are discussed.

DISCUSSION

Summary and Implications

The professional literature indicates that graduate social work education can be stressful. It has been acknowledged that this stress can be related, in part, to a self-awareness process that occurs during the clinical phase of training. Authors have offered various suggestions regarding the schools' role in facilitating this process and channeling this stress positively. According to the present study, few of these methods are required by schools of social work, although quite a few are encouraged and used informally. A large majority of schools agreed that preparation of MSW students for this stress is the schools' responsibility, but little is being done about it in a formal way.

Much of the existing literature emphasizes the importance of supervision in helping students resolve issues related to stress of self-awareness. The results of this study indicate that this emphasis is prevalent in the majority of schools and may indeed account for the lower levels of stress reported by some students during the field instruction period of training (Munson, 1984).

The field instructor is seen by some respondents as the most appropriate person to help students deal with the stress of self-awareness; respondents felt that the field placement is the time to deal with this issue. As Directors of Field Instruction stated, students could "be intellectually aware of the possible stressfulness but really cannot be prepared for the possible impact" before placement.

Other respondents seemed to feel that there was a rationale for this intellectual preparation before placement, even though students might not be able to emotionally prepare themselves. One wrote that "simply informing students that this is to be expected as part of the educational process" is important. Another respondent said that "as adults they should be aware of what they are getting into," while a second commented that "as adult learners, we hope the stress this creates will be channelled into helping them be open to, and excited about, the learning that lies ahead."

Social work educators may wish to examine some of the implications and attitudes reflected in this study. For example, students were not required or encouraged to seek therapy by most of the schools participating in this study, while other helping professions have required their students to do so. What does this indicate? Is it, for example, the perception that therapy is only for the "sick," or is it simply a statement that seeking therapy is not an educational decision but an individual issue to be decided by the student? Other questions might be asked concerning the contradictions between what is required by schools and what is felt should be done in helping students with the stress that may accompany self-awareness. Is this issue being neglected, or is it that this issue affects individual students in different ways and, therefore, is better dealt with individually than by making school policy?

Limitations

This study sought to determine the methods used (or not used) by schools of social work in preparing MSW students to deal with the potential stress of self-awareness. It did not attempt to assess whether these methods are effective.

Although there were some advantages to the self-administered nature of the questionnaire, it has some limitations. Respondents were unable to ask questions and to clarify items which they did not understand. In turn, ambiguous answers could not be clarified.

Another limitation is that one person was asked to represent each school in completing the questionnaire. It is difficult to determine whether the information given was totally accurate, since it may have been based on the perceptions of the Director of Field Instruction rather than on the actual experiences of those supervising the students.

Suggestions for Future Research

Given the limitations of this exploratory study and the relative lack of literature in this area, there is need for further investigation. For example, eliciting students' perceptions of stress of self-awareness, and how their schools have prepared and/or assisted them with it, would add to the results of this study. Such research would help educators to get a clearer picture of students' needs, what is being done, and changes that may be needed.

It would be useful for schools of social work to study the effectiveness of various methods for dealing with the stress of self-awareness. This study only determined which methods are being used. It is important to examine how these methods are implemented and to measure their utility.

Research also could examine other stresses in social work students and could include a broader range of students. Several respondents observed that other potential stressors exist for social work students, and that clinically-oriented students are not alone in being affected by stress. All aspects of stress in social work students are important enough to warrant further research.

CONCLUSION

The high response rate and positive attitudes toward the schools' role indicate a genuine enthusiasm for the issue of preparing MSW students to deal with the potential stress of self-awareness in clinical practice. The geographic distribution of responses indicates that the results probably are representative of all areas of the United States. The main weakness indicated by this study seems to be in the formal implementation of the schools' role, especially in preparing students prior to their actually entering clinical work. Hopefully, this study will lead to more inspired strategies and continued research.

REFERENCES

Atwood, J. D. (1986). Self-awareness in supervision. *The Clinical Supervisor, 4*(3), 79-96.

Balgopal, P. R. (1974). Sensitivity training: A conceptual model for social work education. *Journal of Education for Social Work, 10*(2), 5-11.

Barnat, M. R. (1973). Student reactions to the first supervisory year: Relationship and resolutions. *Journal of Education for Social Work, 9*(3), 3-8.

Beck, D. L. (1976). A counseling program for social work students. *Social Casework, 57*, 651-655.

Bruck, M. (1963). The relationships between student anxiety, self-awareness, and self-concept and student competence in casework. *Social Casework, 44*, 125-131.

Coombs, R. H., & Fawzy, F. I. (1982). The effect of marital status on stress in medical school. *American Journal of Psychiatry, 139*, 1490-1493.

Council on Social Work Education. (1981). *Schools of social work with accredited master's degree programs*. New York: Author.

Davenport, J. J. (1984). The Saturday center: A training institution in process. *Clinical Social Work Journal, 12*, 347-355.

Gaensbauer, T. J., & Mizner, G. L. (1980). Developmental stresses in medical education. *Psychiatry, 43*, 60-70.

Hamilton, G. (1954). Self-awareness in professional education. *Social Casework, 35*, 371-379.

Kagwa, W. G. (1976). Utilization of racial content in developing self-awareness. *Journal of Education for Social Work, 12*(2), 21-27.

Lammert, M. (1986). Experience as knowing: Utilizing therapist self-awareness. *Social Casework, 67*, 369-376.

Mayer, J. E., & Rosenblatt, A. (1974). Sources of stress among student practitioners in social work: A sociological view. *Journal of Education for Social Work, 10*(1), 56-66.

Munson, C. E. (1984). Stress among graduate social work students. *Journal of Education for Social Work, 20*(3), 20-29.

Nichols, E. (1970). *A primer of social casework*. New York: Columbia.

Nichols, W. C., Jr. (1968). Personal psychotherapy for marital therapists. *The Family Coordinator, 17*(2), 83-88.

Pascoe, W. (1975). Education for clinical practice. *Clinical Social Work Journal, 3*(1), 46-54.

Pines, A., & Kafry, D. (1978). Occupational tedium in the social services. *Social Work, 23,* 499-507.

Rahe, R. H., & Holmes, T. H. (1967). The social readjustment rating scale. *Journal of Psychosomatic Research, 11,* 213-218.

Reid, K. E. (1977). Nonrational dynamics of the client-worker interaction. *Social Casework, 58,* 599-606.

Sacks, M. H., Frosch, W. A., Kesselman, M., & Parker, L. (1980). Psychiatric problems in third-year medical students. *American Journal of Psychiatry, 137,* 822-825.

Schwartz, M. C. (1978). Helping the worker with counter-transference. *Social Work, 23,* 204-209.

Selye, H. (1978). *The stress of life*. New York: McGraw-Hill.

Spira, L. (1986). MSW's speak: Experiences in agency and private supervision. *Clinical Social Work Journal, 14*(1), 79-91.

Factors Associated with Student Satisfaction in Undergraduate Social Work Field Placements

Miriam S. Raskin

ABSTRACT. There has been an increasing emphasis and focus on undergraduate education, including the field work course. To determine the factors that contribute to student satisfaction in field placement, the Student Practicum Satisfaction Questionnaire (SPSQ) was developed and utilized to survey students in the eleven accredited undergraduate programs in Virginia. This study reports on the demographic and attitudinal variables which related to student satisfaction in practicum. Implications for placement decisions, for the field curriculum, and for agency personnel are addressed.

During the last decade there has been an increasing professional focus on undergraduate social work education. Two major reasons for this growing interest are a continued shortage of trained personnel in the human services occupations and a decision by the National Association of Social Workers to admit to full membership Bachelor of Social Work (BSW) graduates of programs accredited by the Council on Social Work Education (CSWE).

The field placement experience is an integral and possibly the most important part of social work training (Anderson, 1979). Roberts (1978) has observed the near unanimity of students in selecting the practicum as the single most useful social work course. The content and quality of instruction and learning in field placement

Reprinted by permission of the College of Social Work, University of South Carolina, from *Arete*, Vol. 7 No. 1, 1982, pages 44-55.

experiences are perceived as critical elements in the development of the professional baccalaureate social worker. As Abbott (1931) observed, "Without supervised field work the social worker is not only not expert, but she (sic) is positively dangerous" (p. 114).

Tyler's (1950) theory of learning indicates that satisfaction of the student with the learning experience (i.e., field work) is a necessary condition for the desired learning and behaviors to take place. However, the issue of job satisfaction, which has become increasingly important to the professional social worker, has been virtually neglected as the student prepares for a professional role in the field placement (Pines & Kafry, 1978). The field instruction component, seen as a quasi-work situation by Berengarten (1957), has been found to be an essential key to bridging the gap between student and professional status (Ormsby, 1977; Vinter, 1967). If the student is to be successful in making the transition to professional status, social work educators must consider not only the development of student knowledge and skills necessary for practice but also the important element of satisfaction students derive from their (field) work.

To determine the factors which are associated with student satisfaction in field placement, a pilot study was conducted by this researcher in the fall of 1978 at George Mason University. As an outgrowth of the pilot study, an original survey instrument, the Student Practicum Satisfaction Questionnaire (SPSQ), was subsequently developed.[1] The SPSQ was used to examine the factors that are associated with student satisfaction and dissatisfaction in undergraduate social work field placements in the eleven accredited social work programs in Virginia.

THE PROBLEM AND RELEVANT QUESTIONS

In 1977, a group called Social Work Educators Council of Virginia (SWEC-VA) was formed to address some of the common concerns of undergraduate faculty in Virginia. This group expressed the need to have comprehensive, statewide demographic data for the students, field instructors, and agencies in the state. In addition, questions were raised regarding students' perceptions of the factors that contribute to optimum satisfaction in field placement. As a result of these concerns, the present study was designed to do the following: (1) expand the present limited body of knowledge in the area of undergraduate field instruction; (2) supply empirically based knowledge to social work educators in the area of curriculum development; (3) enhance the selection of optimum field learning experiences by delineating those significant variables or characteristics which students found satisfying and dissatisfying in field placement; and (4) provide information to agency administrators and field instructors which enables them to better assess the educational opportunities provided by their agency to undergraduate social work students.

Eight research questions were framed to guide the investigation of the concerns of the Virginia educators:

1. What are the demographic characteristics of students who were enrolled in a field placement in the participating Virginia institutions during the spring quarter/semester of 1979?
2. How are the demographic characteristics of these students related to their satisfaction in the undergraduate social work field placements?
3. What are the demographic characteristics of the field instructors as reported by the students?
4. How are the demographic characteristics of the field instructors (as reported by the students) related to the expressed satisfaction of the students who were enrolled in the undergraduate social work field placements?
5. What are the demographic characteristics of the field placement agencies as reported by the students?
6. How are the agency characteristics (as reported by the students) related to the expressed satisfaction of the students who were enrolled in the undergraduate social work field placements?
7. How are the expressed explanations of the students' perceptions related to their level of satisfaction or dissatisfaction?
8. What factor or factors make the greatest contribution in explaining the variance of the expressed satisfaction of undergraduate social work students who are completing a field placement?

THE VIRGINIA STUDY

The study population consisted of the undergraduate senior social work students in Virginia who were completing a senior year practicum during the spring quarter/semester of 1979. Only students from the eleven accredited undergraduate programs were surveyed. Of the 216 students in field placement at these institutions in the spring of 1979, a total of 170 (78 percent) responded to the study questionnaire.

The SPSQ underwent two revisions prior to its use with the Virginia students. The first occurred after the completion of the pilot study at George Mason University; the second after the revision received feedback with regard to the accuracy and clarity of questionnaire items from students in two accredited undergraduate programs outside Virginia. In final form, Part I of the SPSQ contained 27 demographic variables (12 were student specific, 4 related to the field instructor, and 10 pertained to the agency); Part II contained 73 Likert-type satisfaction items and 73 corresponding explanations ("amounts") for the expressed satisfaction items. Figure 1 shows how the second part looked, using two items from the scale.

As can be seen from Figure 1, the student was asked to make two responses. On the left hand side of the questionnaire, the student indicated his/her level of satisfaction (from "Very Dissatisfied" to "Very Satisfied") or indicated that the question was not applicable to one's experiences. On the right hand side of the survey instrument, the student explained the level of satisfaction for each question by indicating whether he/she was satisfied or dissatisfied because there was "Too much," "Too little," or "Just the right" amount of the experience in the placement.

Two items on the SPSQ (74 and 75) asked the students if they would accept a job at their agency and recommend the agency as a field placement. The last item solicited additional comments through an open-ended question. Seventy-one students (41.7 percent) responded to the open-ended question. Reliability coefficients of .94 and .95 were determined for the questionnaire by calculating Cronback's (1951) "Coefficient Alpha."

The SPSS program Frequencies was used to address Research Questions 1, 3, and 5. The relationship between demographic char-

FIGURE I

Sample Items from Part II, SPSQ

In my field placement, this is how

I feel about............

		Very Dissatisfied	Dissatisfied	Neither Satisfied nor Dissatisfied	Satisfied	Very Satisfied	Not Applicable	Much Too Little	Too Little	Just Right	Too Much	Much Too Much	Not Applicable
1.	The number of individuals I was assigned to work with during field placement.	1	2	3	4	5	NA	6	7	8	9	10	NA
2.	The number of groups I was assigned to work with during field placement	1	2	3	4	5	NA	6	7	8	9	10	NA

325

acteristics and student satisfaction (Research Questions 2, 4, and 6) was addressed through the use of SPSS programs for the t-test and Multiple Regression Analysis. Research Question 7 was investigated by using the SPSS program Pearson Correlation, while Research Question 8 was addressed by means of the program Factor Analysis.

FINDINGS

Analysis of Research Questions 1, 3, and 5, which provided demographic characteristics of the senior undergraduate students completing a field placement, their field instructors, and the agencies in which they were placed, found that: (1) the majority of the undergraduate social work students in Virginia who were completing a field placement were female and between the ages of 19 and 29; (2) slightly under half of the students were in concurrent placements; and (3) the majority of the students had GPAs which ranged from 2.6 to 3.0 and did not receive remuneration for field work. The field instructors were described by the students as primarily being employees of the agency where they worked and having a social work degree (BSW, MSW, DSW) with some previous supervisory experience. The agencies where the students were trained were primarily large (more than 20 professional staff) public agencies in which the majority of the professional staff were not social workers (host agencies).

Analysis of the final three questions showed that the majority (60 percent) of the students would accept a job at the agency in which they completed their field work, and that 86 percent would recommend their agencies to other students. Seventy-one students provided responses to an open-ended item. The comments indicated that students appeared to assess the field work experience as overall positive. These results seem to be in agreement with the research findings of Galambos and Wiggins (1970), Walton and Walz (1971), and Ormsby (1977). Just as the percentage of satisfied and dissatisfied workers has remained fairly stable over time (80-85 percent satisfied), the limited research on social work student satisfaction seems to also show some consistency (overall, 65-75 percent satisfied with their placements).

A second finding comes from the t-test and multiple regression analysis which were used to examine Research Questions 2, 4, and 6. These three questions were concerned with the relationship between demographic characteristics and student satisfaction. All demographic characteristics (except for field work grade, which could not accurately be ascertained) were included in the full regression model. Demographic characteristics accounted for 27.2 percent of the variance of the dependent variable Average Student Satisfaction; the overall F-ratio for the regression equation was significant at the .01 level. The demographic variable which explained the greatest percentage of the variance of student satisfaction was Type of Placement (Block). The following nine demographic variables were found to be significantly related to Average Student Satisfaction with the field placement; (1) Type of Placement (Block); (2) Grade Point Average (lower the average, the more satisfied); (3) Remuneration (if paid, more satisfied); (4) Field Instructor Degree (lack of social work degree, more satisfied); (5) Social Work/Host Agency (more satisfied in Social Work Agency); (6) Location of Agency (urban); (7) Training at the Field Work Agency of Social Work Graduate Students (previous training of graduate social work students, the more satisfied the undergraduate respondents); (8) Training at Field Placement Agency of Undergraduate Social Work Students (previous training of undergraduate students, the less satisfied); and (9) a Variety of Task Assignments, such as crisis, long-term and contract work (more varied the tasks, the more satisfied).

In all but one case (grade point average), the variables are subject to external manipulation or control. For example, the director of field instruction can institute block placements if none exist or increase the number which already exist. More placements that offer remuneration or grants for undergraduates can be sought and utilized. Placing students in urban, social work agencies where previous graduate students have been trained is a further example of how these characteristics could be utilized to enhance student satisfaction in field placement.

The variables GPA and Variety of Tasks have been reported in the literature as contributing to student satisfaction (Galambos & Wiggins, 1970); these earlier findings are supported in this study.

The following sets of demographic variables were found not to be significantly related to student satisfaction in field placement: (1) Student variables — age, marital status, preference for type of agency, previous paid or volunteer experience, and sex; (2) Field Instructor variables — employment status, previous supervisory experience, and sex; and (3) Agency variables — previous training of students from other fields, size of agency, size of work unit, and type of funding. The variables employment status of field instructor, size of agency, and size of work unit have been reported in the literature as not being associated with student satisfaction (Ormsby, 1977); these earlier findings are supported by this study.

A third major finding of this study deals with the relationship between the expressed explanations ("amounts") of the student's perceptions and level of satisfaction or dissatisfaction (Research Question 7). Seventy (70) satisfaction items and their corresponding explanations ("amounts") were significantly and positively correlated at the .01 level. Students were satisfied when the variables were present in the field experience at the "Just right" amount. On the other hand, the corresponding explanations ("amounts") indicated that students were dissatisfied when the items were present "Too little" or "Too much" in the field experience. The three variables that were present "Too much" were red tape, paperwork, and tension between individuals and groups in the agency. In general, students tended to have "Too little" work rather than "Too much."

Factor analysis was the mathematical tool used to analyze Research Question 8. This procedure helped to highlight the factors which made the greatest contribution to student satisfaction in field placement. Seven factors accounted for 81.5 percent of the variance of the dependent variable specifically used for the factor analysis (Overall Student Satisfaction). Agency climate factors were found to contribute 5.8 percent of the variance, while combined Supervisory factors (Factors 2 and 3) accounted for 13.7 percent of the variance of the dependent variable. Factor 5 contributed almost 60 percent of the variance of the dependent variable. This factor was best explained as a "New Learning" factor and primarily consists of: (1) the agency as a place to learn about social work; (2) the feelings of accomplishment the student gets from the work; and (3) the chance to use one's abilities and skills.

The literature has shown that some of the factors that influence professional social worker satisfaction are related to agency climate, supervision, working conditions, autonomy, agency policies, responsibility, and achievement. The findings of this study seem to confirm that some of the same factors impact upon undergraduate social work student satisfaction in field placement (e.g., climate, supervision, and achievement). However, the factor which made the largest contribution to the variance of the dependent variable in this study was New Learning (59.3 percent). That is, the actual achievement of field work objectives (new learning) is strongly and positively associated with student satisfaction. In turn, student satisfaction is a necessary condition for the occurrence of appropriate student behaviors in the learning process.

The major factor associated with student satisfaction, "New Learning," is itself a desired outcome of field placement. Consequently, measuring the relative attainment of student satisfaction may help to predict the relative attainment of certain field work objectives. In classroom courses, achievement of educational objectives can be assessed through exams, term papers, class presentations, and group discussion. In field work, these methods are not appropriate. Factor analysis of the responses to the SPSQ may provide undergraduate programs with a vehicle for determining the fulfillment of selected field work program objectives.

DISCUSSION

Although the students who participated in this study were from Virginia, the findings from the demographic data appear to be in agreement with the findings of Galambos and Wiggins (1970) and with Ormsby (1977), whose populations were drawn from other sections of the country. The limited available data point to a consistency in the demographic characteristics of undergraduate social work students, their field instructors, and the agencies utilized for field placement.

The inverse relationship found between GPA and student satisfaction may indicate that students with higher GPAs have higher expectations and are more demanding of their field placements and their field instructors. These students may be more critical of agency policies and the abilities and skills of their field instructors. Since there generally seems to be "Too little" for students to do rather than "Just the right amount" or "Too much," perhaps higher GPA students are bored and need more of a challenge. The study found that academically weaker students were generally more satisfied. Therefore, the placement experiences of the academically stronger student may need more attention and careful planning. In addition, if future studies support the finding that students are more satisfied with field instructors without social work degrees, further work would be needed to determine the implication of such findings.

The finding that students were satisfied in agencies where graduate social work students had been previously placed, but not where undergraduates have been trained, can possibly be understood as a function of time. Agencies have had a great many years of experience in the training of graduate students but very limited time in training undergraduate students. An agency that has had experience with graduate level performance can perhaps better select appropriate assignments for undergraduate students. The statistical significance of this finding could be expected to disappear with time and increased interaction between undergraduate students and field work agencies. Another factor that will possibly aid in diminishing the significance of this finding is the ability of undergraduate educators to better define field work objectives.

Although demographic characteristics are often difficult to manipulate, those characteristics included in this study which were significantly related to student satisfaction are subject to external control (except for GPA). This means that, to some extent, student satisfaction in field work may be enhanced through the use of significant demographic characteristics in placement decisions.

Since there are demographic characteristics which have not yet been studied, conclusions regarding the relationships found between demographic characteristics and student satisfaction should be considered tentative and used with some caution, especially by programs outside of Virginia.

Findings from Research Question 7 indicate that there are specific areas in the field work experience that could be improved. Unless supervisors, agencies, and the faculty have concrete systematic feedback from student experience, changes or improvement in curriculum might not occur or are likely to occur in inappropriate areas. Students have indicated that they have "Too little" to do in the placement. They also are lacking in enough opportunities for direct observation of their field instructors. The expressed explanation ("amount") for student satisfaction and dissatisfaction with specific elements of the field placement can guide the appropriate increase or decrease of certain experiences in order to increase the level of student satisfaction and decrease the level of dissatisfaction.

Although the literature points to the importance of the relationship between agency climate, supervisory factors (Galambos & Wiggins, 1970), and the job satisfaction of professional social workers, these factors contributed a total of 19.5 percent to the variance of the dependent variable in this study. The most important factor (Factor 5) to the student was "New Learning." It was shown that similar factors contribute to both worker and student satisfaction, but there seems to be a major difference. The focus of students' satisfaction is related to achieving their objectives as students — New Learning.

IMPLICATIONS

The subject of job satisfaction has been under investigation and close scrutiny for approximately 80 years. Each research effort on the subject has contributed to the understanding of the larger unfolding picture. The insights gained from the findings of this study have implications for: (1) the general knowledge base of job satisfaction and, more specifically, for student satisfaction in undergraduate social work field instruction; (2) instituting curriculum changes; and (3) CSWE accreditation guidelines with respect to undergraduate field instruction.

A satisfaction instrument which addressed the special needs of students in a quasi-work setting did not exist when this study was undertaken. Tailoring an instrument to this unique group has had some definite benefits. First, an instrument is now available which can be adapted by other social work programs that wish to assess the level of student satisfaction in field placements in their programs and to explore the achievement of field work objectives. More importantly, the findings from this study's unique instrument

(SPSQ) can be used by social work faculty, field instructors, and agency administrators in their ongoing efforts to develop, improve, and change curriculum. The issue of validity would require further study by those using the SPSQ on populations outside Virginia.

The nine demographic characteristics which were found to be significantly related to student satisfaction can be of use to undergraduate social work faculty presently involved in placement decisions. For example, the accredited social work program in this study that had the highest mean satisfaction score (338) was a rural school which utilized only block placements. (The placements were in both rural and urban locations.) Traditionally, rural programs have used block placements because of the distance between the school and the field work agencies. However, in schools located in urban areas (where there are a larger number of social agencies and the students commute to school) block placements are often not seen as necessary. Usually, the type of placement offered is based on faculty teaching schedules or administrative decisions made outside the social work programs.

The finding that students are more satisfied with field instructors without social work degrees leads to additional research questions. This variable was found to contribute less than 1 percent (0.64) to the variance of Average Student Satisfaction. Since its contribution (although statistically significant) was so negligible, perhaps the field instructor's skills and abilities in technical, evaluative, and human relations areas are the key factors rather than educational degree. If future studies support this finding, implications would exist for criteria to be used in the selection of field instructors and for the re-evaluation of accreditation guidelines as presently established by CSWE with regard to undergraduate field work.

Demographic characteristics contributed approximately 27 percent of the variance of student satisfaction. Their importance in student placements needs to be kept in perspective and utilized in placement decisions according to their relative contribution to student satisfaction. Since there are also demographic characteristics which have not yet been studied, conclusions regarding the relationships found between demographic characteristics and student satisfaction should be considered tentative and used with some caution, especially by programs outside of Virginia.

Students were most dissatisfied with variables that related to bureaucratic issues (red tape, paperwork, tension between individuals and groups). Since the majority of students are placed in large urban agencies, the programs need to incorporate into the curriculum issues and problems that relate to bureaucratic survival. Coping mechanisms should be taught both in class and in the field work agencies.

RECOMMENDATIONS

This study was a beginning step in the investigation of the complex issue of work satisfaction as it applies to undergraduate students. Several recommendations for future and improved research efforts can be derived from the findings. Specific recommendations follow:

1. National surveys which would include data on undergraduate social work student, field instructor, and agency characteristics need to be undertaken. Since demographic characteristics are related to student satisfaction, additional variables not included in this study should be collected and statistically tested for their relationship to student satisfaction.
2. Increasing the number of New Learning variables on the SPSQ should be considered. These variations could then account for an even higher percentage of the variance of Average Student Satisfaction.
3. There is a general lack in the literature of information about both undergraduate field instruction and student satisfaction. A contribution to the literature could be made by building on the present study and engaging in further empirical work in the area of field instruction. For example, the level of satisfaction of graduate social work students in field placements could be explored.

Utilizing Tyler's (1950) educational model, this study investigated the factors which are associated with student satisfaction in undergraduate social work field placements. The beginning insights provided by this research can stimulate changes in the field work curriculum, in placement decision, and in the training of future BSW practitioners.

NOTE

1. This questionnaire has been copyrighted by the author. Copies can be obtained by writing the author at George Mason University, Fairfax, VA.

REFERENCES

Abbott, E. (1931). *Social welfare and professional education*. Chicago: University of Chicago Press.

Anderson, W. A. (1979). *Education for employment: BSW graduates' work experiences and the undergraduate curriculum*. Paper presented at the Annual Program Meeting of the Council on Social Work Education, Boston, Mass.

Baer, B. L., & Federico, R. (1978). *Educating the baccalaureate social worker, report of the undergraduate social work curriculum development project*. Cambridge: Ballinger.

Berengarten, S. (1957). Identifying learning patterns of individual students: An exploratory study. *Social Service Review, 31*, 407-417.

Beverly, D., & Dickman, J. (1981). A systems model: The Virginia state manpower study. *Journal of Education for Social Work, 17*(2), 106-112.

Closing the gap in social work manpower. (1965). Washington, D.C.: Government Printing Office.

Cronback, I. (1951). Coefficient alpha and the internal structure of tests. *Psychometrika, 16*, 297-334.

Galambos, E. C., & Wiggins, X. R. (1970). *After graduation: Experiences of college graduates in locating and working in social welfare positions*. Georgia: Southern Regional Education Board. Atlanta.

Meyer, C. H. (1976). *Social work practice*. New York: Free Press.

Olmstead, J. A. (1973). *Organizational structure and climate: Implication for agencies*. HumRRO Working Papers (73-05-403), Human Resources Research Organization, Alexandria, Va.

Ormsby, H. (1977). The impact of the field work placement on professional attitudes of baccalaureate degree social work students (Doctoral dissertation, University of Denver 1977). *Dissertation Abstracts International, 38*, 3057-A.

Pines, A., & Kafry, D. (1978). Occupational tedium in the social services. *Social Work, 23*, 499-507.

Roberts, R. W. (1973). An interim report of the development of an undergraduate-graduate continuum of social work education in a private university. *Journal of Education for Social Work, 9*(3), 58-64.

Tyler, R. W. (1950). *Basic principles of curriculum and instruction*. Chicago: University of Chicago Press.

Vinter, R. D. (1967). The social structure of service. In T. J. Edwin (Ed.). *Behavioral sciences for social workers*. (pp. 193-206). New York: Free Press.

Walton, E., & Walz, T. (1971). A follow-up study of graduates of a pre-social work program: Implications for education and practice. *Social Work Education Reporter, 19*, 54-57.

Factors Associated
with Fieldwork Performance
in a Social Work Course
in Hong Kong

Nai-ming Tsang

ABSTRACT. This paper reports the findings of research which identifies possible factors affecting students' performance in fieldwork. Four independent variables were examined: demographic variables of students; structural variables of placements; modes of study; and the academic score of students. Female students appeared to perform better than male students, and part-time students did better than full-time students. Students using macro-intervention also attained higher average fieldwork grades. Academic score was found to have the highest association with fieldwork performance. Implications for social work education are drawn from the findings.

BACKGROUND

The Department of Applied Social Studies (known as the School of Social Work prior to 1986) at Hong Kong Polytechnic is in one of the six post-secondary colleges, Polytechnics, and Universities that are recognized by the Government of Hong Kong as formally offering social work education. Social work graduates from these institutions are eligible for full membership in the Hong Kong Social Workers' Association and are certified for employment in the field.

A Diploma in Social Work Course is one of the programmes offered by the Department. This requires two years of study designed to provide basic and practical training in social work. A programme requiring three years of part-time study with a similar syllabus also is offered. It is designed to enable those already em-

© 1989 by The Haworth Press, Inc. All rights reserved.

337

ployed in social welfare agencies, and who have demonstrated commitment and potential for a career in social work, to be released from work during the day to pursue formal social work training. Agency sponsorship is a necessary condition for the part-time programme in addition to other similar requirements of the full-time course with respect to age, academic standard, suitability in personality, and dedication to social work (Hong Kong Polytechnic, Prospectus, 1986/87, pp. 198-200).

Fieldwork is regarded as very important in social work education. In addition to satisfactory performance, a social work student must be able to demonstrate ability to apply theory and knowledge, commitment to social work values and assumptions, and satisfactory performance in the various roles of a social worker in providing effective service to clients in fieldwork practice. The importance of fieldwork is increasingly recognized, as reflected in a growing number of publications in this area (Wilson, 1981; Butler & Elliott, 1985; Sheafor & Jenkins, 1982).

The performance of a social work student in fieldwork is often measured by an evaluation form on which the fieldwork instructor makes an assessment of the student in different areas. There are six major areas for assessment that are contained in the evaluation form for fieldwork in the Diploma in Social Work Course: involvement in practice; practice competence; working relationships; integration; service accountability; and learning accountability.

Qualitative assessment in written form and grades are given in each area. An overall grade also is given. The completed form reflects the strengths and weaknesses of the student in different areas and in overall performance. Information on the nature of the placement (e.g., the setting of the agency, assignment given to students, or major methods of intervention used) also can be found on the evaluation form.

Possible Factors Associated with Students' Fieldwork Performance

Among the field instructors in the Department, there seems to be a general impression of the differences in the strengths and weaknesses between the full-time and part-time (day release) students in their fieldwork performance. The part-time group appears to be better in handling inter-personal relationships, administrative duties, and program skills, but less able to analyze, conceptualize, and generalize from their practice situation. Such differences may have something to do with different characteristics of the two groups of students. A possibly lower academic standard attained before admission,[1] and the number of years elapsed since they last attended formal education, could hinder the ability of the part-time students to conceptualize and generalize their practice experience in more theoretical terms, or to apply appropriate theories and concepts in specific practice situations. On the other hand, their longer years of working experience and their concomitant role as workers in welfare agencies are definite advantages to equip part-time students with the knowledge and skills involved in handling administrative duties, inter-personal relationships, and programme implementation.

Speculation on this has focused our attention on the possible association between characteristics of students and their fieldwork performance. For example, Raskin (1982) included a set of demographic characteristics of the students in a study of factors associated with student satisfaction in fieldwork. Further exploration of the possible relationship between fieldwork performance and student demographic variables such as age, sex, working experience, and educational standards is a useful empirical endeavor.

A previous study by the author on students' perspective on field instruction called our attention to another set of variables which may affect the performance of students in fieldwork. The nature of placement (block or concurrent), the status of the field instructor (a school or agency field instructor), and the agency setting were felt by students to have different impact on their fieldwork experience. Raskin (1982) also included a set of "demographic characteristics" of the field instructors and field placement agencies and examined their effect on students' satisfaction in fieldwork placement. Her study suggests that there are seven factors related to the fieldwork agencies or field instructors that are significantly related to average student satisfaction with field placement.

This set of variables, which is concerned with the arrangement of fieldwork placement, its nature, the agency setting, the status of fieldwork instructors, and the types of assignments, can be categorized as a set of structural variables. The possible association of these variables with students' performance in fieldwork can be tested. An interesting study by Merriam (1972) on the relations between scholastic achievement in a School of Social Work and six factors in the background of students is of similar nature, but it uses the scholastic achievement of the students as the dependent variable. The six factors are: graduation from college; undergraduate courses in sociology; participation in undergraduate activities involving sociology; related work and/or voluntary service experience during the interim between college and professional school; size of students' home community; and undergraduate grades in courses in the social sciences. The relationship between these six factors and fieldwork performance, and between performance in fieldwork and classroom study of students, also were compared.

The current study compares the academic and fieldwork performance of students in the Diploma Course. Will those students with high academic scores also achieve relatively higher scores in fieldwork? What relationship exists between the learning ability in the cognitive domain, an essential requirement in academic study, and the ability to handle feelings, tasks, and other practice skills essential for social workers in practice? Examination of this relationship can provide some interesting information useful in understanding the learning patterns of students in a social work course.

Research Design

The focus of this study is the fieldwork performance of students in the Diploma Course. The dependent variable is the average of grades received for each placement taken by a student. Four types of independent variables which may affect students' fieldwork performance are examined: demographic, structural, mode of study, and academic score.

The first type of independent variable includes the following personal demographic data of students (demographic variables):

- age
- sex
- marital status
- highest academic qualification obtained prior to study for the Diploma in Social Work Course
- working experience, including those related to social work
- experiences in voluntary services
- sponsorship for study by a welfare agency during the course of study

The second type of independent variable takes into account the various aspects of the structure of a fieldwork placement. These structural variables include:

- the nature of placement (e.g., block/concurrent)
- the status of field instructors (e.g., school/agency)
- the nature of the placement agency (e.g., voluntary agency/ Social Welfare Department)
- the major social work methods employed in the placement (e.g., casework/groupwork)

These variables are placement-specific since each student has one set of structural variables for a particular placement. A student with two placements would have two sets of structural variables.

The third independent variable is the mode of study for the student (i.e., full-time or part-time). The fourth independent variable is the academic score of the student at the end of the course for all academic subjects, and it is calculated by the cumulative grade point average.[2]

The student population includes 459 graduates of the full-time program and 149 graduates of the part-time program for the Diploma in Social Work Course in the School of Social Work, Hong Kong Polytechnic, during the years 1978 to 1985.

The effects of four types of independent variables on the combined fieldwork grade point average, and their possible association, are examined in this study by employing primarily the Statistical Package for the Social Sciences using a VAX-11/750 (DEC) computer system.

Fieldwork Performance and Demographic Variables

Student profiles can be drawn by examining and comparing the demographic data of the students in the full-time and part-time study modes. The typical student in the Diploma in Social Work Course (both modes of study) is likely to be a female student, in her early twenties, single, has passed the High/Advance Level Examinations,[3] and has about 3 years of working experience and a half year of voluntary experience.

A typical student in the Diploma in Social Work Course (full-time) is even more likely to be a female, in her early twenties, single with a high probability of passing the High/Advance Level Examinations, and has 2 years of working experience and about half year of voluntary experience.

A typical student in the Diploma in Social Work Course (part-time, day release) is more likely to be a male student, in his late twenties, single, has passed the School Certificate Examinations[3] (minimum entrance qualifications), and has 6 years of working experience and about 9 months of voluntary experience.

The differences between full-time and part-time students for each of these demographic characteristics, except voluntary experience, were statistically significant (Chi-Square test or t-value with p less than .001). The set of six demographic variables (age, sex, academic qualification, social work-related working experience, non-social work experience, and marital status) were examined for their possible association with the student's fieldwork performance. In examining these relationships, the combined fieldwork grade (the dependent variable) is measured on an interval scale, while the independent variables are either nominal or ordinal. Analysis of variance is used to test the level of significance in terms of the F-value. A η value is calculated to show the correlation or the strength of association between one variable on an interval scale and another variable on a nominal scale. This value indicates the percentage of variation in fieldwork grades which can be explained by any one of the demographic characteristics of the student. Table 1 shows the results of this analysis.

The pattern of scores for combined fieldwork grades is more or less the same for both single and married students. However, sex,

Table 1

Analysis of Variance of Combined Fieldwork

Performance by Demographic Variables

	F-ratio	Significance	η
Sex (M/F)	21.94	$p < .001$ (yes)	0.035
Age (years)	0.704	$p < .1$ (no)	0.002
Marital Status (M/S)	3.35	$p > .05$ (no)	0.006
Academic Qualification (High Level/Certificate)	2.65	$p < .05$ (yes)	0.013
Working Experience (Yes/No)	4.925	$p < .05$ (yes)	0.008
Social Work-Related Experience (Years)	2.69	$p < .05$ (yes)	0.013
Non-Social Work Experience (Years)	1.03	$p > .1$ (no)	0.005
Combined Working Experience (Years)	3.65	$p < .05$ (yes)	0.018

level of academic qualification, working experience, and social work-related experience are significantly associated with student performance in fieldwork (all at $p < .05$). The sex of a student is able to explain about 3.5 percent of the variation in fieldwork performance, while the academic qualification of a student can explain about 1.3 percent of this variation. Working experience explains about 0.8 percent of the variation of student performance in fieldwork, and social work-related working experience explains about 1.3 percent of this variation.

Female students appeared to perform better, scoring more As in their combined fieldwork grade. Students with working experience performed better than those without working experience, but the relationship between combined fieldwork grades and the length of working experience is weak. Students with different academic qualifications performed differently in their fieldwork performance. However, students with minimum qualifications (School Certificate Examination) did quite well in their fieldwork performance having the highest total percentage of As and Bs.

Overall, the results indicate that a female student who has passed the School Certificate Examination qualifications, and who has a number of years of social work or combined with other work experience, has a higher probability of doing better in fieldwork performance. Her age and marital status will not affect her fieldwork performance significantly.

Fieldwork Performance and Structural Variables

Statistical analysis of the structural variables associated with student placements helps to describe typical placement profiles (TPP). For example, a typical placement in the Diploma Course (full-time and part-time) can either be of block or concurrent nature, is likely to be in voluntary agencies and supervised by a member of staff from the School, and will use casework and groupwork as the major methods of intervention.

A typical placement for a full-time student is likely to be of concurrent nature, in voluntary agencies, supervised by a member of staff from the School, and use casework and groupwork as the major methods of intervention.

A typical placement for a part-time, day release student is likely to be in the form of a block nature, even more likely for the full-time student to be in voluntary agencies and to be supervised by a member of staff from the School, and will use casework and group-work as the major methods of intervention.

There are statistically significant differences between full-time and part-time students with respect to these structural characteristics of field placement. The next four sections explore the effects of these structural variables on students' performance in fieldwork. Analysis of variance is used.

Agency and Fieldwork Performance

The nature of placement agencies can be classified into three categories. The first category, voluntary agencies, generally has less rigid and bureaucratic administrative procedures, and adopts a more flexible and innovative approach in service delivery. The second category, Social Welfare Department, has statutory functions (e.g., in probation, care, and protection of women and children) and has a more formal and bureaucratic structure. The third category of agencies includes organizations that do not primarily provide social work services but have a social work component in their service provision (e.g., Correctional Services Department, City District Offices, Education Department, and Labour Department). Each of these organizations is a secondary setting since each has its own primary function but is willing to provide opportunities for social work students to do their fieldwork placement as a supplement or complement to their provision of service and achievement of organizational goals.

The mean fieldwork grades were similar in the Social Welfare Department and secondary settings (2.993 and 2.994, respectfully), reaching 3.093 in the voluntary agency setting.

The nature of agency can only explain roughly 1 percent of the variation of fieldwork grade of students. Multiple-group comparison shows significant differences in the mean value of combined fieldwork grade by students placed in voluntary agencies and the Social Welfare Department ($p < .01$), and between voluntary agencies and secondary setting ($p < .01$), but there is no significant difference between mean scores by students placed in the Social Welfare Department and a secondary setting.

Nature of Placement, Fieldwork, Supervisor, and Fieldwork Performance

Similar testing was done to determine any significant differences between the grades given in concurrent and block placement, and by school and agency supervisors. No significant differences were found for any of the possible combinations of placement type, supervisor, and fieldwork performance.

Major Methods of Intervention and Fieldwork Performance

Table 2 illustrates the relationship between the fieldwork grades given when selected social work methods are used as the major tools for intervention. These methods range from micro-intervention (casework) through macro-intervention (group and community work).

The mean value of grades is in ascending order from Method I to Method V, where group and community work methods are combined. It seems that it is less difficult to get higher grades in field placement when using macro-intervention skills. The strength of association between grade and intervention, however, is very weak. Only 0.6 percent of the variation in the fieldwork grades can be explained by the method of intervention used. Multiple comparisons using Scheffe's Method also were made. Table 3 shows the F-values and levels of significance reached in such comparison.

From the multiple comparisons in Table 2, it appears that only the F-values between Groups I and III, Groups I and IV, and Groups I and V are greater than F^1 at $p = 0.01$.[4] The mean value of grades given in settings that employ casework methods only (I) differs significantly from all other settings using different methods, except in those settings that employ the group work method of intervention only (II).

At this stage, two structural variables — the nature of fieldwork agencies and the major methods of intervention used in placement — appear to be associated with significantly different mean values for fieldwork grades. However, the strength of association

Table 2

ANADVA of Fieldwork Grade by Major Methods of Intervention

	CASE (1)	GROUP (II)	GROUP (III)	COMMUNITY (IV)	COMMUNITY (V)
Mean	2.971	3.037	3.076	3.079	3.11
F-value		2.377			
Level of Significance			p < .05		
			0.006		

Table 3

Multiple Group Comparison of Fieldwork Grade in Placement

Using Different Methods of Intervention

COMPARISON	F-VALUE	SIGNIFICANCE
I & II	8.465	not significant (p > .05)
I & III	27.78	p < .01
I & IV	34.62	p < .01
I & V	27.812	p < .01
II & III	3.308	not significant (p > .05)
II & IV	6.923	not significant (p > .05)
II & V	7.157	not significant (p > .05)
III & IV	1.113	not significant (p > .05)
III & V	1.882	not significant (p > .05)
IV & V	0.249	not significant (p > .05)

between these structural variables and fieldwork grades is weak. These independent (structural) variables do not explain much of the variation in fieldwork grades. Moreover, there is no statistically significant difference between the mean value of fieldwork grades in various categories of the other two structural variables (types of fieldwork supervisor and nature of placement).

The pattern of relationships between the fieldwork grades and the structural variables suggests that a student has a greater chance to score a higher grade in placements in voluntary agencies using macro-intervention. In contrast, students placed in the Social Welfare Department or secondary settings, and using casework as the major method of intervention, have a higher probability of scoring lower grades in fieldwork.

Test of Differences in Fieldwork and Academic Performance

The combined average fieldwork grade for part-time students (3.151) is significantly higher than the average for full-time social work students (3.064). A t-value of 2.09 is calculated at a level of $p < .05$. Part-time students do better in fieldwork. With respect to academic performance, however, the reverse seems to be true. The average academic score is 2.754 for full-time students compared to 2.643 for part-time students. There is a statistically significant difference between the mean value of academic results for the two types of students (t-value of 3.68 at the level of $p < .001$).

Association Between Combined Fieldwork Grades and Academic Scores

The empirical association between the two variables is examined using the combined field grade as the dependent variable (Y) and the academic score of the student as the independent variable (X). A simple bivariate regression computed $Y = 3.18(X) - 5.6$. The value of Pearson's r is 0.431, indicating a moderate and positive linear relationship between the combined fieldwork grades and academic scores of students. The r^2 value of 0.186 indicates that the academic score of a student explains about 19 percent of the total variation in the combined fieldwork grades.

This value of $r = 0.431$ is higher than the value of $r = 0.395$

found in Merriam's study in 1972. Following Merriam's interpretation, it indicates that both academic score and combined fieldwork grade measure something common in the student. The qualities required for outstanding academic performance (e.g., comprehension, organization, memory, reading ability, logical thinking, and fluency in written presentation) may, in part, enable the student to do well in some areas of fieldwork performance (e.g., integration of theory and practice, writing up records, analyzing and evaluation, and generalization from working experience) but possibly not in the areas of practice skills and performance. Ability in academic study, however, is a definite advantage in helping a student to perform well in fieldwork.

DETECTING THE SINGLE AND COMBINED EFFECT OF VARIABLES ON FIELDWORK PERFORMANCE

The effects of full-time and part-time modes of study, academic performance, and other demographic and structural variables on the fieldwork performance of students have been identified in the preceding. More refined statistical analysis (analysis of covariance) is used to test the relationship between fieldwork performance and modes of study when the academic score of students is controlled as a covariate. The results of this analysis indicate significant difference between the fieldwork performance of full-time and part-time students when their academic performance is held constant ($p <$ .001). But the modes of study explain only about 2 percent of the variation in students' fieldwork performance.

Sex and Fieldwork Performance
When Academic Score Is Controlled

Similarly, there is a statistically significant difference in the fieldwork performance of male and female students when academic performance is held constant ($p <$ .05). The sex factor also explains very little variation in the fieldwork performance of students (less than 1 percent).

Finally, a similar test is done on the relationship between fieldwork performance and the highest academic qualification reached before admission, the academic score held constant. A significant difference at $p < .001$ is obtained. Academic qualifications explain about 4 percent of the variation in fieldwork performance.

Multiple Regression — Combined Fieldwork Grade

Multiple regression is used to detect the relationship between the combined grades for fieldwork performance and the several demographic variables. The dependent variable is the combined fieldwork grade, and the independent variables include: academic score, social work experience, combined working experience (on an interval scale), mode of study, sex, and highest academic qualification prior to admission. Dummy variables $(0,1)$ are used for data measured on a nominal scale. A stepwise regression is performed. The regression equation is:

Y (Combined fieldwork grade) $= 0.610$ (X_1: academic score) $+ .026$ (X_2: social work related experience in years) $- 0.101$ (X_3: if male $= 1$, female $= 0$) $+ 0.101$ (X_4: minimum entrance qualification $= 1$, if not $= 0$) $+ 1.39$.

Each of the coefficients (X_1 through X_4) are significant at $p < .05$. The multiple $R^2 = 0.244$. The F-value of R is 48.69, significant at $p < .001$. That is, 24.4 percent of the variation in the fieldwork performance is explained by variation in academic score, sex, social work-related experience, and academic qualifications prior to admission.

Multiple Regression — Academic Score

The regression coefficient is a partial regression coefficient which refers to the variation of the dependent variable and a specific independent variable, when all the other independent variables in the equation are held constant. As shown in the equation just given, the value of the regression coefficient for academic score is the highest; the academic score appears to be the most powerful predictor of a student's fieldwork performance. What are the factors associated with a student's academic score? A regression equation is computed with academic score as a function of several demographic variables:

Y (Academic score) = 2.84 − 0.175 (X_1: if male = 1, if female = 0) − .04 (X_2: voluntary experience in years) − .121 (X_3: if sponsored = 1, if not = 0).

Each of the coefficients (X_1 through X_3) are significant at $p < .01$. The computed R^2 indicates that three demographic variables explain approximately 19 percent of the variation in the academic score of students. The F-value of R is 15.86, significant at $p < .001$.

Using the previously mentioned two equations, the academic score and the combined fieldwork grade are estimated for three hypothetical students with different demographic characteristics. Table 4 summarizes the results.

Table 4 shows that the female student passing in the High/Advance Level Examinations and admitted directly into the Social Work Course will have the best score in academic study; however, the female student with minimum academic qualifications, and with several years of social work-related working experience and voluntary service, will do best in the combined fieldwork grade and in the overall average grade. It seems that this category of student is the most ideal for social work training. The mature male student sponsored by the agency will be at a disadvantage in terms of academic score, probably because he has left formal school for a number of years. However, he does measurably better in his fieldwork performance. The new female graduate, who enters the Course without any working or voluntary experience, has the smallest difference between her fieldwork and academic score, and she can achieve a fairly high average grade.

SUMMARY AND CONCLUSION

The major findings of this study are summarized in the following.

Student Profiles

The full-time and part-time (day release) students differ significantly in their age, marital status, sex, highest academic qualification attained before admission, and length of working experience. The part-time student is likely to be male, older in his late 20s,

Table 4

Simulation of Combined Fieldwork Grade and Academic Score for

Three Hypothetical Cases

Hypothetical Case	Academic Score	Combined Fieldwork Grade	Average Grade
Female, minimum academic quali-fications, 2 years voluntary experience, 3 years social work-related experience, nonsponsored	2.76	3.25	3.01
Male, without minimum academic qualifications, 5 years of voluntary and social work-related experience, sponsored	2.344	2.85	2.6
Female, no voluntary or social work-related experience, high advanced level, non-sponsored	2.84	3.12	2.98

single, with minimum academic qualification, and with about 6 years of working experience. The full-time student is likely to be female, somewhat younger in her early 20s, single, with High/Advance Level qualification, and about 2 years of working experience.

Placement Profiles

The full-time and part-time (day release) student placements differ significantly in the nature of placement and agency, type of supervisor, number of supervisors, and the major methods of intervention used in the placement. The part-time student placement is likely to be of a block nature, in a voluntary agency, under a supervisor from the School of Social Work, and to use casework and/or groupwork as the major methods of intervention. The full-time student placement is likely to be of a concurrent nature, in a voluntary agency, under a supervisor from the School of Social Work, and also use casework and/or groupwork as the major methods of intervention, but to a lesser degree than in the part-time student's placement setting.

Fieldwork and Academic Performance by Modes

Significant differences between the mean value of combined fieldwork grade and academic score of the two modes of students have been identified. The part-time day release students are stronger in their fieldwork performance, while the full-time students are stronger in their academic score.

Demographic Variables and Fieldwork Performance

There are significant differences between the mean values of combined fieldwork grades of students for different categories of the following demographic variables: sex, highest academic qualification attained, and social work-related working experience. However, only a very small percentage of variation in the combined fieldwork grades (a maximum of less than four percent) can be explained by variations in these demographic variables.

Structural Variables and Fieldwork Performance

Statistically significant differences were computed in the mean value of grades given to student placements for different categories of the two structural variables, nature of fieldwork agencies, and major methods of intervention used. The relationship between fieldwork grades and two other structural variables (nature of placement and fieldwork supervisor) was not significant. However, variations in these structural variables explained a very small percentage of variation in fieldwork grades.

Factors Associated with Fieldwork Performance

This study found that academic score had the highest association with the student's fieldwork performance. Together with a student's social work-related experience, sex, and highest academic qualification attained, academic score was able to explain 24.4 percent of variation in a student's combined fieldwork grades. One can predict that a female student who passes the School Certificate Examinations, who has 3 years of social work-related experience and 2 years of voluntary work experience, and who is nonsponsored will achieve the best results in fieldwork and in overall performance. This type of student seems to be most "ideal" for social work training.

Implications for Social Work Education

This study describes the association of fieldwork and academic performance with the personal characteristics of students. The findings can serve as useful references for the selection of students in order to enhance the probability of better academic and fieldwork grade achievement. The quality of graduates, of course, needs improvement from the perspective of both the scholar and the practitioner. It is interesting to note, however, that raising the minimum academic qualifications required prior to admission may not be important. If the objective is to maximize overall grade average, younger female students, with some years of social work-related experience and with the minimum acceptable academic qualifications, would seem to be the best candidates for the Social Work Course.

The findings also provide rich information for fieldwork supervision. They direct the attention of supervisors to the differential ability of students in different categories. The comparatively weaker fieldwork performance of the full-time student, in spite of stronger academic ability, requires the supervisor to pay more attention to the student's learning about the attitudinal, feeling, and behavioural domains in fieldwork and student development in the areas of working relationship, practice skills, and work management. The comparatively weaker academic ability of the part-time (day release) student requires the supervisor to emphasize the understanding and application of theoretical concepts and knowledge in guiding professional practice.

The fieldwork supervisor also can use the results of this study to identify potentially weaker students in fieldwork performance; preparations can then be made to improve the effectiveness of fieldwork teaching. For example, single male students, without any social work experience and with higher academic qualification prior to admission but weak academic performance, will likely merit attention from the field work supervisor in fieldwork learning and performance.

Finally, the fieldwork supervisor can pay attention to the nature of the fieldwork placement. The relatively lower mean value of grades received in the Social Welfare Department and secondary setting may require the supervisor to be less strict in his/her grading in these placements. The lower mean value may reflect an assignment of a more difficult and complicated nature, and effort is necessary to normalize the average grade. The lower mean value of grades given in placements that emphasize casework and other micro-interventions may reflect the higher level of inter-personal skills demanded by the fieldwork supervisor. This may be necessary in settings that deal with the family and the personal problems of clients. The supervisor should be aware if a more intensive review of the student is being made with respect to inter-personal skills, sensitivity to feelings, and ability in problem-solving, all required for effective casework practice. There is greater possibility for the student's weaknesses to be revealed under such intense and close supervision.

CONCLUSION

It is hoped that the results of the research can be useful in the selection of students, the arrangement of fieldwork placements, and the ability of fieldwork supervisors to enhance their sensitivity to the effect of different demographic and structural variables on the students' performance in fieldwork. The specific findings of this research cannot be generalized to other social work courses. Cross-cultural comparison can be made when more findings using a similar research design are available in different cultures. It is hoped that this research will stimulate insights, innovations, and more in-depth investigation in this vital area of social work education.

NOTES

1. All part-time (day release) students admitted must be sponsored by their own agency, and sponsored students can be exempted from the academic qualifications required for admission.

2. The grading system for fieldwork and academic grades was slightly different during 1978-80 and 1980-82. The School has a conversion table which enables the grades obtained in these years to be made comparable. All the fieldwork grades and academic grades of students in this study are made comparable by this conversion table. They are represented by a 5-point scale of 0 through 5, for F through A grades, respectively.

3. The School Certificate Examinations are taken by middle school Form 5 graduates, while the High Level and Advance Level Examinations (higher academic qualifications) are taken by students in Matriculation classes as entrance requirements to 4-years and 3-years of University undergraduate study.

4. $F^1 = F(k-1) = 9.48$ at level of $p = .05$ and 13.28 at level of $p = .01$, where k is the number of groups.

REFERENCES

Blalock, H. M., Jr. (1979). *Social statistics*, (rev. 2nd ed.) McGraw-Hill International.

Butler, B., & Elliot, D. (1985). *Teaching and learning for practice*. Gower.

Ferguson, G. A. (1981). *Statistical analysis in psychology and education*, 5th ed. McGraw-Hill International.

Healey, J. E. (1984). *Statistic—a tool for social research*. Wadsworth.

Hong Kong Polytechnic (1986/87) *Prospectus*.

Merriam, T. W. (1972). *The relations between scholastic achievement in a school of social work and six factors in students' background*. AMS.

Raskin, M. (1982). Factors associated with student satisfaction in undergraduate social work field placement. *Arete*, 7(1), 44-53.

Sheafor, B. W., & Jenkins, L. E. (1982). *Quality field instruction in social work program development and maintenance*. New York: Longman.

Tsang, N. M. (1983). *Students' perspectives of field instruction in undergraduate social work education in Hong Kong*. Master's Thesis, Unpublished. Hong Kong University.

Wilson, S. J. (1981). *Field instruction techniques for supervisors*. New York: Free Press.

Student Satisfaction with Field Placement

Anne E. Fortune
Candace E. Feathers
Susan R. Rook
Rita M. Scrimenti
Paula Smollen
Barbara Stemerman
Eleanor L. Tucker

ABSTRACT. Students' perceptions of their field placements rarely are taken into account in the literature on field practicum and supervision. This survey of MSW students at a southern university examines factors associated with student satisfaction with field agency, field instructor, and field learning. The survey covers student and agency characteristics, learning goals and structure, supervision, and school-agency linkages. Students associated the quality of supervision and relevance of learning most highly with satisfaction in their placement experiences. Being treated as a professional in the agency, school-agency linkages, student characteristics, and amount of time engaged in specific social work activities were found not to be major factors in student satisfaction with field work.

INTRODUCTION

In social work education, field placement is a major vehicle for professional development. The supervised practicum is intended to help students translate theory into practice and learn practice techniques and skills in an agency, rather than academic, setting. While there is extensive literature on field placement, most of it is from

Reprinted with permission of the Council on Social Work Education, from the *Journal of Social Work Education*, Vol. 21, No. 3, Fall 1985, pages 92-104.

the point of view of educators and agency personnel. Little attention has been paid to the students' perceptions (Rosenblatt & Mayer, 1975). Student satisfaction, however, is an important element and, some argue, a necessary condition for appropriate learning (Raskin, 1982). This paper examines student satisfaction with field placement and factors contributing to satisfaction.

Satisfactory Field Placement

The study focused on five areas related to "satisfactory" field placement and learning experiences for social work students: student characteristics, agency characteristics and climate for learning, learning goals and structure for learning, supervisors and supervision, and the school-agency link.

Student characteristics—personality, experience, knowledge, and skills—all are important factors in planning field learning (Dea, Grist & Myli, 1982; Goldmeir, 1983), but little is known about how they influence the field experience for students. Experience is the only factor explored consistently: More experienced students generally have the same expectations and evaluation of supervision as do less experienced students, although they do report different supervisor behaviors (Heppner & Roehlke, 1984; Raskin, 1982; Rotholz & Werk, 1984; Worthington, 1984).

Agencies which provide field instruction for students have three major responsibilities: to make a commitment to the educational process at all levels within the agency, to provide a positive educational climate for the student, and to provide adequate learning experiences (Selig, 1982). Principles of adult learning suggest that the learner must be treated as a mature, self-directed person who learns by dealing with self-recognized problems and interests (Hersh, 1984). This implies that the agency should recognize the student as an adult, a "professional-to-be," through support and involvement in professional activities, while at the same time protecting its administrative functions and its clients.

Expectations also relate to "agency climate"—for specific learning goals and for professional behavior—and the structure of learning opportunities. Brennen says that the most pervasive learning problem for social work students in the field is not knowing what they should learn (Brennen, 1982). Two studies confirm that both students and supervisors consider it important to set clear learning goals and specific agenda for supervisory conferences (Peaper, 1984). In addition, students need structure and guidelines to help them reach their goals and to learn new counseling skills (Berg & Stone, 1980; Brennen, 1982; Cassidy, 1982).

Supervision and the competence of the field instructor are the crucial mediators between agency climate, clear goals and structure, and the students' actual experiences in the practicum. The instructor-student relationship often is the most intense, growth-producing (or growth-retarding), and memorable experience of a student's education.

However, supervisors and students often disagree on what supervisory behaviors are desirable. For example, in one study, they agreed that emotional support is important, but students valued autonomy more than did supervisors while supervisors valued cognitive structuring more than did students (Rotholz & Werk, 1984). In another study, behaviors which field instructors thought important to good supervision did not always correlate with what supervisees rated as "important" — counseling skills, supervisor competence, and satisfaction with supervision (Worthington & Roehlke, 1979). Rosenblatt and Mayer, focusing solely on students' views, found that students objected to four behaviors: (1) constrictive supervision, in which the student is not given enough autonomy; (2) amorphous supervision, in which the student gets too little direction; (3) unsupportive supervision, in which field instructors are cold, aloof, and sometimes hostile; and (4) therapeutic supervision, in which the supervisor ascribes deficiencies to the students' personality and conducts supervision as a form of therapy to work on the student's supposed personality deficiency (Rosenblatt & Mayer, 1975).

The school-agency relationship is a crucial and difficult link in the educational process. The school must prepare and support students for responsible fieldwork through academic coursework, must keep the agency and supervisor up-to-date on curriculum and expectations, and must maintain a sense of "morale" or reward for the agency's service to the school and profession by accepting student trainees (Gordon, 1982). Many schools designate a faculty role of Field Liaison to carry out the necessary facilitative, monitoring, and evaluative roles (Rosenblum & Raphael, 1983; Raphael & Rosenblum, in press). Although the field liaison usually is intended as a resource for students as well as agencies and instructors, students often do not use the liaison appropriately (Rosenblatt & Mayer, 1975).

The five areas — student characteristics, agency characteristics, learning goals and structure, supervision, and school-agency link — were selected for examination in relation to student satisfaction with fieldwork. Since the study was exploratory, no hypotheses were formulated. The basic research question was whether student perceptions of the five areas relate to their satisfaction, as the literature suggests they should.

RESEARCH PROCEDURES

The sample consisted of master's students attending Virginia Commonwealth University School of Social Work. Immediately after the 1984 spring vacation, approximately 300 students at the central Richmond campus and at five off-campus sites received questionnaires. Of the 155 who returned the questionnaire, 101 were in field practica; they are included in this study.

The survey instrument was a lengthy, self-report questionnaire about many aspects of students' experiences in graduate school. Three items served as dependent variables in this study: satisfaction with field agency, satisfaction with field instructor, and satisfaction with field learning. The survey used 7-point scales (7 = very satisfied) embedded in a section dealing with satisfaction with life at the university, including classes, faculty, and student body, as well as field.

In a separate section, there were 19 more specific statements about practicum. Students were asked to consider their field placements over the past six months (since the beginning of the school year) and respond using a scale anchored with 1 = strongly disagree and 7 = strongly agree (some items were reversed so that a higher score always is more positive). These statements, given in Table 1, were drawn from the literature on attributes of successful field learning and involved perceptions of the agency, supervisor, treatment of students, field liaison, and school-agency links.

Agency and school characteristics were derived from a series of multiple-choice questions. Students evaluated content, temporal structure of placement, and learning opportunities by the amount of time they spend in activities such as direct client contact, supervision, and paperwork. Finally, an open-ended question elicited factors that contributed positively and negatively to students' field experience.

At the university under study, first-year MSW placements were 14 hours a week and engaged students in a generic spectrum of individual, family and group treatment activities, administration, planning, community organization, and policy analysis. Students were assigned to agencies by the school. Second year placements were 20 hours a week, with students selecting agencies from approval lists organized by method (casework, groupwork, administration, or planning) and field-of-practice specializations (mental health, family and public social services, health, and justice). Most full-time students took placement concurrent with coursework, while part-time students had a choice of concurrent or block field placement.

RESULTS

Student Agency Characteristics

Of the 101 students in practica, 87 percent were female and 94 percent white. Age ranged from 21 to 55 years, with a mean of 29.3 years; 33 percent had BSW degrees while 60 percent had prior social work experience. Of the sample, 17 percent were from one of the off-campus sites and 24 percent were first-year students. Most (91 percent) were in, or planning to, specialize in "micro" methods (individual, family, and group treatment) in the second year; 51 percent were in, or planning to, specialize in mental health in their second year; 29 percent were in family; 14 percent in health; and 4 percent in justice.

Placements involved 67 percent of students in public agencies, 19 percent in private not-for-profit agencies, and the rest in sectarian, for-profit, and other agencies. In terms of client age groups, 40 percent of the students worked primarily with young adults and 26

Table 1

Average Item Scores and Factor Loadings For Satisfaction

and Perceptions of the Field Placement

	Item	Item Mean
Satisfaction with field agency	5.25.	
Satisfaction with field instructor	5.28	
Satisfaction with field learning	5.42	
		Factor Loading
Factor 1: School-Agency Liaison		
My contact with my field liaison has been satisfactory to meet my learning needs.	4.10	.918
If there are problems at my field placement, I am comfortable consulting with my field liaison.	4.01	.873
When I have problems in my placement I go to my field liaison.	3.05	.838
I am aware of the possible roles of my field liaison	4.68	.708
Communication between the school of social work and my agency is adequate.	3.99	.663

Factor 2: Professional Role

I have the same responsibilities as the professional
staff at my agency.   5.44   .859

I am included in all agency activities that professional
staff are expected to attend.   5.54   .825

I have the same privileges as the professional staff
at my agency   5.23   .779

I have been able to meet the expectations of my field
placement   6.13   .636

I agree with my agency's policies   5.00   .457

Factor 3: Relevant Learning

I enjoy working with the type of client I serve at my
agency   5.94   .840

My field work assignments this year have been relevant
to my learning goals.   5.64   .751

I was able to actively participate in designing my learning
experience.   5.54   .616

Factor 4: Supervision

My field instructor enjoys his/her role as "teacher"   5.79   .770

I have been encouraged to express new or different ideas in
my practicum setting.   5.30   .654

365

TABLE 1 (continued)

	Item	Factor Loading
Factor 5: Practicality		
My agency provides adequate physical facilities (i.e., desk, office, supplies) for students.	5.11	.727
My courses this year have been relevant to my field experience.	4.75	.536
Factor 6: Evaluation Anxiety		
There is conflict between the agency and the school's policies concerning expectations for students in the field.*	4.39	.716
Having a "pass/fail" system reduces my anxiety concerning my field placement.	5.74	.668

* Scoring is reversed (higher=less perceived conflict). On all other items, higher scores indicate more of the quality.

percent with middle-aged adults; the rest were split among children, adolescents, elderly, whole families, and a mixture of age groupings. Clients were unemployed or had very low incomes (32 percent); low income (30 percent); middle income (33 percent); and "other" (5 percent). No students reported having upper income clients.

The time spent by students in various social work activities was converted to proportions of total practicum hours. Direct contact with clients was the predominant activity for most students (mean = 39 percent of time), followed by planning for such contact (excluding supervisory time) which averaged 15 percent of time. Paperwork averaged 14 percent of time, supervision 11 percent, and staff meetings 10 percent. Two "macro" activities consumed relatively little time: The average time in internal administration, budgeting, and planning was 5 percent for all students. External-to-agency activities — outreach, education, publicity, interagency coordination, legislative planning and lobbying, etc. — averaged 4 percent of time. Finally, "other" activity, the nature of which was not specified, averaged 4 percent of practicum time.

Of eight social work activities listed on the questionnaire, most students engaged in five or six, with a range from four to all eight. Consistent with student interests, the two "macro" activities were least frequent.

Perceptions of Placement, Agency, Supervision, and School-Agency Links

On the average, students were "somewhat satisfied" with their field agency, field instructor, and learning in the field (means near 5.0 on 7-point scales; see Table 1). Between 71 (field instructor) and 81 percent (field learning) were satisfied (scores of 5 or higher), which compares favorably with Raskin's (1982) report that 65 to 75 percent of Virginia BSW seniors were satisfied with placement. Not surprisingly, the three satisfaction scales were related, with correlation coefficients between .53 (instructor satisfaction and learning satisfaction) and .70 (agency satisfaction and learning satisfaction).

Factor analysis with principle components analysis and varimax rotation reduced the number of survey items to manageable proportions. This yielded six factors with eigenvalues above 1.0. The factors were converted to scales for further data analysis by taking the average of each student's responses to the items in the factor.

Factor 1, School-Agency Liaison, consisted of five items about the faculty liaison and school-agency communication (see Table 1 for mean scores and factor loadings). These included the items receiving the lowest ratings on the questionnaire (see Table 1 for mean scores and factor loadings). These included the items receiving the lowest ratings on the questionnaire (scale mean = 3.9).

Factor 2 included five items related to students being treated as professional staff, agreeing with agency policy, and meeting agency expectations. This factor, Professional Role, appeared to reflect the professional-to-be treatment that is considered appropriate for adult learners. The scale mean was 5.5; students agreed most strongly with the item on meeting agency expectations.

Factor 3, Relevant Learning, included three items on the student participating in designing practicum experiences, meeting individual learning goals, and enjoying work with the type of clients served by the agency. This factor appears to measure a second aspect of treatment as an adult learner — involvement in setting goals and making learning relevant to interests. Students generally agreed with items on the scale (mean = 5.7).

The fourth factor included two items, the instructor enjoying a teacher role and the student being encouraged to express new ideas. While these do not represent a full array of supervisory behaviors, they were the only items directly relevant to supervision; hence, the factor was called Supervision. Average scores were moderately high (mean = 5.5). Factor 5, including adequacy of physical facilities and relevancy of course to field, appeared to reflect an important practical element to performing well in the field and thus was called Practicality. It was the second-lowest-rated factor (mean = 4.9).

The final factor, Evaluation Anxiety, included anxiety in a "pass/fail" grading system (a policy introduced that year for field courses only) and conflict between school and agency over expectations for students. While students agreed that pass/fail reduced anxiety, they were relatively likely to perceive conflict between school and agency expectations for students. Since the items loaded in different directions, scores on pass-fail anxiety were reversed to compose the scale. Thus, high Evaluation Anxiety scores indicate *less* perceived conflict and higher anxiety. This is a discrepancy from what might be considered "normal" (nondiscrepant situations—high conflict combined with high anxiety and low conflict combined with low anxiety—yield low scores on the Evaluation Anxiety Scale). The mean was 3.2.

Factors Related to Satisfaction with Field Placement

The survey examined relations between field satisfaction and student demographic characteristics, agency characteristics, and student perceptions of practicum, using, as appropriate, students' t, ANOVA, Pearson's correlation, and partial correlation (Bartlett, 1947). In the partial correlation, analyses were conducted for "micro" students only to control for students' "micro-macro" specialization, since there were too few "macro" students for similar analyses. Other variables selected as controls were those most highly correlated with the independent variable and with each other. Through such statistical controls, one can examine the relationship between two variables without the influence of other variables.

Student Characteristics. Most of the student characteristics did not relate to satisfaction with field placement: age, gender, marital status, length of previous social work experience, undergraduate degree (BSW or non-BSW), year in graduate school, status as full- or part-time student and campus attended (central versus off-campus site). Satisfaction did vary somewhat by students' choice of method and substantive specialization. Those in, or planning to be in, "macro" methods (administration and planning) were more satisfied with field learning than those in "micro" methods (mean = 6.3 to 5.3), but there were no differences in satisfaction with the field instructor or field agency. Students in health were less satisfied with their instructors (mean = 4.3) than those in family (5.7) or justice (6.8); they also were slightly less satisfied with other aspects of fieldwork. Since students were placed in agencies based on specialization, this may be a characteristic of the setting—usually large, interdisciplinary medical facilities which may devalue the social worker—rather than a difference among students or quality of field instructors.

Placement Characteristics. Auspices of the agency (public versus private and sectarian agencies) and age group of clients had no impact on satisfaction. Client income related to some measures of satisfaction. Students working with unemployed or very low income clients were least satisfied with the agency (mean = 4.7), while those serving middle income clients were most satisfied with the agency (5.7). Similarly, those serving very low income clients were less satisfied with field learning (mean = 4.8) than those working with middle income clients (5.9). However, when the client income scale was treated as interval-level data (omitting "other") and controlled for related factors, the partial correlations indicated little association (see Table 3).

Table 2 gives the correlations for the temporal structure of practicum, noting proportions of time in social work activities and satisfaction. The scatterplots for each pair of time-satisfaction variables were examined for curvilinear or other nonlinear patterns. For example, it was possible that satisfaction increased with amount of client contact until a student was overwhelmed, could not cope, and thus became dissatisfied. However, since no nonlinear patterns were evident, linear analysis was used.

Client contact, the predominant activity for most students, related negatively to agency satisfaction; those with more client contact were less satisfied ($r = .21$). However, when related variables were controlled by partial correlation for "micro" students, there was no relationship (partial $r = -.07$; see Table 3), nor did the amount of client contact relate to satisfaction with field instructor or field learning.

Supervision time, expected to contribute to satisfaction, did not relate to it directly, although there were some moderate relationships when other activities were controlled (partial r for satisfaction with the field instructor = .21; for field learning = .20).

There was direct, relatively high correlation between time spent in internal administrative activities and all three satisfactions scales (Table 2). However, removing the influence of other factors reduced most of the correlations considerably. Similarly, time spent in external-agency activities had modest direct relationships to satisfaction (Table 2), but these relationships disappeared when other activities were controlled (Table 3). None of the remaining activities — planning for client contact, attending meetings, paperwork, or "other" — correlated highly with satisfaction with agency, in-

Table 2

Relationship of Time in Social Work Activities and Student

Perceptions of Placement to Field Satisfaction:

Simple Correlation Coefficients

	SATISFACTION WITH:		
	Field	Field	Field
TIME SPENT IN:	Agency	Instructor	Learning
Client contact	−.210°	−.155	−.084
Planning for client contact	−.105	−.025	−.075
Supervision	.069	.165	.124
Staff meetings	.033	.006	.129
Administration and planning	.300°	.251°	.237°
Community organization, outreach, publicity	.189⁺	.192⁺	.202°
Paperwork	.009	.006	−.084
Other	−.176⁺	.029	−.112
TOTAL NO. SOCIAL WORK ACTIVITIES	.036	.196°	−.084
STUDENT PERCEPTIONS OF FIELD:			
Liaison Scale	.103	.100	.083
Professional Role Scale	.457°	.362°	.322°
Relevant Learning Scale	.532°	.390°	.557°
Supervision Scale	.496°	.648°	.414°
Practicality Scale	.197⁺	.010	.241°
Evaluation Anxiety Scale	.141	.131	.200°

°Probability less than or equal to .05.

⁺Probability between .051 and .10

structor, or learning, nor did total number of activities relate to satisfaction when other variables were controlled.

Perceptions of Agency, Supervision, and School-Agency Links

Table 2 also gives the correlations between satisfaction and the six scales derived from the factor analysis. The Relevant Learning Scale related directly to all three measures of satisfaction. When controlled, it retained moderate correlations for two measures: Stu-

TABLE 3. Partial correlations of selected variables with field satisfaction (micro students only).

PARTIAL CORRELATION COEFFICIENTS
SATISFACTION WITH:

INDEPENDENT VARIABLE	Field Agency	Field Instructor	Field Learning	CONTROLLING FOR:
Client Income	.156	.099	.176	Time In: administration relevant learning; eval. anxiety
Client contact	-.072	-.112	.163	Time In: agency; practicality
Planning for client	-.099	-.007	-.111	Time In: client contact, contact supervision, staff meetings
Supervision	.033	.208[+]	.199[+]	Time In: client agency; staff
Staff meetings	.042	-.029	.126	Time In: client contact, supervision, administration

372

INDEPENDENT VARIABLE	Field Agency	Field Instructor	Field Learning	CONTROLLING FOR:
Administration and Planning	.180	.233°	-.041	Time In: client contact, supervision, external-agency; liaison
Community Org. outreach, publicity	-.072	.037	-.060	Time In: client contact, administration, paperwork, practicality; eval. anx.
Paperwork	.048	.126	.026	Time In: administration, external-agency; social work activities
Other	-.088	-.021	-.065	Time In: client total social work activities
Total no. social	-.060	.194+	-.152	Time In: paperwork; prof. anxiety; supervision
Liaison Scale	.018	.061	-.041	Time In: administration; supervision scale
Professional Role Scale	.129	-.127	-.089	Rel. learning; supervision scale; practicality; social work activities

373

TABLE 3 (continued)

INDEPENDENT VARIABLE	Field Agency	Field Instructor	Field Learning	CONTROLLING FOR:
Relevant Learning Scale	.387°	.144	.385°	Time In: admin.; prof. role; supervision scale
Supervision Scale	.245°	.596°	.189⁺	Prof. role; rel. learning; total social work activities
Practicality Scale	-.095	-.240°	.040	Prof. role; rel. learning; total social work activities
Evaluation Anxiety Scale	.075	.072	.145	Time In: admin., external- agency; liaison; client age

°Probability less than or equal to .05

⁺Probability between .051 and .10.

dents associated more relevant experiences with greater satisfaction with the agency and with learning. On the other hand, other dimensions of the adult-learner role, being treated as a professional (the Professional Role Scale), were not associated with satisfaction after related factors were controlled, despite direct correlations. Most of the original, direct relationship was due to associations of Professional Role Scale with the Relevant Learning and Supervision Scales.

More positive perceptions on the Supervision Scale were associated with greater satisfaction with the agency and with the field instructor, both directly and when controlled. However, a direct relationship with learning satisfaction dropped when the effects of other variables were taken into account. Again, the associations with Professional Role and Relevant Learning reduced the relationships. However, the magnitude of the correlation between the Supervision Scale and satisfaction with the field instructor was relatively unaffected by adding the two dimensions of being treated as an adult learner.

The Practicality Scale — adequate physical facilities and relevant coursework — demonstrated an interesting reversal when controlled. There was no direct relationship with field instructor but, after adding control, the students associated greater perception of adequate facilities and courses with *dissatisfaction* with the field instructor. That is, other factors — Professional Role, Relevant Learning, and the total number of social work activities — suppressed a negative relationship between practicality and satisfaction with the field instructor. On the other hand, uncontrolled positive associations with agency and learning satisfaction disappeared when the effects of the same three variables were taken into account.

SUMMARY

Satisfaction with the agency correlated only moderately with the Relevant Learning and Supervision Scales, while satisfaction with field learning related only to the Relevant Learning Scale and to being in the "macro" specialization. However, students associated satisfaction with field instructor with several factors: more positive scores on the Supervision and Practicality Scales, more time in administrative activities, and students being in substantive specializations other than health.

Many of the relationships evident with simple correlation disappeared or dropped substantially when other variables were taken into account (for example, satisfaction and client income or being treated as professionals). In general, the most powerful variables were the Relevant Learning Scale and the Supervision Scale; these items retained their relationships to satisfaction but reduced the relation of other variables to satisfaction when used as controls.

DISCUSSION

The two factors most highly correlated with satisfaction with field work were the Relevant Learning Scale and the Supervision Scale. Social work educators often assert but seldom test the importance of relevant learning and student involvement in designing practicum experiences. This survey provides some confirmation that it is, indeed, a major factor, at least in student satisfaction with the agency and with learning. Interestingly, Relevant Learning did not relate to satisfaction with instructor when other variables, including the Supervision Scale, were controlled, even though the supervisor presumably influences (or allows) the student to set goals and assigns cases or tasks.

The Supervision Scale, not surprisingly, was the single factor associated most highly with satisfaction with the supervisor. This scale measured student perception of whether the instructor enjoyed teaching and encouraged ideas. Thus, it is an indirect measure of quality and perhaps of the appropriate "equality" documented by Nelsen (1974). The only other measure related to supervision, the *amount* of time spent in supervision, did not relate directly to satisfaction, but did have a modest correlation when time in other activities was controlled. Thus, more "quality" supervision relates somewhat to student satisfaction with instructor, but time devoted to supervision alone does not measure quality supervision adequately; it may even detract from other relevant activities, such as administration. However, student responses to the open-ended question about important positive and negative contributors to their field experience confirmed the general importance of the instructor. The most frequent positive factor was the field instructor, while poor field instruction was the second-most mentioned negative factor.

The Supervision Scale also correlated with satisfaction with field agency and with learning. These correlations are lower than that of Relevant Learning, which suggests that "quality" supervision has a direct bearing on agency and learning satisfaction but is not as important as being involved in designing practica, enjoying clients, and engaging in goal-relevant experiences. Ironically, students rarely made comments on the open-ended question that could be interpreted as "relevant learning." Their spontaneous remarks gave the supervisor more importance than suggested by these data.

A similar anomaly is that students most often mentioned respect and support of agency staff and independence and responsibility accorded to them by the agency. These aspects were measured by the Professional Role Scale, but Professional Role did not relate to satisfaction when the influence of other factors, such as relevant learning and supervision, were removed. Thus, it appears that students spontaneously focus on relationship aspects of fieldwork — good interpersonal and professional relations with supervisor and agency staff — when in actuality the conceptualization and relevance of learning is more important to their own satisfaction. Such an interpretation is consistent with Rotholz and Werk's (1984) finding that students undervalued cognitive structuring and overvalued autonomy.

In terms of the five areas investigated, neither student demographic characteristics nor the Evaluation Anxiety Scale related to satisfaction with practica. However, some career-choice factors did relate to satisfaction: "macro" students were more satisfied with field learning than "micro" students. Those choosing a health specialization were less satisfied with their field instructor than students in other specializations. The number of "macro" or health students was too small to explore the reasons for this further. However, with the possible exception of experience, no theoretical rationale or previous research suggest a relationship between student characteristics and satisfaction (Heppner & Roehlke, 1984; Raskin, 1982; Rotholz & Werk, 1984). Especially if, as the literature suggests, the field instructor takes individual differences into account when planning students' learning experiences (Goldmeir, 1983).

Of the relatively objective agency characteristics, auspices and age group of clients did not relate to student satisfaction. Client income did relate directly to agency satisfaction, but not when other factors were controlled. It is, however, sobering to realize that students with higher income clients were more likely to perceive their learning as relevant.

Agency climate and the structure of learning were measured, in part, by student perceptions on three scales: Professional Roles, Relevant Learning, and Practicality. As mentioned, Relevant Learning was a fairly powerful predictor of satisfaction with agency and learning. It also was a major factor in explaining relationships between satisfaction and other variables. However, Professional Role, or treatment as a professional, a dimension of treatment as an adult learner, did not relate to satisfaction when controlled. The direct relationship suggests this factor may indicate other, more relevant, factors (such as relevancy of learning or quality of supervision), but itself is not the crucial factor the literature suggests.

The Practicality Scale — adequacy of physical facilities for students and relevancy of courses to fieldwork — also was unrelated to satisfaction with agency and learning when controlled. Its direct relationship, before applying statistical controls, suggests that physical facilities could be a concrete, easy-to-observe indicator for the more important abstract concepts involved in Professional Role and Relevant Learning. On the other hand, the negative partial correlation of Practicality with instructor satisfaction is puzzling; perhaps students relied more on the instructor and were less willing to be critical when facilities were inadequate.

The temporal structure of practicum — time devoted to various social work activities — generally did not relate to student satisfaction or related in unexpected ways. When controlled, more time in administration related to greater satisfaction with supervisor, perhaps an indicator of the supervisor's role in involving students in agency activity. Supervision time was expected to relate to satisfaction but, as discussed, did so marginally at most when quality and other factors were controlled. Similarly, students almost universally request more time with clients, but this also did not relate to satisfaction. Time spent on paperwork, which students usually consider excessive, did not relate to dissatisfaction (Raskin, 1982).

The total number of activities in which a student engaged also did not relate to satisfaction. Based on Raskin's (1982) findings that new learning opportunities were a major predictor of BSW student field satisfaction, this factor was intended to measure breadth of opportunity, along with time-in-activities. In retrospect, the factor appears inadequate to capture the scope and variety of experiences important to satisfactory field placement. On the open-ended questions, students identified "variety of clients" and "breadth of opportunities" as the second-most-mentioned positive contributors to field experience. In fact, they often cited lack of particular opportunities as a negative factor. Since student responses generally were idiosyncratic—where one desired more family contact or crisis counseling, another wanted more individual, group, or long-term treatment, for example—it may be difficult to measure "variety" and "breadth" in terms that would have common meaning to all students. This again underscores the importance of Relevant Learning and especially of student involvement in designing practica and participating in assignments relevant to individual interests and goals.

The importance of the Supervision Scale to satisfaction was discussed earlier. The questionnaire did not include many items about supervisors, so the survey cannot determine what supervisory behaviors or characteristics contribute to more positive student perceptions on the Supervision Scale. For example, previous studies suggest that specific supervisor behaviors and student opportunities to observe treatment interactions contribute to student satisfaction (Barth & Gambrill, 1984; Raskin, 1982; Richards, 1984; Rotholz & Werk, 1984; Worthington & Roehlke, 1979), but this study did not measure any of these areas. However, it is clear from this study that the supervisor is a key link to student satisfaction with practicum, although not the sole one.

Despite the importance placed on the school-agency linkage in the literature, the items which measured it in this study had little bearing on student satisfaction. The key indicator, the School-Agency Liaison Scale, was unrelated totally to satisfaction. The items on that scale were among those with which students expressed the least agreement. On the open-ended question, complaints about the liaison were the single largest category of negative factors in the field experience.

Consequently, it is not clear if the students perceived poor agency-school linkage but were able to divorce that from their evaluations of the field experience, or whether the school-agency link is indeed irrelevant to student experience. Rosenblatt and Mayer (1975) also found that students generally were unconcerned with the liaison. However, even if such linkages are irrelevant for students, they remain important to the agency and to integrating the curriculum, which this study did not address.

Major limitations of this study should be noted: the large number of variables examined and using a sample drawn from only one school of social work. Further, all measures were student perception, which potentially is distorted and subject to a "halo" effect. For example, one cannot be certain that there were actual differences in "quality" of supervision or if students who were more satisfied generalized their satisfaction to their supervisors, regardless of what the supervisor did.

For similar reasons, the data cannot address whether students actually learned or performed competently in field; satisfaction with field learning is not necessarily the same as competent professional conduct. However, as mentioned, satisfaction is assumed to facilitate learning. Clearly, the most important factors in student satisfaction with fieldwork are relevant learning experiences and supervision.

REFERENCES

Barth, R. P., & Gambrill. (Ed.). (1984). Learning to interview: The quality of training opportunities. *Clinical Supervisor, 2*, 3-14.

Bartlett, M. S. (1947). The use of transformations, *Biometrics, 3*, 39-52.

Berg, K., & Stone, G. (1980). Effects of conceptual level and supervision structure on counselor skill development. *Journal of Counseling Psychology, 27*, 500-509.

Brennen, E. C. (1982). Evaluation of field teaching and learning. In B. W. Sheafor & L. E. Jenkins (Eds.), *Quality field instruction in social work* (pp. 76-97). New York: Longman.

Cassidy, H. (1982). Structuring field learning experiences. In B. W. Sheafor & L. E. Jenkins (Eds.), *Quality field instruction in social work* (pp. 198-214). New York: Longman.

Dea, K. L., Grist, M., & Myli, R. C. (1982). Learning tasks for practice competence. In B. W. Sheafor & L. E. Jenkins (Eds.), *Quality field instruction in social work* (pp. 237-261). New York: Longman.

Goldmeier, J. (1983). Educational assessment, teaching style and case assignment in clinical field work. *Arete, 8*, 1-12.

Gordon, M. S. (1982). Responsibilities of the school: Maintenance of the field program. In B. W. Sheafor & L. E. Jenkins, (Eds.), *Quality field instruction in social work* (pp. 116-135). New York: Longman.

Heppner, P. P., & Roehlke, H. J. (1984). Differences among supervisees at different levels of training: Implications for a developmental model of supervision. *Journal of Counseling Psychology, 31*, 76-90.

Hersh, A. (1984). Teaching the theory and practice of student supervision: A short-term model based on principles of adult education. *Clinical Supervisor, 2*, 29-44.

Nelson, J. C. (1974). Relationship communication in early fieldwork conferences. *Social Casework, 55*, 237-243.

Peaper, R. E. (1984). An analysis of student perceptions of the supervisory conference and student developed agendas for that conference. *Clinical Supervisor, 2*, 55-69.

Raphael, F. B., & Rosenblum, A. F. (in press). An operational guide to the faculty field liaison role. *Social Casework*.

Raskin, M. S. (1982). Factors associated with student satisfaction in undergraduate social work field placements. *Arete, 7*(1) 44-54.

Richards, L. D. (1984). Verbal interaction and supervisor perception in counselor supervision. *Journal of Counseling Psychology, 31*, 262-265.

Rosenblatt, A., & Mayer, J. E. (1975). Objectionable supervisory styles: Students' views. *Social Work, 20*, 184-189.

Rosenblum, A. F., & Raphael, R. B. (1983). The role and function of the faculty field liaison. *Journal of Education for Social Work, 19*(1), 67-73.

Rotholz, T., & Werk, A. (1984). Student supervision: An educational process. *Clinical Supervisor, 2*, 15-27.

Selig, A. L. (1982). Responsibilities of the field instruction agency. In B. W. Sheafor & L. E. Jenkins (Eds.), *Quality field instruction in social work* (pp. 136-143), New York: Longman.

Worthington, E. L., Jr. (1984). Empirical investigation of supervision of counselors as they gain experience. *Journal of Counseling Psychology, 31*, 63-75.

Worthington, E. L., Jr. & Roehlke, H. J. (1979). Effective supervision as perceived by beginning counselors-in-training. *Journal of Counseling Psychology, 26*, 64-73.

Bibliography

Abbott, E. (1931). *Social welfare and professional education*. Chicago: University of Chicago Press.

Ackerman, N. (1954). Systems concepts in casework theory and practice. *Social Casework, 50*, 74-82.

American Association of Schools of Social Work. (1943). *Accreditation Manual*. New York: Author.

Anderson, W.A. (February 1979). *Education for employment: BSW graduates' work experience and the undergraduate curriculum*. Paper presented at the annual program meeting, Council on Social Work Education. Boston.

Atwood, J.D. (1986). Self-awareness in supervision. *The Clinical Supervisor, 4*(3), 79-96.

Austin, L.N. (1979). Basic principles of supervision. In C.E. Munson (Ed.). *Social work supervision classic statements and critical issues* (pp. 56-69). New York: Free Press.

Baer, B.L., & Federico, R. (1978). *Educating the baccalaureate social worker, report of the undergraduate social work curriculum development project*. Cambridge: Ballinger.

Balgopal, P.R. (1974). Sensitivity training: A conceptual model for social work education. *Journal of Education for Social Work, 10*(2), 5-11.

Barnat, M.R. (1973). Student reactions to the first supervisory year: Relationship and resolutions. *Journal of Education for Social Work, 9*(3), 3-8.

Barrett, M. & McKelvey, J. (1980). Stresses and strains of the child care worker: Typologies for assessment. *Child Welfare, 59*, 277-285.

Barth, R.P., & Gambrill, (Ed.). (1984). Learning to interview: The quality of training opportunities. *The Clinical Supervisor, 2*, 3-14.

Bartlett, H. (1950). Responsibilities of social work practitioners

© 1989 by The Haworth Press, Inc. All rights reserved.

and educators toward building a strong profession. *Social Service Review*, *24*, 379-391.

Bartlett, M.S. (1947). The use of transformations, *Biometrics*, *3*, 39-52.

Beck, D.L. (1976). A counseling program for social work students. *Social Casework*, *57*, 651-655.

Behling, J., Curtis, C., & Foster, S.A. (1982). Impact of sex-role combinations on student performance in field instruction. *Journal of Social Work Education*, *18*(2), 93-97.

Berengarten, S. (1962). Educational issues in field instruction in social work. In *Field Instruction and Casework*. New York: The Jewish Guild for the Blind.

Berengarten, S. (1961). Educational issues in field instruction in social work. *Social Service Review*, *XXXV*(3).

Berengarten, S. (1957). Identifying learning patterns of individual students: An exploratory study. *Social Service Review*, *31*, 407-417.

Berg, K., & Stone, G. (1980). Effects of conceptual level and supervision structure on counselor skill development. *Journal of Counseling Psychology*, *27*, 500-509.

Beverly, D., & Dickman, J. (1981). A systems model: The Virginia state manpower study. *Journal of Education for Social Work*, *17*(2), 106-112.

Billingsley, A. (1964). Bureaucratic and professional orientation patterns in social casework. *Social Service Review 38*, 400-407.

Bisno, H. (1959). *The place of the undergraduate curriculum in social work education*. New York: Council on Social Work Education.

Black, H.C. (Ed.). (1979). *Black's law dictionary*. (5th ed.) St. Paul: West Publishing.

Blackey, E. (1967). *Field learning and teaching*. New Orleans: Tulane University School of Social Work.

Blalock, H.M., Jr., (1979). *Social statistics*, (rev. 2nd ed.) McGraw-Hill International.

Bloom, T. (1963). Untitled Paper, In *The future for field instruction: Agency-School commitment and communication*. New York: Council on Social Work Education.

Boehm, W. (1959). *Objectives of the social work curriculum of the future*. New York: Council on Social Work Education.

Boyd, L.H., Jr., Hylton, J., & Price, S. (1978). Computers in social work practice: A review. *Social Work, 23,* 368-371.

Brackett, J. (1983). Training for work. In C. E. Munson, (Ed.). *Social work supervision, classic statements and critical issues* (pp. 6-17). New York: Free Press.

Brager, G., & Michael, J.A. (1969). The sex distribution in social work: Causes and consequences. *Social Casework, 50,* 595-601.

Bregman, H., & Salasin, J. (1977). *The Delphi technique: Analysis of responses to a survey of children's mental health services development*. Mitre Corp. McLean, Virginia.

Brennen, E.C. (1982). Evaluation of field teaching and learning. In B.W. Sheafor & L.E. Jenkins (Eds.), *Quality field instruction in social work* (pp. 76-97). New York: Longman.

Brieland, D. (1959). *An experimental study of the selection of adoptive parents at intake*. New York: Child Welfare League of America.

Broverman, I., Vogel, S.R., Broverman, D.M., Clarkson, F.E., & Rosenkranz, P.S. (1972). Sex-role stereotypes: A current appraisal. *Journal of Social Issues, 28,* 59-78.

Brown, E.G. (1970). Selection of adoptive parents — A videotape study, PhD Thesis, School of Social Service Administration, University of Chicago.

Brownstein, C. (1981). Practicum issues: A placement planning model. *Journal of Education for Social Work, 17*(3), 52-58.

Bruck, M. (1963). The relationships between student anxiety, self-awareness, and self-concept and student competence in casework. *Social Casework, 44,* 125-131.

Butler, B., & Elliott, D. (1985). *Teaching and learning for practice*. Gower.

Cassidy, H. (1982). Structuring field learning experiences. In B.W. Sheafor & L.E. Jenkins (Eds.). *Quality field instruction in social work* (pp. 198-214). New York: Longman.

Child Welfare League of America. (1959). *Child welfare league of America standards for foster family care services*. New York: Author.

Clincht, B.M., Belenky, M.F., Goldberger, N., & Tarule, J.M.

(1985). Connected education for women. *Journal of Education*, *167*(3).

Closing the gap in social work manpower. (1965). Washington, D.C.: Government Printing Office.

Coombs, R.H., & Fawzy, F.I. (1982). The effect of marital status on stress in medical school. *American Journal of Psychiatry*, *139*, 1490-1493.

Corwin, R.G. (1961). The professional employee: A study of conflict in nursing roles. *American Journal of Sociology*, *66*, 604-615.

Council on Social Work Education. (1984). *Accreditation standards and procedures for master's degree and baccalaureate degree programs in social work education*. New York: Author.

Council on Social Work Education. (1984). *Handbook of accreditation standards and procedures*. New York: Author.

Council on Social Work Education. (1982). *Curriculum Policy Statement*. New York: Author.

Council on Social Work Education (1982). Curriculum policy for master's degree and baccalaureate degree programs in social work education. *Social Work Education Reporter*, September, 5-12.

Council on Social Work Education. (1981). *Schools of social work with accredited master's degree programs*. New York: Author.

Council on Social Work Education. (1974). *Accreditation manual*. New York: Author.

Council on Social Work Education. (1971). *Manual of accrediting standards for graduate professional schools of social work*. New York: Author.

Council on Social Work Education. (1971). *Manual of accrediting standards*. New York: Author.

Council on Social Work Education. (1969). *Curriculum Policy Statement*. New York: Author.

Council on Social Work Education. (1953). *Curriculum Policy Statement*. New York: Author.

Cronback, I. (1951). Coefficient alpha and the internal structure of tests. *Psychometrika*, *16*, 297-334.

Cronian, D.L. (March, 1977). *A contractual approach to practicum learning*. Paper presented at the Council on Social Work Education Annual Program Meeting, Phoenix, Arizona.

Cunningham, M. (1982). Admission variables and the prediction of success in an undergraduate field work program. *Journal of Social Work Education*, *18*(2), 27-33.

Dailey, D. (1970). The validity of admissions predictions: Implications for social work education. *Journal of Social Work Education*, *10*(2), 12-19.

Daley, M. (1979). Burnout: Smoldering problem in protective services. *Social Work*, *24*, 375-379.

Dalkey, N., & Helmer, O. (1963). An experimental application of the Delphi method to the use of experts. *Management Science*, (3).

Dana, B.S., & Sikkema, M. (1964). Field instruction, fact and fancy. In *Education for social work, proceedings, twelfth annual program meeting*. New York: Council on Social Work Education.

Davenport, J.J. (1984). The Saturday center: A training institution in process. *Clinical Social Work Journal*, *12*, 347-355.

Davidson, J.H., & Trueblood, R. (1970). Accounting for decision-making. In A. Rappoport (Ed.). *Information for decision-making: Quantitative and behavioral dimensions*. New Jersey: Prentice-Hall.

Davis-Sacks, M.L., Jayaratne, S., & Wickess (1985). A comparison of the effects of social support on the incidence of burnout. *Social Work*, *3*, 240-244.

Dea, K.L., Grist, M., & Myli, R.C. (1982). Learning tasks for practice competence. In B.W. Sheafor & L.E. Jenkins (Eds.). *Quality field instruction in social work* (pp. 237-261). New York: Longman.

Dewey, J. (1938). *Experience in education*. New York: MacMillan.

Diangson, P., Kravetz, D.E., & Lipton, J. (1975). Sex role stereotyping and social work education. *Journal of Education for Social Work*, *11*(3), 44-49.

Dolgoff, R. (1974). *Report to the task force on social work practice and education*. New York: Council on Social Work Education.

Dorland's Illustrated Medical Dictionary. (1974). (25th ed.) Philadelphia: Saunders.

Engle, P.R. (1977). *Supervision of the baccalaureate social worker*. New York: University of Syracuse School of Social Work.

Faherty, V. (1979). Continuing social work education: Results of a Delphi survey. *Journal of Education for Social Work, 15*, 12-19.

Faver, C., & Fox, M.F. (1984). Publication of articles by male and female social work educators. *Social Work, 29*, 488.

Fellin, P.A. (1982). Responsibilities of the school: Administrative support of field instruction. In B.W. Sheafor & L.E. Jenkins (Eds.), *Quality field instruction in Social Work* (pp. 101-115). New York: Longman.

Ferguson, G.A. (1981). *Statistical analysis in psychology and education*, 5th ed. McGraw-Hill International.

Finestone, S. (1967). Selected features of professional field instruction. *Journal of Education for Social Work, 3*(2), 14-26.

Fletcher, H.J. (1981). Reporting explained variance. *Journal of Research in Science Teaching, 18*, 1-7.

Fortune, A.E., Feathers, C., Rook, S.R., Scrimenti, R.M., Smollen, P., Stemerman, B., & Tucker, E.L. (1985). Student satisfaction with field placement. *Journal of Social Work Education, 21*(3), 92-104.

Freudenberger, H. (1977). Burnout: Occupational hazard of the child care worker. *Child Care Quarterly, 6*, 90-99.

Frumkin, M.L. (1980). Social work education and the professional commitment fallacy: A practical guide to field-school relations. *Journal of Education for Social Work, 16* (2), 91-99.

Gaensbauer, T.J., & Mizner, G.L. (1980). Developmental stresses in medical education. *Psychiatry, 43*, 60-70.

Galambos, E.C., & Wiggins, X.R. (1970). *After graduation: Experiences of college graduates in locating and working in social welfare positions*. Georgia: Southern Regional Education Board. Atlanta.

Gartner, A. (1976). *The preparation of human service professionals*. New York: Human Sciences Press.

George, A. (1982). A history of social work field instruction. In B.W. Sheafor & L.E. Jenkins (Eds.), *Quality field instruction in social work* (pp. 37-47). New York: Longman.

Gilpin, R. (1963). *Theory and practice as a single reality*. Chapel Hill: University of North Carolina Press.

Gitterman, A. (1975). The faculty field instructor in social work education. In *Dynamics of field instruction: Learning through doing*. New York: Council on Social Work Education.

Gitterman, A. (1972). The field instructor in social work education: A study of role strain. Doctoral Dissertation, Columbia University, Teachers College.

Gizyniki, M. (1978). Self awareness of the supervisor in supervision. *Clinical Social Work Journal, 6*(3).

Glicken, V. (1980). Enhancing work for professional social workers. *Administration in Social Work, 4*(3), 61-74.

Goldmeier, J. (1983). Educational assessment, teaching style and case assignment in clinical field work. *Arete, 8,* 1-12.

Good, C.V. (Ed.). (1973). *Dictionary of education*. New York: McGraw-Hill.

Gordon, W.E., & Gordon, M.S. (1982). The role of frames of reference in field instruction. In B.W. Sheafor & L.E. Jenkins (Eds.), *Quality field instruction in social work* (pp. 21-36). New York: Longman.

Gordon, M.S. (1982). Responsibilities of the school: Maintenance of the field program. In B.W. Sheafor & L.E. Jenkins, (Eds.). *Quality field instruction in social work* (pp. 116-135). New York: Longman.

Gordon, W.E., & Schutz, M.L. (1969). *Final report: Field instruction research project*. St. Louis: George Warren Brown School of Social Work, Washington University.

Grosser, C.F. (1976). *New directions in community organization: From enabling to advocacy*. New York: Praeger.

Hackman, J.R., & Lawler, E.E. (1971). Employee reactions to job satisfaction characteristics. *Journal of Applied Psychology, 55,* 259-286.

Hamilton, G. (1954). Self-awareness in professional education. *Social Casework, 35,* 371-379.

Harris, L.H., & Lucas, M. (1976). Sex role stereotyping. *Social Work, 21,* 390-395.

Harrison, D.W. (1980). Role strain and burnout in protective service workers. *Social Service Review, 54,* 31-44.

Haynes, K. (1979). Job satisfaction of mid management social workers. *Administration in Social Work, 3,* 207-217.

Healey, J.E. (1984). *Statistic—a tool for social research.* Wadsworth.

Heppner, P.P., & Roehlke, H.J. (1984). Differences among supervisees at different levels of training: Implications for a developmental model of supervision. *Journal of Counseling Psychology, 31,* 76-90.

Hersh, A. (1984). Teaching the theory and practice of student supervision: A short-term model based on principles of adult education. *Clinical Supervisor, 2,* 29-44.

Holloway, W. (no date). The underlying information system. (Available from Cynthia Brownstein, Bryn Mawr College, The Graduate School of Social Work and Social Research, 300 Andale Road, Bryn Mawr, Pennsylvania, 19010).

Hong Kong Polytechnic. (1986/87) *Prospectus.*

Janchill, M.P. (1969). Systems concepts in casework theory and practice. *Social Casework, 50,* 74-82.

Jayaratne, S., Chess, W., & Kunkel, D. (1986). Burnout: Its impact on child welfare workers and their spouses. *Social Work, 1,* 53-59.

Jayaratne, S., Tripodi, T., & Chess, W. (1983). Perceptions of emotional support, stress, and strain by male and female social workers. *Social Work Research and Abstracts, 19,* 19-27.

Judah, E.H. (1979). Values: The uncertain component in social work. *Journal of Education for Social Work, 15*(2), 79-86.

Kadushin, A. (1985). *Social work supervision.* New York: Columbia University Press.

Kadushin, A. (1976). Men in a woman's profession. *Social Work, 21,* 440-447.

Kadushin, A. (1980). *Child welfare.* New York: McMillan.

Kadushin, A. (1976). *Supervision in social work.* New York: Columbia University Press.

Kagan, J. (1964). Sex typing and sex role identity. In L. Hoffman & M. Hoffman (Eds.), *Review of child development research* (p. 144). New York: Russell Sage.

Kagwa, W.G. (1976). Utilization of racial content in developing self-awareness. *Journal of Education for Social Work, 12*(2), 21-27.

Kahn, S.L. (1981). An analysis of the relationship between social work schools and field placement agencies in their joint task of educating social workers. Doctoral Dissertation, Columbia University School of Social Work.

Kendall, K.A. (1959). Selected issues in field instruction. *Social Service Review*, *33*, 1-9.

Kendall, K.A. (1953). A conceptual framework for the social work curriculum of tomorrow. *Social Service Review*, *28*, 15-26.

Kimberley, M.D. (Ed.). (1984). *Beyond national boundaries: Canadian contributions to international social work and social welfare*. Ottawa: Canadian Association of Schools of Social Work.

Kirk, S.A., & Rosenblatt, A. (1984). The contribution of women faculty to social work journals. *Social Work*, 67-69.

Kirk, S.A., & Rosenblatt, A. (1980). Women's contribution to social work journals. *Social Work*, *25*, 204-209.

Kolevzon, M.S. (1979). Evaluating the supervisory relationship in field placements. *Social Work*, *24*, 241-244.

Kostin, L.B. (1972). *Child welfare: Policies and practice*. New York: McGraw-Hill.

Kravetz, D.E. (1976). Sexism in a woman's profession. *Social Work*, *21*, 421-426.

Lammert, M. (1986). Experience as knowing: Utilizing therapist self-awareness. *Social Casework*, *67*, 369-376.

Larsen, J. (1980). Competency-based and task-centered practicum instruction. *Journal of Education for Social Work*, *16*(1), 87-94.

Lipset, S.M., Trow, M.A., & Coleman, J.S. (1956). *Union democracy: The internal politics of the international typographical union*. New York: Free Press.

Lodge, R. (1975). Foreword. *The dynamics of field instruction: Learning through doing*. New York: Council on Social Work Education.

Lowy, L. (1983). Social work supervision: From models towards theory. *Journal of Education for Social Work*, *19*(2), 55-61.

Lowy, K., Blackberg, L.M., & Walbert, H.J. (1971). *Integrative learning and teaching in schools of social work: A study of organizational development in professional education*. New York: Associated Press.

MacDonald, M.E. (1961). Major current issues in curriculum policy. In *Major issues in curriculum policy and current practices in accreditation*. New York: Council on Social Work Education.

Manis, F. (1979). *Openness in social work field instruction: Stance and form guidelines*. California: Kimberly Press.

Manis, F. (1972). *Field practice in social work education: Perspective from an international base*. California: Sultana.

Maslach, C. (1976). Burn-out. *Human Behavior*, *5*, 16-22.

Matson, M.B. (1967). *Field experience in undergraduate programs in social welfare*. New York: Council on Social Work Education.

Mayer, J.E., & Rosenblatt, A. (1974). Sources of stress among student practitioners in social work: A sociological view. *Journal of Education for Social Work*, *10*(1), 56-66.

McGowan, B.G., & Meezan, W. (1983). *Child welfare current dilemmas, future decisions*. Itasca: Peacock.

Mere, A. (1981). Field work instruction in Nigerian schools of social work. *International Social Work*, *XXIV*(3), 41-45.

Meredith College self-study and application for reaccreditation.(1981). Raleigh: Meredith College Social Work Program.

Merriam, T.W. (1972). *The relations between scholastic achievement in a school of social work and six factors in students' background*. AMS.

Merton, R.K. (1964). The role set: Problems in sociological theory. In L.A. Coser & B. Rosenberg (Eds.), *Sociological theory: A book of readings* (pp. 379-384). New York: MacMillan.

Merton, R. (1957). *Social Theory and Social Structure*. Glencoe, IL: Free Press.

Meyer, C.H. (1976). *Social work practice*. New York: Free Press.

Miller, I. (1974). Supervision in social work. *Encyclopedia of social work*, (pp. 1494-1501), *16*, Washington, D.C.: N.A.S.W.

Morales, A., & Sheafor, B.W. (1983). *Social work: A profession of many faces*. (3rd ed.). Boston: Allyn & Bacon.

Munson, C.E. (1984). Stress among graduate social work students. *Journal of Education for Social Work*, *20*(3), 20-29.

Munson, C.E. (1981). Style and structure in supervision. *Journal of Education for Social Work*, *17*(1), 65-72.

Munson, C.E. (1979). Evaluation of male and female supervisors. *Social Work*, *24*, 104-110.

Munson, C.E. (1979). *Social work supervision, classic statements and critical issues*. New York: Free Press.

Murphy, C.G. (1957). Community organization for social welfare. *Social work year book*. New York: National Association of Social Workers.

Namboodiri, N., Carter, L., & Blalock, H. (1975). *Applied multivariate analysis and experimental design*. New York: McGraw-Hill.

National Association of Social Workers. (1980). *Code of ethics*. Washington, D.C.: Author.

Nelsen, J.C. (1974). Relationship communication in early fieldwork conferences. *Social Casework, 55*, 237-243.

Nichols, E. (1970). *A primer of social casework*. New York: Columbia.

Nichols, W.C., Jr. (1968). Personal psychotherapy for marital therapists. *The Family Coordinator, 17*(2), 83-88.

Ohlin, L.E., Piven, H., & Papenfort, D.M. (1958). Major dilemmas of the social worker in probation and parole. (pp. 251-262). In H. D. Stein & R. A. Cloward (Eds.). *Social perspectives on behavior*. Glenco, Ill: Free Press.

Olmstead, J.A. (1973). *Organizational structure and climate: Implication for agencies*. HumRRO Working Papers (73-05-403), Human Resources Research Organization, Alexandria, Va.

Ormsby, H. (1977). The impact of the field work placement on professional attitudes of baccalaureate degree social work students (Doctoral dissertation, University of Denver 1977). *Dissertation Abstracts International, 38*, 3057-A.

Orzek, A.M. (1984). Mentor-mentee match in training programs based on Chickering's vectors of development. In C. E. Munson (Ed.), *Supervising student internships* (pp. 71-77). New York: The Haworth Press, Inc.

Oswald, I. (1966). Field instruction: Facts and outlook. In *Trends of field work instruction* (p. 7). New York: Family Service Association of America.

Papell, C.P. (1978). A study of styles of learning for direct social work practice. (Doctoral dissertation, Yeshiva University, 1978). *Dissertation Abstracts International, 39*, 182A-183A.

Pascoe, W. (1975). Education for clinical practice. *Clinical Social Work Journal, 3*(1), 46-54.

Peaper, R.E. (1984). An analysis of student perceptions of the supervisory conference and student developed agendas for that conference. *Clinical Supervisor, 2,* 55-69.

Perlman, H. (1962). Intake and some role considerations. In C. Kasius (Ed.). *Social Casework in the Fifties.* New York: Family Service Association of America.

Pettes, D.E. (1979). *Staff and student supervision.* London: George Allen & Unwin.

Pfouts, J., & Hinley, H.C., Jr. (1977). Admission roulette: Predictive factors for success in practice. *Journal of Social Work Education, 13*(3), 56-62.

Pines, A., & Aronson, E. (1981). *Burnout: From tedium to personal growth.* New York: Free Press.

Pines, A., & Kafry, D. (1978). Occupational tedium in the social services. *Social Work,* 6, 499-507.

Pines, A., & Maslach, C. (1979). Characteristics of staff burnout in mental health settings. *Hospital and Community Psychiatry,* 29, 233-237.

Pines, A., & Ginsberg, L. (1971). New developments in social work education and their impact on Jewish communal service and community center work. *Journal of Jewish Communal Services,* XLVIII(1).

Rahe, R.H., & Holmes, T.H. (1967). The Social readjustment rating scale. *Journal of Psychosomatic Research,* 11, 213-218.

Ramsay, W.R. (1974). Role of the agency supervisor. *New directions for higher education,* 2, 45-54.

Raskin, M. (1983). A Delphi study in field instruction: Identification of issues and research priorities by experts. *Arete, 8*(2), 38-48.

Raskin, M.S. (1982). Factors associated with student satisfaction in undergraduate social work field placements. *Arete, 7*(1), 44-54.

Reid, K.E. (1977). Nonrational dynamics of the client-worker interaction. *Social Casework,* 58, 599-606.

Reid, W.J. (1974). Developments in the use of organized data. *Social Work,* 19, 585-593.

Reisman, L. (1949). A study of role conceptions in bureaucracy. *Social Focus,* 25, 305-310.

Reynolds, B.C. (1965). *Learning and teaching in the practice of social work.* New York: Russell.

Richards, L.D. (1984). Verbal interaction and supervisor perception in counselor supervision. *Journal of Counseling Psychology*, *31*, 262-265.

Ripple, L. (1968). A follow-up study of adopted children. *Social Service Review*, *42*, 479-497.

Roberts, R.W. (1973). An interim report of the development of an undergraduate-graduate continuum of social work education in a private university. *Journal of Education for Social Work*, *9*(3), 58-64.

Rodgers, A., & Williams, E.G. (1977). Field instruction and evaluation: Some continuing and some new issues. *Arete*, *4*(4), 225-234.

Rose, S. (1965). Students view their supervision: A scale analysis. *Social Work*, *10*, 90-96.

Rosenblatt, A., & Mayer, J.E. (1975). Objectionable supervisory styles: Student views. *Social Work*, *20*, 184-188.

Rosenblatt, A., & Mayer, J. (1970). Reduction of uncertainty in child placement decisions. *Social Work*, *15*, 525-529.

Rosenblum, A.F., & Raphael, F. (1983). The role and function of the faculty field liaison. *Journal of Education for Social Work*, *19*(1), 67-73.

Rothman, J., & Jones, W.C. (1971). *A new look at field instruction: Education for application of practice skills in community organizing and social planning*. New York: Association Press & Council on Social Work Education.

Rothman, J. (1966). Working paper on field instruction in community organization. *Community organization curriculum development project*. New York: Council on Social Work Education.

Rotholz, T., & Werk, A. (1984). Student supervision: An educational process. In C.E. Munson (Ed.), *Supervising student internships in human services* (pp. 15-27). New York: The Haworth Press, Inc.

Rotholz, T., & Werk, A. (1984). Student supervision: An educational process. *Clinical Supervisor*, *2*, 15-27.

Ryan, A.S. (1981). Asian-American students. *Social Casework*, *62*, 95-105.

Schein, V.E. (1973). The relationship between sex role characteristics and requisite management characteristics. *Journal of Applied Psychology*, 57, 95-100.

Schein, V.E. (1975) Relationships between sex role sterotypes and requisite management characteristics among female managers. *Journal of Applied Psychology*, 60, 340-344.

Schoech, R., & Arangio, T. (1979). Computers in the human services. *Social Work*, 24, 96-102.

Schubert, M. (1983). *Field instruction in social casework*. Chicago: University of Chicago.

Schubert, M. (1963). Admissions decisions. *Social Service Review*, 37, 154-165.

Schutz, M. (1969). The potential of concurrent field instruction for learning. In B.L. Jones (Ed.). *Current patterns of field instruction in graduate social work education* (pp. 99-107). New York: Council on Social Work Education.

Schutz-Gordon, M. (1975). *Current issues in field instruction*. Paper presented at the Annual Program Meeting of the Council on Social Work Education. New York.

Schwartz, M.C. (1978). Helping the worker with counter-transference. *Social Work*, 23, 204-209.

Schwartz, M.C. (1974). Importance of the sex of worker and client. *Social Work*, 19, 177-185.

Scotch, C.B. (1971). Sex status in social work: Grist for woman's liberation. *Social Work*, 16, 5-11.

Selig, A.L. (1982). Responsibilities of the field instruction agency. In B.W. Sheafor & L.E. Jenkins (Eds.). *Quality field instruction in social work* (pp. 136-143), New York: Longman.

Selye, H. (1978). *The stress of life*. New York: McGraw-Hill.

Sheafor, B.W., & Jenkins, L.E., (1982). *Quality field instruction in social work program development and maintenance*. New York: Longman.

Shinn, E.B. (1968). Is placement necessary: An experimental study of agreement among caseworkers in making foster care decisions, PhD Thesis, New York: Columbia University.

Shulman, L. (1983). *Teaching the helping skills of field instructors guide*. Illinois: F.E. Peacock.

Shulman, L. (1982). *Skills of supervision and staff management*. Illinois: F.E. Peacock.

Shulman, L. (1981). *Identifying, measuring, and teaching helping skills*. New York: Council on Social Work Education.

Simon, B.K. (1959). Field instruction as education for practice: Purposes and goals. In K. Wenzel (Ed.). *Undergraduate field instruction programs: Current issues and predictions*. New York: Council on Social Work Education.

SPSSX Users Guide. New York: McGraw-Hill.

Starr, P., Taylor, D.A., & Taft, R. (1970). Early life experiences and adoptive parenting. *Social Casework*, 51, 491-500.

Statistics on social work education in the United States. (1977). New York: Council on Social Work Education.

Sterne, R. (1967). The initial influence of structural variations in casework field instruction upon students' mastery of classroom knowledge (Doctoral dissertation, Washington University, 1967). *Dissertation Abstract International*, *28*, 3268-A.

Thomas, C.L. (Ed.). (1977). *Taber's cyclopedic medical dictionary* (14th ed.). Philadelphia: F. A. Davis Co.

Thomlison, B., Watt, S., & Kimberley, D. (1980). *Trends and issues in the field preparation of social work manpower*. Ottawa: Canadian Association of Schools of Social Work.

Thyer, B.A., Sowers-Hoag, K.M., & Love, J.P. (1986). The influence of field instructor-student gender combinations on student perceptions of field instruction quality. *Arete*, *11*(2), 25-30.

Torre, E. (1974). Student performance in solving social work problems and work experience prior to entering the MSW program. *Journal of Social Work Education*, *10*(2), 114-117.

Towle, C. (1954). *The learner in education for the professions as seen in social work education for social work*. Chicago: University of Chicago Press.

Tropman, E.O. (1977). Agency constraints affecting links between practice and education. *Journal of Education for Social Work*, *13*, 8-14.

Tsang, N.M. (1983). *Students' perspectives of field instruction in undergraduate social work education in Hong Kong*. Master's Thesis, unpublished. Hong Kong University.

Tuggle, F.D. (1978). An analysis of employee turnover. *Behavioral Sciences*, *23*(1), 32-37.

Turner, J.B. (June, 1984). *Excellence in field education*. Paper presented at the New England Conference of Field Education. West Hartfort, Connecticut.

Turoff, M. (1971). Delphi and its potential impact on information systems. *AFIPS conference proceedings*, *39*, 317-326.

Tyler, R.W. (1950). *Basic principles of curriculum and instruction*. Chicago: University of Chicago Press.

United Nations. (1958). *Training for social work*. New York: Author.

Van der walls, J. (1974). Die frage nach dem lehrinhalt (The problem of the teaching content). In E.M.J. Siegers, (Ed.), *Praxisberatung* (pp. 123-151). West Germany: Lambertus Verlag.

Vigilante, J.L., Lodge, R., Lukton, R., Kaplan, S., & Mason, R. (1980). *Searching for theory: Following Hearn*. Unpublished Manuscript, Adelphi University School of Social Work, Garden City.

Vinter, R.D. (1967). The social structure of service. In T.J. Edwin (Ed.), *Behavioral sciences for social workers*. (pp. 193-206). New York: Free Press.

Walton, E., & Walz, T. (1971). A follow-up study of graduates of a pre-social work program: Implications for education and practice. *Social Work Education Reporter*, *19*, 54-57.

Wasserman, H. (1971). The professional social worker in a bureaucracy. *Social Work*, *1*, 89-95.

Watson, K.W. (1973). Differential supervision. *Social Work*, *18*, 80-88.

Wayne, J., Skolnik, L., & Raskin, M.S. (this issue). Field instruction in the United States and Canada: A comparison of studies. In M.S. Raskin (Ed.). *Empirical studies in field instruction*. New York: The Haworth Press, Inc.

Wayne, J. (1982). *A survey of field instruction: Department directors' views of supervisors of micro and macro practice*. Unpublished paper, Boston University School of Social Work.

Wijnberg, M.H., & Schwartz, M.C. (1977). Models of student supervision: The apprentice, growth, and role systems models. *Journal of Education for Social Work*, *13*(3), 107-113.

Williams, M., Ho, L., & Fielder, L. (1974). Career patterns: More grist for women's liberation. *Social Work*, *19*, 463-466.

Wilson, S.J. (1981). *Field instruction techniques for supervisors*. New York: Free Press.

Worthington, E.L., Jr. (1984). Empirical investigation of supervision of counselors as they gain experience. *Journal of Counseling Psychology*, *31*, 63-75.

Worthington, E.L., Jr., & Roehlke, H.J. (1979). Effective supervision as perceived by beginning counselors-in-training. *Journal of Counseling Psychology*, *26*, 64-73.

Zietz, D., & Erlich, J.L. (1976). Sexism in social agencies: Practitioners' perspectives. *Social Work*, *21*, 434-438.